D0425526

"As Others See Us." Cartoon by Morris published in the *Tampa Tribune,* Tampa, Florida, n.d. Reprinted by permission.

Peace
Moveme
in
America

Peace Movements in America

Edited with an Introduction by
CHARLES CHATFIELD

SCHOCKEN BOOKS · NEW YORK

For David and Carol

74-2612

With the exception of the newly added Introduction and Preface, this book is a reprint of the Spring 1972 issue of *American Studies*.

First SCHOCKEN edition 1973

Contents

Preface

Peace Movements in America is a comprehensive survey of the twentieth-century antiwar movements in the United States. It is not complete; there are inevitable gaps in coverage. But it is interpretive and it does develop fresh understanding of the generations of peace advocates who were active before the recent antiwar campaign coalesced in the shadow of the Indochina War.

The essays in this volume are the product of recent research. With one exception, they were first published in a special issue of *American Studies* (12, No. 1 [Spring, 1972]), an interdisciplinary journal sponsored by the Midcontinent American Studies Association and the University of Kansas.

The volume is arranged in roughly chronological order, leading up to interpretations of peace education, Cold War historiography, and the concept of internationalism. The reader may find it useful, however, to begin with the symposium. It is based on the conceptual analysis of internationalism in the pre-World War I period by Sondra Herman. Rather than attempt to frame an abstract definition of internationalism, the respondents to the symposium were invited to discuss the concept functionally, in terms of the roles that its various interpretations have played. Their comments thus complement the other essays, and together they suggest a useful interpretive distinction.

These essays demonstrate the variety of wings and factions in organized struggle against war—diversity so great as to call into question the existence of a single peace movement. The authors illustrate the contexts in which men and women have sought to abolish war or mitigate its results. They document the range and variety of social and cultural traditions involved in the peace movement, and they suggest the effects of the varying factions on the movement itself and on its relation to the public. What is more, the articles taken together suggest several broad frames of reference from which to interpret the specific facets of the peace movement recounted here, perspectives from which we can explore further aspects of the search for peace.

I am indebted to *American Studies* for the opportunity to fashion this collection—to the editor, Stuart Levine, and especially to the associate editor, Norman T. Yetman. I am most appreciative of the help of the journal's editorial assistant, Mary Jane Harmon. She put the issue together in a manner at once thoroughly professional and sensitive to the feelings of all concerned. It is a pleasure to acknowledge, too, the help of Beverly Colman who has guided me in the necessary revision for this edition.

CHARLES CHATFIELD

Introduction

Charles Chatfield

Recently a search for photographs of events and leaders in the history of peace movements in America led me to the pictorial division of the Library of Congress. In its photograph index, I found two items listed under "disarmament," and a single card entry for "pacifism." The latter was a cross reference to an entry in the regional files: "7665 (agitation)." The National Archives has a large collection of recently deposited World War I photographs. The index lists several boxes of pictures of "peace parades," and so I made an anxious search, only to find that they are records of Armistice Day parades—Victory parades— around the country. This blind alley gave me pause. Who assembled and deposited this fine collection? The War Department General Staff of 1917–19. How would the War Department have classified the pacifists and peace advocates whose pictures I wanted to find? A moment's reflection led me to photographs of just the people I was after, filed under such designations as "Arrest of Alien Enemies in U.S." and "Antiwar Agitators."

To an archivist this story would illustrate the importance of assessing the perspective of whoever organizes collections. To a historian it should illustrate the importance of reassessing the historical perspective on the American peace and antiwar movements. That is the purpose of this volume. It is addressed to participants in the peace movement no less than to students of it, for ignorance of past efforts, successes, and failures is a barrier to effectiveness as well as to understanding.

I

What were the peace movements in America? Who led them and how far back did they reach? Were they occasional outbursts against specific wars or did they have continuity? What were their goals and objectives, their tactics, and their sense of history? Were they similar in any respect to the recent campaigns of the 1960's? A survey of the story of peace efforts in the United States may supply a useful canvas for the essays in the book.

Organized antiwar protest accompanied the War of 1812, the Mexican-American War of 1846, and the Spanish-American War of 1898, as Samuel Eliot Morison and others have shown in *Dissent in Three American Wars* (1970). There was war resistance, too, on both sides of the Civil War. The official policy in each of these wars was challenged, along with the patriotic rationale and rhetoric in which it was clothed. Opposition led to political activity and even created an antiwar literature, represented in this volume by Perry Gianakos' essay on Ernest Howard Crosby. For the most part, wartime resistance in the nineteenth century was a spontaneous reaction to political and social grievances. In 1812 and 1846 it was largely geographical and political in orientation. Centered in New England, it was given coherence by the Federalist and Whig parties respectively. There was more protest of the imperialist crusade to subdue the Filipinos than of the Spanish-American War itself, and that too appears to have been based largely in New England. Most important, wartime opposition in the nineteenth century was usually dissipated in peacetime. It was rarely connected with any view of the world larger than an idealistic version of our continental destiny. It was more nearly a political expression than an ideological commitment.

By contrast, organized peace activity began in nineteenth-century America as a largely religious phenomenon. It was built upon religious tradition dating from biblical times and defined in terms of the so-called peace churches: the Brethren, Mennonites, and Society of Friends. "War, considered in itself, is the premeditated and determined destruction of human beings, of creatures originally formed after the image of God," wrote Quaker Anthony Benezet in 1778. Nineteenth-century peace advocates were rarely sectarians, however. They represented instead the influence of Protestant denominations, and their societies were among those reform agencies that sought to inculcate religious values in a secular society. In this respect they built also upon the optimistic humanitarian sentiments and peace projects of the seventeenth and eighteenth centuries, a tradition represented in 1798 when Philadelphia physician Benjamin Rush proposed the appointment of a Secretary of Peace with cabinet rank.

Early peace advocates also responded to the dark side of history—to a century of European wars culminating in the continental struggles of the Napoleonic era and their extension to the New World in the War of 1812. Indeed, the first peace societies were formed in the last year of that war which had aroused such bitter opposition. Of the several local groups initiated then, two represent the beginning of a continuous peace movement in America. The first was the New York Peace Society formed by David Low Dodge in August, 1815. It was absolutely pacifist—opposed to all warfare—and it had a decidedly religious basis. By the mid-1820's it had declined to obscurity. The second was the Massachusetts Peace Society formed by the indefatigable Noah Worcester in December, 1815. It became a broad-ranging and ecumenical organization, and it fed into the American Peace Society (1828) which was based in New York and given vigor and scope by brusque, robust William Ladd.

The American Peace Society challenged a nearly suffocating public apathy to international issues. Its agents traversed the hinterland of American consciousness, seeking support. They made some inroads in the churches, established a regular peace journal, and stimulated interest in some colleges. They paid close attention to foreign affairs, stimulating friendly exchanges between Americans and Britons, and they helped to organize opposition to the Mexican War of 1846. They responded to domestic injustice, too, especially slavery. Their movement was given impetus in the 1840's by a "learned blacksmith," Elihu Burritt, who worked both sides of the Atlantic with organizational and rhetorical effectiveness.

But by that time the American Peace Society was being polarized by a tension that would recur throughout the history of the peace movement: the advocates of absolute opposition to all war and a personal position of total non-resistance to violence fought for leadership in the organization against a moderate wing interested in political action, international relations, and gradual reform. Peace advocates were divided also over other burning social issues, notably slavery and the status of women. The Society declined in influence until during the Civil War it became virtually inoperative. Leading members even supported what they believed was a holy war against slavery. The official line of the Society was that the Civil War was not a proper war at all; it was a rebellion against rightful authority or an assertion of Southern iniquity which would have to be quashed in order to make peace possible. The testimony of even the traditional peace churches was tested as never before by the contradictory moral claims of that conflict, as Peter Brock has shown in *Pacifism in America to 1914* (1968). Here and there individuals kept the faith of absolute pacifism, but organized work abated.

It was revived shortly after the war. The American Peace Society was reactivated along its traditional lines and with its implicit religious emphasis. New leaders succeeded old ones, and prestigious figures were enlisted as at least honorary officers. In reaction to the moderate leadership of the Society and to its compromising history during the Civil War, a new organization, the Universal Peace Union, was formed in 1866. Thus, the division over tactics that had divided the Society before was represented by two cohesive groups which were for the most part complementary.

The Universal Peace Union was uncompromising in its non-violence, and it extended its opposition to aggressiveness and hatred on the domestic scene, even lending support to the labor movement upon occasion. It supported a wide range of foreign-policy positions, from arbitration to anti-imperialism, because it derived its coherence from "universal" principles rather than from specific programs. Its president from 1866 to his death in 1913 was Alfred Love, a man who, however modest, was a vigorous organizer and who, however romantic and sentimental, attended to practical foreign-policy problems. Love introduced symbolism into the movement as an alternative to the patriotic pageantry of the era and, most important, he forged organizational ties with the burgeoning peace movement in Europe.

The work of these two broad organizations was supplemented in the half-century before World War I by specialized approaches to peace—notably arbitration, and international law and organization. These lines were developed together because of the nature of international relations and because all peace advocates appealed largely to a constituency representing the upper-middle and intellectual classes of the country. Peace workers engaged in political as well as evangelical activity; but they did not challenge political leadership so much as they tried to work through it for their own ends.

The idea of arbitration rested on the assumptions that conflicts of national interest can be resolved equitably, that a negotiated settlement best serves the national interest in an interdependent world, and that a neutral third party can help to define equity. It was a popular concept with nineteenth-century peace movements, and groups in Europe and America worked in tandem to achieve arbitration both of national claims and of personal claims across national lines. In 1874 both houses of Congress passed a resolution that requested the President to include arbitration clauses in future treaties. A stronger resolution passed in 1890. The principle had been accepted by the Pan-American Congress the year before, but the State Department ignored it. In the 1890's, on the other hand, an arbitration treaty written by the McKinley Administration was rejected by the Senate. Despite the fact that Theodore Roosevelt submitted specific cases to arbitration, Senate resolutions continued to be hedged about with reservations exempting matters of national honor and security. They violated the spirit and intent of the concept.

Although arbitration did not prove to be the systematic alternative to arms that its proponents hoped for, it did provide them with a principle of organization. Lobbying in Congress and among the people created an informal coalition of peace advocates and kept them in touch with their European colleagues. It spawned new, specialized organizations: the National Arbitration League (1882), the Christian Arbitration Association (1886), the International Arbitration League (English-initiated, 1880), and the Lake Mohonk Arbitration Conferences (1895–1916). The latter brought together each year businessmen, clergymen, diplomats, lawyers, and educators for discussion of arbitration and related subjects. Two kinds of things were happening. On one hand, the broader implications and requirements of international arbitration were being explored. On the other, a new constituency was being formed for the peace movement in America—one that was respectable, with inestimable resources in money and prestige. The extent to which this expansive constituency stifled perceptions is suggested by David Patterson in "An Interpretation of the American Peace Movement, 1898–1914."

The broader requirements of arbitration were codes and institutions of international law. The search for a body of general principles and specific rules that are binding upon the members of the international community in their mutual relations antedates the modern period of history. It was given form in the work of Hugo Grotius, *De Jure Belli ac Pacis* [*The Rights of War and Peace*], 1625. Jeremy Bentham advocated the codification of international law, assuming that once understood it would be enforced by the power of public opinion. Americans such as Ladd and Burritt concurred, and jurists such as William Jay, Francis Lieber, and especially David Dudley Field explored the concept of international law systematically. The secretary of the American Peace Society, James B. Miles, formed an American Code Committee and proselytized Europe for codification, finding there a receptive base of understanding. Partly as a result of his initiative, a congress of jurists was held in Brussels in 1873, from which emerged the Institut de Droit International and another organization which eventually (in 1895) became known as the International Law Society. American participation in this movement became increasingly incidental in the last quarter of the century, until interest was revived in negative reaction to the Spanish-American War and in positive affirmation of the First Hague Conference of 1899.

Called by Czar Nicholas II to deal with armaments and the rules of war, the Hague Conference caught the imagination of American peace advocates. They popularized it and used what influence they had to secure an official delegation sympathetic to their views. The American government counseled its delegates to avoid disarmament negotiations and to work for arbitration, including some sort of international court. Most other nations wanted to avoid disarmament, too, but agreed to establish a Permanent Court of International Arbitration —actually a panel of judges to which nations might voluntarily take disputes. It certainly did not threaten national sovereignty, and it was approved by the Senate.

The Hague Convention generated unwarranted optimism, visions of a reign of international law. But it led, too, to clearer notions of the international institutions required to support it. Americans began to shift their attention from arbitration treaties to a world court and a congress of nations, a movement of thought and organization narrated by Warren F. Kuehl in *Seeking World Order: The United States and*

International Organization to 1920 (1969). By the time of the Second Hague Conference in 1907, the influence of legalists had placed special emphasis on the formation of codes and of an international court in conjunction with arbitration procedures. The Conference was disappointing in these respects. It left arbitration largely as it stood in 1899, and it treated international law mainly in terms of the rules of warfare and neutral rights (rather as Grotius had done in the third book of *De Jure Belli*).

Nonetheless, the American peace movement found a program of organization in preparing public opinion and expert analysis for the Hague Conferences. Eminent jurists, including especially James Brown Scott, Theodore Marburg, and Elihu Root, led an American Society for the Judicial Settlement of International Disputes in an attempt to follow up the Permanent Court with a truly international court of justice. Hundreds of peace advocates attended a national congress called in 1907 to give public support to the Hague program, and the congress became an annual affair until 1915. An American School Peace League was formed to influence public-school curricula, and shortly cosmopolitan clubs were organized on college campuses. The established peace societies—the American Peace Society and the Universal Peace Union—grew in strength, if not influence; and they were supplemented by new organizations with permanent endowments: the World Peace Foundation (1910), handsomely provided for by publisher Edwin Ginn, and the Carnegie Endowment for International Peace (1910) and the Church Peace Union (1914), both endowed by Andrew Carnegie. The future seemed auspicious indeed if one contemplated the mushrooming of societies and prominent support and paid less attention to the mounting arms and naval race, expanding colonial pretensions, military alliances, and endemic crises of the international order.

THE IMPACT OF WORLD WAR I

Then, in August, 1914, a shot fired in Sarajevo cracked the dikes of complacency. War engulfed much of the world, peace movements and all. American leaders reacted predictably at first, expressing shock and abhorrence. But as outstanding peace advocates of all classes came to the defense of one warring power or another, the established peace societies wavered or (like the Carnegie Endowment) actually supported the Allied cause. Impatient pacifists formed new organizations. They related to those Europeans who held out against war, and they opposed American involvement. The peace movement was restructured as those who supported the war and those who adamantly opposed it aligned into two wings.

A Woman's Peace Party convened early in 1915, and it worked with women abroad in the cause of neutral mediation. Jane Addams and other women tried to secure Wilson's leadership. Failing in this, they organized an expedition financed by Henry Ford to join their European colleagues in a private continuous committee for mediation. Meanwhile, American pacifists formed a branch of the English-initiated Fellowship of Reconciliation (1914), a home for absolute religious objectors to war. Antimilitarists also responded to the preparedness drive of the Wilson Administration and emerged in 1916 as the vigorous American Union Against Militarism (AUAM). It not only conducted a massive public campaign against armaments and military training, but effectively intervened in an incident on the Mexican border that might have led to war. The leaders of these three organizations introduced a new constituency to peace work. Progressives all, they included numerous social workers, reformers, and social-gospel ministers, together with liberal Quakers, who were united in opposing American intervention in the European war. They were politically oriented, too, ready to mobilize public pressure, intent on influencing the course of events.

Three events in 1917 shook the peace movement to its foundations and sifted the new constituency of all but the most resolute opponents of war. In February, President Wilson responded to the resumption of unrestricted submarine warfare by severing relations with Germany. With the loss of a few leaders, the progressive peace advocates formed a new coalition to oppose intervention—the Emergency Peace Federation. In vain they conducted a massive program to hold the line for neutrality. The United States entered the war in April. More peace advocates reluctantly accepted the national course; but those remaining formed a new coalition with antiwar Socialists, the People's Council of America for Peace and Freedom, which mounted pressure for open discussion of peace aims and protection of civil liberties. During the summer there was a serious division within the AUAM over affiliation with the People's Council and, more seriously, over efforts of some leaders on behalf of conscientious objectors. By fall it was no longer a real coalition, and a new alignment of the peace movement had congealed.

On one hand, there were those progressives who remained adamantly against the war. They were organized in the Fellowship of Reconciliation, the American Civil Liberties Bureau (it became independent of the AUAM), and the American Friends Service Committee which was formed in 1917 to give Quaker conscientious objectors options for alternative service. They were joined by antiwar Socialists, some members of the Woman's Peace Party, literary radicals like Randolph Bourne and Max Eastman, and by new recruits to the cause of peace. Together they gave an altogether new dimension to the American peace movement. Now it included organized opponents of a national war effort who also were committed to an enduring search for peace and international order. It had leaders who were both socially conscious activists and absolutely opposed to war. It had a wing that conceived of warfare as being inextricably linked to arbitrary authority and which, therefore, felt a commitment to work for both international peace and social justice. This essentially pacifist group was solidified by the very wartime persecution in which pro-war peace advocates all too often acquiesced, as Blanche Wiesen Cook suggests in "Democracy in Wartime: Antimilitarism in England and the United States, 1914–1918." It became the nucleus of the most vigorous and aggressive peace movement in the wake of the war.

On the other hand, those advocates of peace who felt obligated to support World War I did not abandon their international vision. Indeed, they attributed to the war the very values for which they had worked before—the search for international equity, law, and order. The American Peace Society and the Carnegie Endowment worked on the assumption that the collapse of the German imperial government was requisite for peace. But, looking beyond victory, numerous leaders tried to fashion the elements of a new world order.

Their views diverged, as Warren F. Kuehl has shown, although there was a core of unanimity in them. The goal of arbitration was for the most part superseded by that of international organization; and it was over the elements of organization—the terms on which nations would be related to one another—that differences occurred. It was commonly agreed that a world court should be created through which international law might be developed and applied. In May, 1915, a World's Court League was formed to explore and propagate this view. But already an important group of internationalists had gone beyond it; about a month later they launched the League to Enforce Peace. Its intellectual antecedents were hundreds of years old, but its organization began with the leadership of Hamilton Holt, editor of *The Independent,* and largely in response to his views. The League conducted a huge public campaign to popularize the notion of a league of nations loosely bound to respect pacific procedures, and its leaders conducted study groups to explore details. William Howard Taft became its president, and in May, 1916, President Wilson subscribed to its goals. When the nation entered the war, Wilson sought to stifle public discussion of the terms of a league, but his chief advisor, Col. Edward House, relied much upon the thinking and influence of the League to Enforce Peace leaders. Unfortunately, perhaps, Wilson did not keep in close touch with developing thought on international organization, and the league for which he fought in Paris neglected key elements of internationalist thought—notably the universal membership of nations, and the development of judicial institutions.

Indeed, the League to Enforce Peace plans were opposed by some peace advocates. The American Peace Society refused to support any program embodying economic and military sanctions, for example, and the World's Court League held to its narrowly judicial concept of world order. A few individuals dissented because the League did not go far enough toward supranational government or even a federation of nations. Considering the fact that the League to Enforce Peace could not unite internationalists behind a comprehensive plan, and the fact that Wilson's program aroused opposition within this strongest body of pro-war peace advocates, it is no wonder that the League of Nations divided the peace movement when it came before the United States Senate. The general idea had been given a stronger base of public support than its specific terms could carry. However, the goal had provided a wartime principle of organization.

THE MODERN DIVISION

The alignment created in World War I roughly characterized peace forces until the mid-1950's. Organizationally, peace movements continued to develop from the separate experiences of the pacifists who had opposed that war and the internationalists who had supported it. Neither wing formed a unified whole. Each represented a loose and shifting coalition. Both advocated some of the same alternatives. For a generation, however, they remained distinct and occasionally conflicting movements.

In the 1920's, as Charles DeBenedetti has suggested in "Alternative Strategies in the American Peace Movement," the internationalists were most sharply divided by the question of strategy. One legacy of the League of Nations controversy was division of opinion among even advocates of world organization, together with public apathy or antagonism to the whole idea. A second legacy was a continuing League of Nations Non-Partisan Association. Its leaders, particularly James T. Shotwell, worked for changes that would make the international experiment more effective at the same time that they sought to make it more acceptable to the public. Although the Association supported full American participation, it joined other League supporters—the World Peace Foundation, the Foreign Policy Association (formed during the war), the Woodrow Wilson Foundation, and the Carnegie Endowment —in an informal coalition to increase the involvement of the United States in an advisory capacity. Their campaign was low-keyed and all but drowned out by vociferous debates over the World Court and the Outlawry of War.

Operative international law was a well-established goal of juridically oriented internationalists in the United States, as we have seen. The divisive question was one of strategy. One group of legalists promoted American entry into the International Court of Justice. They mobilized public and congressional support but failed largely because of the wily maneuvering of irreconcilable Senators who saw beyond the Court the specter of League and a diminution of American sovereignty. Another group of legalists supported the notion of outlawing war as an instrument of national policy, on the grounds that law had to be codified before it could be applied, and that an international treaty agreement would alleviate American apprehensions of involvement with the League. However compatible the Outlawry of War and the World Court might have been in theory, politically they came to have alternative priorities. Internationalists were unable to form a working coalition to secure them both, and isolationists used each alternative to weaken the other. The outlawry idea was disembodied in the Kellogg-Briand Pact without visible means of enforcement. The World Court did not gain a sufficient base of support to pass the Senate even in 1935.

That fact, viewed against rising totalitarianism and disintegrating international relations, convinced leading internationalists of the need to organize a more effective political coalition. Initially they designed it to support disarmament negotiations and liberal economic policies abroad, but the new coalition was soon converted to the cause of collective sanctions against aggressor states. Increasingly, it competed with a well-developed pacifist coalition, as I have argued in "Alternative Antiwar Strategies of the Thirties." Some important legalists came to support a policy of strict neutrality, but the most active internationalists accepted the direction of the Committee to Defend America by Aiding the Allies, directed by Clark Eichelberger.

The same men who were urging that America help in the defense of Western Europe participated in the planning of the world after the war. In this respect they duplicated the World War I experience of internationalists. No sooner had war burst upon Europe in 1939 than James T. Shotwell created a Commission to Study the Organization of Peace. The Federal Council of Churches and the Council on Foreign Relations sponsored similar groups, and Cordell Hull set up a study committee in the Department of State. After the United States entered the war in 1941, postwar planning became a more formal function of the Department and of the internationalist associations alike, and some of the same leaders—Shotwell and Eichelberger, for example—worked on both fronts. The complex planning in private and public agencies, and the difficulties of relating to the executive branch, are described in detail by Robert A. Divine in *Second Chance: The Triumph of Internationalism in America During World War II* (1967). The internationalists did not just plan, however—they propagated; and in this regard the developing United Nations plan provided the organizing program for one of the major peace movements in American history.

Throughout the war the goal of a united nations organization was advanced by the League of Nations Association and other internationalist groups: the Carnegie Endowment, the Church Peace Union, and the Woodrow Wilson Association, for example. In June, 1944, most of these groups joined a formal coalition called Americans United for World Organization in order to coordinate their efforts. That fall, Clark Eichelberger and his colleagues began to prepare a mammoth campaign to sell the Dumbarton Oaks proposals—the heart of the emerging covenant—to the American people. Their effort was launched in February, 1945, as the League of Nations Association converted itself into the American Association for the United Nations. Civic and religious bodies were brought along, and even the Americans United overcame its initial reluctance. Every avenue of public opinion-formation was utilized, although attention centered upon the educated middle classes. The State Department maintained a close working relationship with the private organizations during the campaign, and the final adoption of the U.N. covenant seemed like a victory for all concerned, the more especially because serious differences in approach had been subsumed by the coalition.

In the United Nations Organization of 1945 the concentration of power resulting from World War II had been grafted onto the old idea of a congress of nations, now much strengthened both by specialized agencies for human welfare and reconstruction and by institutions for collective security. Within three years the division of power had polarized. The specialized agencies of the U.N. continued their constructive work, but the institutions of collective security became converted into agencies of the Cold War. Since the veto power worked to sidetrack critical tests of relative power between the United States and the Soviet Union, these tests took place outside the world organization. They were not only military, as in the case of the formation of NATO (1949), but economic and cultural confrontations, as in the case of the earlier Marshall Plan. Convinced that the Soviet Union menaced not only the status quo but also the operation of U.N. security arrangements, internationalists became Cold Warriors. Jon Yoder interprets this shift in "The United Federalists: Liberals for Law and Order." By the time of the Korean War in 1950, internationalism was widely identified with American national interest and military–political capacity. In this respect the Cold War dramatized the continuity of one wing of American peace movements from its experience in World War I.

There was continuity also in the pacifist wing of the movement. One legacy of the Great Crusade was disillusionment with war itself, and this became widely shared by the American public. A second legacy was the group of pacifist organizations formed during the conflict. The Woman's Peace Party broadened into the Women's International League for Peace and Freedom. The Fellowship of Reconciliation also affiliated internationally, and its magazine, *The World Tomorrow*, became the chief spokesman for the social gospel until its demise in 1934. From the ranks of the FOR came the nucleus of the War Resisters League. The American Friends Service Committee was reorganized with broad social concerns, including especially peace education. The AUAM soon dissolved, but it was replaced by a coalition organization, the National Council for Prevention of War. Through these groups pacifists mounted effective campaigns against naval construction. They fought the introduction of ROTC in schools and colleges, and they publicized the evils and duplicity of warfare. They developed experience in political activity. They worked with churches and with youth, as Patti Peterson shows in "Student Organizations and the Antiwar Movement in America, 1900–1960." Moreover, they became involved in the domestic social-justice movement, especially in the causes of labor and civil rights, where they first formulated the theories of non-violent action that would be applied in the 1950's and 1960's.

Like the traditional internationalists, pacifists responded to the threats of the 1930's by forming coalitions. They worked with other internationalists for disarmament, world economic cooperation, and—in the case of Manchuria—a collective response to aggression. After that failed, however, they turned increasingly to strict neutrality for the United States. In 1937–38 they organized a massive, half-million-dollar Emergency Peace Campaign. Although it propagated programs supported by traditional internationalists, the EPC became a vigorous proponent of neutralism and, therefore, the fulcrum of division within the movement. In the years just before Pearl Harbor, pacifists themselves divided their attention. On one hand, they cooperated in political activity with other neutralist groups. But as well, they turned inward to prepare for the coming war. They strengthened their understanding of the religious principles at the base of their opposition, the convictions explored by Jo Ann Robinson in her essay on "A. J. Muste and Ways to Peace." And they cooperated to secure provisions for conscientious objectors.

During World War II, pacifists generally accepted their status as a minority isolated from public life by its own convictions. A large proportion of their resources were consumed in the administration of programs for conscientious objectors, for which the Friends Service Committee accepted a primary responsibility. The War Resisters League expanded because of its work on behalf of C.O.'s, and it acquired a nucleus of objectors who had been radicalized by their experiences, as Lawrence Wittner showed in *Rebels Against War* (1969). Not only money but unity was taxed because of differences of opinion over what degrees of cooperation with the conscripting state might be ethical. Somehow there was time and money enough for the Fellowship of Reconciliation to launch an ambitious program of publications about pacifism, oppose saturation bombing of German cities, and cooperate with liberal churchmen on behalf of Japanese-Americans. Although leading pacifists accepted their role as a dissenting minority regarding the war, they considered the problems of a postwar settlement, and they anticipated rejoining pro-war internationalists in peacetime.

They expected to return to the politics of pressure groups. Instead, their wartime isolation extended far into the Cold War because the essential characteristic of wartime, insofar as domestic politics are concerned, is that the nation has a nearly ultimate commitment to one side in a polarized world—a position pacifists did not share. A new generation of peace advocates grew up trying to understand and live beyond that fact.

They found themselves still in the role of a minority with little access to the public. They did not share the anti-Communist ideology of the nation, even though most of them had few illusions of Soviet good will. A. J. Muste, among others, was disturbed by the prospect that the developing nations of the "third world" would be polarized in a new international power struggle. Pacifists were unable to acquiesce in the policies of military containment, nuclear deterrence, or calculated limited warfare. They fought peacetime conscription in 1948, but they lost. They challenged the terms of the Cold War, but they were almost without means to affect public policy. In a time known for "McCarthyism" and in a nation at war in Korea, even their numbers dwindled.

Consequently, leading pacifists were receptive to forms of direct action with which they might challenge the prevailing consensus of opinion on foreign policy. Techniques of non-violent action had been developed in India and in the American labor movement, and pacifists had adapted them during World War II and applied them to race relations and civil rights according to theoretical principles worked out before the war. The Congress of Racial Equality was formed in 1942–43 by a nucleus of young pacifists. Its experiments with direct non-violent confrontation during the war were supported by FOR resources. In Civilian Public Service Camps, meanwhile, objectors were experimenting with forms of civil disobedience which they associated with fundamental social change. Whether revolutionary or not, non-violent confrontation was an approach calculated to appeal to a movement without access to public influence.

TOWARD A NEW COALITION

The opportunity to create a new coalition of pacifists and liberal internationalists came with an apparent thaw in the Cold War, signaled by Stalin's death in 1953 and Khrushchev's subsequent denunciation of his regime. In 1957 a small group of pacifists helped to organize the liberal Committee for a Sane Nuclear Policy (SANE) and the radical Committee for Non-Violent Action (CNVA). The CNVA worked independently, its dramatic actions forming a political counterpoint to the traditional approaches of SANE. Pacifists and liberal internationalists were operating in tandem to alter foreign policy, as they had done early in the 1930's, and sporadically attempts were made to formalize the coalition.

SANE brought together internationalists like Norman Cousins and scientists like Linus Pauling who opposed mounting nuclear weapons systems and who had already spoken against the dangers of fallout from bomb tests. Established pacifist organizations lent their resources to a cause they had advocated for years. The campaign burgeoned between 1958 and 1960. Its educational program was dramatized by mass

Easter demonstrations, comparable to the British Aldermasten marches which began in 1958. When progress was interrupted by the resumption of atomic testing in 1960, new protest groups were spawned, notably the Women Strike for Peace. Despite division and sharp controversy within SANE, and although its national policy vacillated, the campaign continued and was credited with having helped to bring about the treaty ratified in September, 1962.

By that time, however, SANE had broadened its policy emphasis to challenge the military terms of the Cold War, and it had begun to develop a politically oriented coalition. It was an agency of the broad shift of opinion among internationalists who, uneasy with the fallout from the Cold War, became ever more skeptical about foreign policy. By 1965 SANE had joined the opposition to President Johnson's escalation of military involvement in Vietnam. Less than two years later, it participated in a broad coalition largely initiated by the peace movement to force the President out of the election of 1968.

Meanwhile, non-violent activists and radical dissenters were brought together in the politics of confrontation, through the Committee for Nonviolent Action and the civil-rights movement. The CNVA was composed of a small band of pacifists who challenged the nuclear arms race directly: climbing fences into restricted military reservations, picketing biological-warfare centers, swimming out to Polaris missile submarines, trying to sail into atomic-testing zones, and demonstrating from San Francisco to Moscow and from Quebec to Guantanamo. These were precursors of larger confrontations in opposition to the Indochina war —draft-card burning, draft-file destruction, mass physical demonstrations.

Pacifists also found an expanding base of activity in the cause of civil rights, with its bold exploration of non-violent action and its commitment to fundamental social redemption. A few of them had been involved before, of course; and they helped Martin Luther King, Jr., in Montgomery, Alabama, in 1956. FOR and CORE provided leaderhip and support in the wake of student sit-ins. Students especially learned non-violent action techniques as they joined the civil-rights movement early in the 1960's.

By the middle of the decade, however, many students and others who had been enlisted as activists through civil rights (or who regretted missing the opportunity) fed into antiwar and youth movements as the Indochina war escalated American consciousness. Students for a Democratic Society, influenced by their experiences in civil-rights and community organization, discovered the moral issue and political potential of the war, and sponsored large demonstrations and teach-ins in 1965. King's own Southern Christian Leadership Conference provided antiwar leadership, and the holder of a Nobel Prize for Peace made an eloquent indictment of the war.

By the time of A. J. Muste's death in 1967, some leaders in FOR and the Peace Education Section of the Friends Service Committee were prepared to join the War Registers League, CORE, and representative groups in the student Left in a broad coalition that launched the Spring Mobilization to End the War. FOR especially began to put Americans in touch with South Vietnamese opponents of the war, and older pacifist groups cooperated with new ones in organized draft resistance (a story recounted by Michael Ferber and Staughton Lynd in *The Resistance,* 1971). By that time, too, there was a major shift in liberal thinking about limited warfare and Vietnam. Journals such as *Christianity and Crisis* and *The Christian Century* reflected opposition to national policy, as did increasing numbers of intellectuals. Clergy and laymen were mobilized into an antiwar group. Political figures, including especially Robert Kennedy and Eugene McCarthy, sensed a shift in public opinion. By 1968 there was a popular base broad enough to support a political movement in opposition to involvement in the war.

This is all the more significant when one considers the enormous access to public opinion available to the government, the duplicity of officials in successive Administrations (reflected in the Pentagon Papers), and covert attempts to divide the movement or to discredit it in the courts. The antiwar movement was not altogether isolated from government, however, as some of its radical members fancied. It provided agencies through which disparate political opposition was rallied, notably in the Democratic Party. And, as Townshend Hoopes has shown in *The Limits of Intervention* (1969), it provided political leverage to those in the State Department and the Department of Defense who were seeking policy alternatives. Not only the public but even the government was divided in its assessment of Indochina policy.

There is no question of the expansion of antiwar activity in the United States at the close of the decade, nor of the evolution of public consensus to reduce American military involvement in Vietnam to a non-controversial minimum. Almost certainly, the continuing pressure of the peace movement accelerated this tendency.

II

What, then, makes a movement? Is the recent antiwar crusade The Movement to which its leaders often refer, or is it but the visible symbol of an idea—the notion of being on the crest of a wave of peace and justice swelling into the future? Is it perhaps a coalition of diverse organizations, the fortuitous conjunction of several historic movements?

Who belongs to a peace movement? Those persons who are against all war? Those who are members of specific groups, or who devote most of their time to the cause? Or perhaps it includes even those persons who work for a "peace candidate" like Eugene McCarthy or George

McGovern, only to disperse after the election, and those who align with antiwar groups on specific issues, only to ignore them with regard to other things.

What are the goals and assumptions underlying the various peace groups and their leaders? Are they sufficiently coherent to define a "movement" or do they differ in significant respects? Perhaps they represent a continuing ideological commitment in American history, or perhaps they are mere eddies in our social life, the passing waves of our dilemmas.

Finally, how effective are peace advocates? Has their influence altered with technological and social changes over the years? Has the role of established peace organizations changed in comparison to the spontaneous outpouring of reaction to specific policies? Perhaps, after all, the history of peace movements in America is significant both for evaluating contemporary activity, and for understanding the course of history.

Questions such as these have been voiced repeatedly with the emergence of broadly based efforts in our time, first in the 1950's to limit the spread of nuclear weapons, and then in the 1960's to curtail American involvement in Vietnam. They are questions asked by persons who have been confronted by antiwar campaigns—public officials and private citizens. They are the reflections of leaders and workers within peace groups, the introspective self-consciousness of people in constant need of reassurance that there is reason to challenge widely accepted policies.

These are the queries also of historians, who, whatever their involvement in current affairs, habitually orient themselves in time. Largely as a result of their questioning, some historians in the past decade or so have probed peace movements of the past which have been largely neglected since their narrative history was established in the 1930's—notably by Merle Curti's *Peace or War: The American Struggle* (1936), A. C. F. Beales's *History of Peace* (1931), and Devere Allen's *Fight for Peace* (1930). Contemporary scholarship is proving fruitful and, although we do not yet have a comprehensive synthesis or narrative interpretation of peace movements in America, some of its terms are becoming clear.

In the first place, it is evident that each peace or reform movement must be defined with respect to the specific issues and choices that engendered it. Opposition to America's earliest wars was so much limited to contemporaneous issues that traditionally it has not even been associated with the peace movements. Much of the activity that is labeled peace work has come in reaction to concrete problems facing society as a whole—the arms race and imperialism at the turn of the century, for example, the European war of 1914, the breakdown of international order and rise of totalitarianism in the 1930's, or the introduction of nuclear arms. War and injustice have presented unique challenges to each generation of peace advocates; indeed, leaders in each case have differed among themselves in assessing massive social crises. Consequently, the response of each peace movement has been distinctive both with regard to policy issues and with respect to the kind of society within which it has operated. The very impulse to become involved in social change precludes isolation from the distributions of power and assumptions which in large measure determine a society and its problems. Peace movements are conditioned by the very crises to which they respond.

Secondly, social-reform groups must be understood in relation to the political processes of which they are a part. A peace movement is composed of at least its workers. The membership of each group is a constituency united by a distinctive point of view (such as pacifism or world government) together with either social characteristics (being Christians, Socialists, or women) or functional programs (dramatizing issues, lobbying, or educating). Each group identifies its own program with the true national interest, and so each one cultivates the support of particular segments of public opinion. They all enlist in their movement people who are interested in it only tangentially, only at the point of some particular issue. In this way an antiwar constituency may attract publics with inconsistent interests, much as opposition to World War I aligned socialists with some moderate liberals, as the position of strict neutrality in the 1930's attracted both isolationists and pacifists, and as people repudiated the Vietnam war from both economic considerations and moral conviction.

In their effort to attract public support, peace and reform groups necessarily form coalitions. Their coalition organizations vie with pro-war groups or with the government itself to influence the public. But because the peace groups do not have identical constituencies, they themselves form a series of publics—segments of potential support— with regard to any given policy. It is necessary to win the antiwar constituencies to a point of view or a political tactic in order to even approach the general public. The more ambitious the movement is for political influence, the more it is dependent upon effective political coalition.

The supportive relationship between the constituencies and publics of coordinating agencies is thus circular. Peace groups cooperate to the extent that a coalition offers access to the general public. And specific publics—civic and interest groups, or ideological groupings such as the New Left—affiliate with a coalition to the extent that it appears to have broad access to the resources of peace-oriented constituencies. Loss of support from these public affiliates, lack of cooperation among the peace groups, or a restricted definition of the public interest served can break the circle.

What is more, coalitions of reform groups are very tenuous. The more publics and the larger resources they can command, the more difficult it becomes to satisfy the restricted tenets and program demands of constituent groups. Always the larger public threatens the narrower constituencies. Such relationships as these have operated most clearly when peace movements have been most explicitly political in program —in the 1930's and 1960's, for example. But to some extent, all peace societies may be understood through the relationship of their constituencies to their publics.

Something like this process seems to have operated in the brief but spectacular coalitions known as the New Mobilization and the Moratorium. The "Mobe" discovered the basis of coalition in opposition to the Vietnam war when it organized massive marches in New York and San Francisco on April 15, 1967. Originally called the Spring Mobilization to End the War in Vietnam, it was a loose coalition of groups whose very eclectic breadth seemed threatening to cautious liberals in the antiwar movement. Nonetheless, thousands of people of all ages and political persuasions invested themselves in activity to bank the fires of military involvement in the months after the marches. Pressures within American society fed the movement, notably black politics and student indignation; and political repression accelerated the New Left thrust, with its politics of confrontation. Frustrated by its failure to capture the Democratic Party for Eugene McCarthy or explicit repudiation of the war, and angered by political persecutions— the Chicago 8, the Black Panthers—the Left gradually found a new basis for coalition in the first year of the Nixon Administration. By the late summer of 1969, it had reformed as the New Mobilization Committee.

Meanwhile, that summer another coalition was taking shape, based largely upon the conjunction of political elements that had been involved in the Kennedy-McCarthy campaigns and established peace groups such as SANE. This was the Moratorium, whose tactic involved a kind of popular strike against business-as-usual for one day in October, to expand in duration each month as long as the war continued. This was a form of consensus politics, the creation of an expanding base of popular awareness and opposition, to exert pressure through normal political channels. The October program generated unexpected support and gave the Moratorium expanded access to the public.

At this point it was a largely self-contained organization. Decisions were made by four coordinators and were based largely upon their calculation of what tactics would win endorsement within the peace movement without alienating political support. In short, the Moratorium promised the organized peace movement access to the public and offered political doves the institutional resources of antiwar groups. Confident that they could build an expanding circle of influence, the leaders planned for nationwide programs in November.

They faced a critical choice of tactics, however, because the New

Mobe called for mass marches in Washington, D.C., and San Francisco at the same time as the Moratorium program. Now a political coalition based on political consensus-forming was faced with the possibility of a major confrontation that might erupt in violence. In that event the Moratorium would lose a large measure of the political credibility it was trying to give the antiwar position. On the other hand, if Moratorium leaders repudiated the March, they would lose the support of the left wing of the antiwar movement and, probably, that of some of the established peace groups which were working with all opponents of the war. The tension was all but intolerable. Two of the coordinators accepted posts on the Mobe executive committee and won votes on the March steering committee for the Moratorium; and at length a decision was reached to cooperate with the March in the expectation of averting either fiasco or violence.

Between 250,000 and 500,000 war protesters marched in Washington on November 15, 1969. Millions watched what appeared to be a cohesive coalition, little knowing that the platform and speakers policy had been determined through frantic negotiation between staffs of organizations which were at the same time cooperating to gain access to the public and competing for constituents within the antiwar movement. The hundreds of thousands of people who flocked to the capital knew nothing of this, of course; but the Administration almost certainly did. Pathetically, it disparaged the greatest outpouring of antiwar sentiment in the nation's history.

The March exhausted the financial resources of the Moratorium, which had provided logistical support, and disrupted the pattern of nationwide local organization. It sapped the precious store of personal amity in its leadership. Already in January, 1970, it was clear that up-coming political campaigns would attract financial backing hitherto available to the committee, and increasingly the staff became active in multi-issue politics. The coalition dissolved formally in April. Although the Cambodian incursion occasioned a brief flurry of activity, mainly initiated by the Mobe, and resulted in senseless deaths at Kent State and Jackson, Mississippi, the movement remained largely dispersed.

What happened to the Moratorium? It suffered the loss of public support from community-oriented groups and from political figures. It suffered from competition among peace groups, and from the rivalry of another coalition with fundamentally alternative tactics. And it suffered from a restricted definition of the public interest served: in place of a national exploration of the complex process of reversing the war policy, the movement succumbed to whatever slogans were broad and general enough to command temporary coalitions. "Stop the Bombing" and "Immediate Withdrawal of Troops" were two such slogans. Under their banner the antiwar movement created large demonstrations and extensive debate on the war from 1965 to 1970. The State Department was forced to abandon its original slogan of simple "aggression from the north." The public began to see the complexity of the war, the impossibility of American military victory, and the tragic cost of persistence. That itself was an impressive achievement— an essential one. But the substitution of one slogan for another was no basis for a continuing coalition when the public began to change its understanding of national interest. As important as it may have been in changing the terms of foreign policy, the politics of coalition had not organized a vision of peace much beyond the curtailment of American involvement in a specific war. The need for peace movements beyond coalitions is obvious: it is their role to translate immediate issues into long-range alternatives, relentlessly assessing political decisions in terms of the values they imply.

This leads us to a third dimension of peace movements in history; for they must be understood in relation to their values and assumptions. They have had continuity beyond spontaneous antiwar campaigns because they have reaffirmed certain values and ideas in different historical contexts.

The very word "peace" has become the subject of searching analysis. Historians and activists alike are trying to replace its negative connotation as the absence of war with a constructive concept—something like: the process of changing the social and international order without violence or arbitrary authority. It has become increasingly apparent, too, that the word "internationalism," with which "peace" so often is associated, needs a great deal of refinement if it is to be a useful tool of analysis. It is a word that, like "nationalism" or "isolationism," has been a counterpane for all sorts of idealistic bedfellows. It is a sort of synonym for the "higher good" to which men might aspire; but it does not express the conceptions of reality upon which their values rest.

The notion of internationalism is explored in the symposium with which this volume concludes, "Internationalism as a Current in the Peace Movement." Probably the spate of histories of the peace and antiwar movements has called attention to the problem of defining this term, if for no other reason than that it causes problems of interpretation. Doubtless, too, the re-evalution of Cold War assumptions has led to reassessment; the internationalism of this period looks increasingly like an extension of collective security.

Following the terminology of German sociologist Ferdinand Tönnies, Sondra Herman has identified two conceptual approaches to world order: those of the "political internationalists" and those of the "community internationalists." Another useful way of making the same distinction, and one with increasing currency among political and social scientists, is to identify internationalists and transnationalists. Most simply, then, internationalists are those for whom the basic unit of reality in international relations is still the nation-state with its existing institutions (including those through which it relates to other nations); and they are realistic in their assessment of political possibilities. Transnationalists are those for whom the basic unit of reality and the ultimate test of policy in international relations is the world (whether conceived of as the mystical body of Christ, or as humanity, or the proletariat, or, ecologically, as a set of interrelated socio-economic systems).

This is but a working definition—one that needs further refinement and testing, and one that may be rejected. But it has the merit of identifying a difference of premises underlying the competing strategies of peace movements as described throughout this volume. The definition is consistent, too, with Manfred Jonas' rejection of the idea that unilateralism is exclusively an isolationist premise. It suggests also what is distinctive about Kenneth Boulding's world view, as described by Cynthia Kerman; for he bases his transnationalism upon a systematic assessment of socio-economic institutions.

That appears to be the characteristic which distinguishes the contemporary movement for peace education from traditional international relations, as discussed by Michael Washburn. Indeed, the confusion in peace education that he describes makes sense in these terms: the contemporary movement derives both from a transnational, largely humanitarian revulsion to the specific war in Vietnam and from a systems-analysis approach to conflict resolution (both of which came to fruition in the 1960's); but it tends to build its curriculum upon the older structure of existing college curricula and training of faculties, which was internationalist in the traditional sense. Thus, whether or not the distinction between transnationalist and internationalist premises involves a true and comprehensive definition of terms, it seems to have utility in evaluating the essays in this book. The application of such a distinction will not prevent conflicting interpretations of internationalism, but it might make the usage less arbitrary. In any case, peace movements must be distinguished in terms of values and assumptions which frequently are only implied.

Fourth, and finally, the significance of peace movements must be measured against the very standards of the historian. There is a contemporary questioning of liberal political processes, for example, that is illustrated with reference to foreign policy in the revisionist histories of the Cold War. These histories reflect a critical interpretation of previous American foreign policy and of domestic liberal institutions, as Norman Wilensky observes in "Was the Cold War Necessary?" In particular, they challenge the long-prevailing consensus of opinion that the underpinning of American foreign policy should be a determination to oppose the expansion of the Communist bloc everywhere. But this challenge to policy leads, in turn, to a challenge to consensus itself, with its assumption that the most meaningful narrative thread of American history has been the formation and reformation of a shifting majority viewpoint.

Such is the accepted test of historical significance: the cause-and-effect relationship of events is biased in favor of the effect. What is normative in ascribing historical importance is that which happened. To this is added the historiographic bias of American historians that what has happened, over the years, is the growth of an ever more complex, pluralistic, and democratic society. However, from the newly revisionist perspective (as always from Marxist and ethnic ones), the essential narrative thread of American history has been the dissenting challenges that have moved, or indeed failed to move, our society off dead center in the interests of justice and peace. From the same point of view, some historians have stressed the institutional weight of those aspects of our society that proscribe movement from the center.

Now, in some measure these are complementary perspectives, matters of relative emphasis. But the priorities of each have led not only to differences in attention but also to conflicts in value. For many historians the mainstream of events is not only the center of attention, but also has a central value: whatever was, somehow was right. From this point of view our wars have always been understandable, if not entirely justified, and opposition to them is interesting but not historically significant. For revisionists, on the other hand, dissent has not only been important (either in shaping events or in defining the tragic meaning of events it failed to shape), but it has also carried values unfulfilled. For liberals the process of consensus-formation not only is characteristic of American society, but must be protected; for radicals the institutions of public consensus must be challenged because they threaten movement by crushing dissenting interests and opinions.

These relative perspectives constitute a frame of reference which is explicit in relation to Cold War historiography and implicit in several other essays in this volume. Even the contemporary movement for peace research and education reflects them. Indeed, the credibility of peace education itself, as interpreted by Michael Washburn, depends upon the resolution of these alternative viewpoints on political action:

> The credibility of the peace approaches [to education] does not depend on their ability to develop right now an obviously workable and comprehensive solution to the world's problems. Peace educators must demonstrate, however, that they recognize the full scope of the problem. . . . Peace educators show very few signs of becoming responsive to the setting within which political action is being and will be taken.

It is just this setting that is explored in these essays on historic peace movements. Clearly, the politics of peace involve the relationship of the organized antiwar movement and public decision-making. This relationship is the setting for political· action; and understanding it will help to clarify the relationship of dissent and consensus in American political institutions. As clearly, the advocates of peace espouse values and visions in their dissent. These are essential reference points for the historian and the activist alike.

In any case, the essays in this volume open new vistas in the history of America and its peace movements. Perry Gianakos' article on Ernest Crosby should be followed by broad studies of war literature both as it has reflected our culture and as it has interacted with events to affect our history. Social psychology can be used to study leaders and organizations for and against war, much as it has been applied to student protest in the 1960's. Suggestions about the apolitical bases of some forms of protest activity made by Sondra Herman and David Patterson (and more recently by Michael Lutzker) can be systematized and evaluated. Institutional analysis can be used to identify more precisely the mechanisms governing the internal politics of protest and the relative effectiveness of various forms of pressure on public policy. Quantitative studies might yield a more reliable index of historic attitudes on war-and-peace issues than we have now. War as portrayed in visual art and the film—the fictional movie, the newsreel, television— offers a virtually untapped approach to American culture.

Perhaps more important than all the specific studies put together, the subject of war and peace offers the study of American society that breadth of outlook that it so desperately needs if it is to overcome its parochial bias. In part this means comparative studies, such as that of Blanche Wiesen Cook. Even more to the point, it implies making value judgments and viewing American culture in terms of its origins in and its impact on world civilization; for the United States and the world share a common past and future.

What happens to a culture that for an extended period of time straddles commitments to peace and war? That question is raised on the frontispiece of this volume, with its cartoon depicting a harassed Uncle Sam trying to ride both a war horse and a dove of peace. Charles Barker has recently called attention to the same dilemma: the conflicts and tensions inherent in valuing both "multilateralism," a notion through which he combines "our federalism at home and our belief in a rational equilibrium of power around the globe," and "unilateralism," by which he refers to the aggressive expansion of our national influence (in his introduction to *Power and Law: American Dilemma in World Affairs*, 1971). Phrased this way, and interpreted in the light of these essays, dilemma characterizes American peace movements as well as national policy. What happens to reform movements that for an extended period of time straddle commitments to both world community and unilateral nationalism, develop strategies of both majority decision-making and minority dissent? The dilemmas of the peace groups are those of the society, and the study of each contributes to our understanding of the other. The United States and its antiwar protest movements hold the past and the future in common trust.

CHARLES CHATFIELD

Wittenberg University
November 1972

Ernest Howard Crosby: A Forgotten Tolstoyan Antimilitarist and Anti-imperialist[1]

Perry E. Gianakos

I

When Ernest Howard Crosby died in 1907, he was eulogized in a memorial service at Cooper Union by the many friends he had made during his career as a reformer in New York City. Among the organizations sponsoring the service were The Social Welfare Club of New York, The Manhattan Single Tax Club, the Society for Italian Immigrants, the Central Federated Labor Union of New York, The Filipino Progress Association, the Anti-Imperialist League

> These are great days, Colonel Jinks . . . . Great Days, indeed, for foreign missions. What would St. John have said on the island of Patmos if he could have cabled for half-a-dozen armies and half-a-dozen fleets, and got them too? He would have made short work of his jailers. As he looks down upon us to-night, how his soul must rejoice! The Master told us to go into all nations, and we are going to go if it takes a million troops to send us and keep us there.
>
> Ernest Howard Crosby,
> *Captain Jinks, Hero*
> (1902), 270-271

and others, some twenty in all.[2] This was quite a tribute for a man who had been engaged in reform for only about ten years. But then Crosby's reforming career, short though it was, was highly unusual.

Born into a patrician New York family in 1856—his father was the popular pastor of the 4th Avenue Presbyterian Church of New York and himself something of a reformer—he was educated in New York City at New York University and Columbia Law School, graduating in 1878. After a brief career as a practicing lawyer, he was elected to the New York Legislature in 1887 as the successor of his friend, Theodore Roosevelt. Two years later he was nominated by President Harrison to sit as a judge on the International Court in Alexandria, Egypt, which nomination was later confirmed by the Khedive. Although this was a lifetime appointment, Crosby remained in Egypt for only four years. Doubtless his work as a judge in the Egyptian Court, which involved the adjudication of disputes between foreigners within the country and between foreigners and natives, readied him for his later career at home; for during these four years he had become keenly aware of the economic injustice and exploitation so blatantly displayed in Egypt by the European powers.[3] But it was another event which precipitated his resignation and return to New York.

Through chance there came into his hands a copy of Count Leo Tolstoy's little book *Life*. Crosby was profoundly impressed:

> For some reason it took hold of me with a strange power. . . . the simple teaching that it is man's higher nature to love—that if he would only let himself love and renounce his selfish aims, he would enter a wider sphere, find his immortal soul, and in fact be born again—all this struck me as a great new discovery. I leaned back in my study chair; I tried to love, and—could I believe my own sensations?—I did actually feel that I had risen to a loftier plane, and that there was something immortal within me. . . . Nor was the change merely temporary, for since that day the world has never looked to me quite as it used to.[4]

Converted to the Tolstoyan philosophy of love, Crosby resigned his post and prepared to return to America. Before returning to New York, however, he determined to journey to Russia to visit Tolstoy. Crosby was known to Countess Tolstoy as a result of his humanitarian acts during the Russian famine of 1892. And so it was through her that he arranged a meeting with her famous husband. After visiting the Countess in Moscow, Crosby then journeyed south to the Tolstoy estate at Toula, where he spent two fruitful days with the Count.[5] The original impact on Crosby of Tolstoy's ideas was greatly reenforced during this visit, for from the evidence of his subsequent writings Crosby was never to forget his brief stay at Yasnaia Poliana. Tolstoy was equally impressed with the young American, as is indicated by the extensive correspondence, which continued until Crosby's death in 1907.[6] In fact, Crosby became Tolstoy's chief defender in America, speaking and writing frequently on behalf of him and his ideas.[7] Upon his return to America, then, Crosby was, as B. O. Flower notes, "imbued as never before with the religion of humanity. Henceforth he could not be other than a democrat . . . and a lover of all his fellowmen."[8]

Taking Tolstoy's advice, Crosby sought out the man whom the Russian reformer had described as "the greatest living American," Henry George, and became an ardent advocate of the single tax. Following the Tolstoyan philosophy of doing service to others, he involved himself in a number of reform movements: the child labor question, settlement work among immigrants, the labor question and industrial arbitration, and civil liberties (writing in defense of aliens arbitrarily detained for alleged anarchist beliefs). For his involvement in these activities Crosby paid a heavy price, since many of his former friends now regarded him as a "traitor to his class."[9] When the war with Spain came in 1898, he based his opposition to militarism and imperialism on the Tolstoyan doctrine of "non-resistance." It is this part of his career which holds the greatest interest for us today.

Crosby's antimilitarist and anti-imperialist writings—consisting of a number of published speeches and letters, essays, columns, three volumes of poetry and one novel—have received consideration in only one historical monograph on anti-imperialism, Fred H. Harrington's essay on "The Literary Aspects of Anti-Imperialism," which appeared in *The New England Quarterly* for 1937. Harrington acknowledges Crosby as the most "prolific" of the anti-imperialist poets and devotes one paragraph to a description of his novel.[10] In part, the neglect of Crosby's writings resulted from the fact that his caustic wit and Tolstoyan views were not representative of the anti-imperialist movement. In part, the neglect can also be traced to the general failure of the anti-imperialist movement itself, which, although it attracted the support of significant elements of the intellectual community, elicited little response from the masses. Though president during his lifetime of the Anti-Imperialist League of New York, Crosby never commanded the kind of attention given to such national figures as ex-Presidents Harrison and Cleveland, Mark Twain, William James, Carl Schurz, Andrew Carnegie and others. Except for short, appreciative works published at the time of his death, Crosby's public life remains unexamined.[11] But aside from William Dean Howells, Crosby was undoubtedly the most prominent of the American disciples of Tolstoy to oppose the war with Spain to free Cuba and the decision to retain the Philippine Islands. When his full career is assessed, he will undoubtedly rank among the most eminent of those Americans who devoted their energies to peace.

A preliminary review of his work seems especially appropriate at this time, since American society is passing through a cultural crisis much like that following the outbreak of the Spanish-American War, which also saw the initiation of the imperialist episode in this country.[12] The similarity between the two periods is most apparent, of course, in the protest movement that in Crosby's day was also directed against overseas involvement. Although dissent then was not nearly so effective nor so widespread as that of the present day, still, much of what Crosby had to say about war, militarism and imperialism has a topicality that is striking now. Consider this poem, published in 1902, one of a series entitled "War and Hell":

3

> Who are you at Washington who presume to declare me
> the enemy of anybody or to declare any nation my
> enemy?
> However great you may be, I altogether deny your author-
> ity to sow enmity and hatred in my soul.
> I refuse to accept your ready-made enemies, and, if I did
> accept them, I should feel bound to love them, and,
> loving them, would you have me caress them with
> bombshells and bayonets?
> When I want enemies, I reserve the right to manufacture
> them for myself.
> If I am ever scoundrel enough to wish to kill, I will do my
> own killing on my own account and not hide myself
> behind your license.
> Before God your commissions and warrants and enlistment
> rolls, relieving men of conscience and independence and
> manhood, are not worth the paper they are written on.
> Away with all your superstitions of a statecraft worse than
> priestcraft!
> Hypnotize fools and cowards if you will, but for my part,
> I choose to be a man.[13]

Substitute a few earthy Anglo-Saxonisms for some of Crosby's more gentlemanly words and the poem could very well pass for a contemporary production. But the sentiments expressed in this poem—familiar to us today—pervade Crosby's work, which suggests that arguments against war and militarism are universal and timeless. Crosby had lived through the Civil War (although he was a child of six at its beginning), the Spanish-American War, the Boer War, the Filipino Insurrection (the proper designation of which should be the Philippine-American War) and the Boxer Rebellion, in all but one of which American troops were involved. These wars and military engagements, their rationales and the behavior of the military became the subject matter of his poetry, his essays, speeches, columns and letters and his one novel, *Captain Jinks, Hero* (1902).

Crosby's novel is the best of the anti-imperialist and antimilitarist novels published during the expansionist period and is still effective as an antiwar document.[14] Since Crosby incorporated in it many of the ideas found in his poetry, essays and speeches, and since the novel is the most sustained prose expression of his views, it provides a useful vehicle for an examination of those of his ideas having contemporary significance. Although not always successful as a satire, the novel makes clever use of contemporary events to indict the militarist and imperialist sentiments supporting the expansionist program, not only in America but also in Great Britain and Germany. And since the novel is about an ostensible "hero," Crosby also makes brilliant satiric use of the highly publicized exploits of the so-called "heroes" produced by the war.

A year before its publication Crosby had attacked support for the war and imperialism in a speech in Boston entitled "The Absurdities of

Militarism," which was subsequently published by the American Peace Society. After General Funston had captured Aguinaldo, the Filipino patriot leader, by employing some highly questionable tactics, Crosby contributed an indignant essay entitled "The Military idea of Manliness,"[15] in which he attacked what appeared to be a new notion of military honor. It was this same incident which later provoked Mark Twain's explosive outburst "In Defence of General Funston," wherein he scathingly denounced both Funston and American imperialism.[16] In that Boston speech and in a later poem Crosby had called for a new Cervantes to "prick this bubble of militarism" and "make the profession of war impossible by opening our eyes to the irresistible comicality of it."[17] He suggested that perhaps Mr. Dooley or Mark Twain might do the job:

> Will not one of these gentlemen, or some other genius yet to be discovered, turn his winged shafts squarely against war and the war-maker? When another Cervantes shall have decked out another soldier Don Quixote in his true colors,—when he shall have laid bare the childishness of the paint and tinsel that have so long held us under their spell,—then indeed the twentieth century will be able to boast of a greater start in literature than has yet appeared, and bold indeed will be the "hero" who will thereafter select war as a career. Such a book would ring down the curtain upon the profession of the soldier.[18]

Doubtless Crosby was also reacting to the continuing flood of romantic war stories and novels (and military memoirs) that started in 1898 and continued well through the turn of the century. In varying degrees, most of the popular fiction (including nickel and dime novels) reflected the influence of Theodore Roosevelt's idea of the "strenuous life" and/or Kipling's notion of "The White Man's Burden." War was a noble endeavor and required all the "manly" attributes. Consequently, if one could meet the test (i.e., prove himself a man) he would return home covered with "glory." (This word occurs repeatedly in the fiction of the Spanish-American War.) Realist Stephen Crane, unreservedly the best of the American writers to cover the Cuban phase of the war, was atypical in that he dwelt on its inglorious aspects.[19] Consequently, it was writers like Richard Harding Davis who captured the public's imagination, since their dispatches and stories most completely mirrored the public's romantic view of the war.[20] William Dean Howells' short story "Editha," published some years after the events, vividly portrays and bitterly indicts this romantic view of war as exhibited by American women of the period.[21]

Since neither Twain nor Finley Peter Dunne, the creator of "Mr. Dooley," chose to take up Crosby's earlier suggestion to expose war and the new heroism along the lines he had suggested, and since the fiction writers of the period continued to celebrate the continuing

American war effort in the Philippines, Crosby decided to attempt the job himself. *Captain Jinks, Hero* was the result.

II

Following Cervantes' famous model, Crosby loosely shaped his novel into the picaresque form.[22] It most closely resembles Cervantes' work in that, as the title indicates, it satirizes the idea of the hero. But while Cervantes and readers of his novel are sympathetic toward Don Quixote and Sancho Panza, the same cannot be said about Crosby's characters. Nor can one say that Cervantes' satire of an outmoded chivalry reaches the level of violence that Crosby depicts in *Captain Jinks, Hero*. But, then, the object of Crosby's satire was an infinitely greater evil. And although Crosby appreciated the comic in the classic Spanish model and had originally called for an exposé of the "comicality" of the profession of war and the modern soldier, his depiction of them in *Captain Jinks, Hero* is grim and sobering. For although the reader can laugh at the absurdities and pomposities of Jinks and his fellow officers, he cannot escape the blood, the cruelty and the destruction that followed in their wake. Herein lies the source of Crosby's biting wit and withering sarcasm, brilliantly combined in a satiric style that stands on their heads all the conventional pieties mouthed by the expansionists. And herein, finally, must lie the power of the novel, for Crosby gives the lie to the romantic and arrogant nonsense that somehow invariably American soldiers and political leaders are exceptions to the general rule applicable to countries that go to war.

Crosby also employs the characteristic picaresque device of telling a story through a series of adventures. From Sam Jinks's childhood, when he acquires his lifelong ambition to become a "hero," Crosby takes him to "East Point," the army academy, and thence to war. The stage for Sam's military adventures is ingeniously set: American intervention in Cuba and the attempt to subjugate the Philippines, followed by American participation in the Boxer Rebellion, are merged into the story of Jinks's search for "glory" in an American campaign to subdue the island nation of the "Cubapines." The last part of the novel depicts Sam's activities in "Porsslania" [China] and his eventual triumphant return to America as a "hero." In all his military exploits, Jinks is accompanied by his trusty companion (another picaresque convention) whose function it is to publicize his hero's deeds. But where Cleary, the companion, evolves from a hawk into a dove (or perhaps a wise owl) during the course of the novel, Jinks remains a committed hawk almost to the very end, when he winds up as something considerably less than a bird of prey.

The novel opens with an amusing and revealing incident, for in linking militarism to the idea of a saving mission Crosby reveals that his anti-imperialist views are inextricably linked to his Tolstoyan views against militarism. Young Sam Jinks is introduced to the idea of militarism and the concept of the "hero" through a gift of some lead soldiers from his father. Determined as a consequence now to become a "hero," young Sam joins the "John Wesley Boys' Brigade" (what Crosby called "militarism in the flesh"), whose marching song, with words adapted by the local Methodist pastor, is sung to the tune of "Onward, Christian Soldiers":

> "Onward, Christian soldiers
> 'Gainst the heathen crew!
> In the name of Jesus
> Let us run them through." (p. 12)

This is the first of several attacks on organized religion's complicity in war and imperialism.[23]

To those anti-imperialists who suggested that America should "haul down the flag" and give the Filipinos independence, the expansionists responded that once the American flag had been raised it should never be lowered. Crosby attacked this expansionist posture in the novel by linking blind patriotism to some dubious benefits of American civilization—prostitution and veneral disease. Sam Jinks, now a Captain in the Army, and his friend Cleary have arrived in "Havilla," the capital city of the "Cubapines," and are being shown around the town by a fellow officer. Sam inquires about a building which has just come into view:

> "What building is that . . . with our flag over it and the nicely dressed young women in the windows?"
> "That?" said Foster, laughing; "Oh, that's the Young Ladies Home. We have to license the place. It's the only way to keep the army in condition. Why, we've got about fifty per cent infected now."
> "Really?" cried Sam. "How our poor fellows are called upon to suffer for these ungrateful Cubapinos! Still they can feel that they are suffering for their country, too. That's a consolation."
> "There's more consolation than that," said Foster, "for we're spreading the thing like wildfire among the natives. We'll come out ahead."
> "I wish, tho, that they wouldn't fly Old Gory [sic] over the house," said Sam.
> "There was some talk of taking it down, but you see it's the policy of the Administration never to haul down the flag when it has once been raised. It presents rather a problem, you see."

Sam, the blind patriot, refusing to see the hypocrisy of the American mission or the absurdity of the slogan, consoles himself by suggesting that "It may wear out in time . . . altho it looks painfully new." (pp. 140-141)

Later Sam and Cleary encounter the white commanding officer of a Negro regiment. Sam is curious about the fighting quality of the Negro soldier and discovers from the colonel that they make much better soldiers than white men. And how does the colonel account for this fact, Sam wants to know.

> Well, they're more impressible, for one thing. You can work them up into any kind of passion you want to. Then they're more submissive to discipline; they're used to being ordered about and kicked and cuffed, and they don't mind it. Besides, they're accustomed from their low social position to be subordinate to superiors, and rather expect it than not. They are all poor, too, and used to poor food and ragged clothes and no comforts, and of course they don't complain of what they get from us. (pp. 190-191)

The colonel's explanation is a damning illustration of the white American's inhumanity to Negroes. To Crosby, a disciple of Tolstoy, it is also damning proof of what militarism does to human beings.

The public relations aspect of heroism and yellow journalism are also satirized. Early in the novel, both Sam and his friend Cleary resign from the "Point" so they can get into the war, Sam as a Captain of Volunteers, and Cleary as a newspaper correspondent for the *Daily Lyre,* a yellow journal that is said to be "largely responsible for the war." The editor plans to publicize Sam's exploits and make him a public hero. But, Sam asks: "Why do you select me instead of one of the great generals at the front?"

> Why, don't you see? . . . The people are half tired of the names of the generals already. They want some new name. It's our business to provide them. Then all the other newspapers are on the track of the generals. We must have a little hero of our own. When General Laughter [General Shafter] or General Notice [General Otis] do anything, all the press of the country have gotten hold of them . . . . We simply can't get ahead of them, and people are beginning to think that it's not our war at all. When we begin to boom you, they'll find out that we've got a mortgage on it yet. (pp. 80-81)

Sam goes on to distinguish himself at the "Battle of San Diego," and becomes the hero he always vowed he would be. The exertions of his publicist friend, Cleary, are crucial to his success. Crosby's account of this battle is a not-too-thinly disguised satire of the exploits of his friend, Theodore Roosevelt, at the Battle of San Juan Hill. While it is the longest of those accounts in the novel that have some basis in the actual events surrounding the actual "heroes" of the actual war, it differs sufficiently in detail from Roosevelt's exploits to allow the President some anonymity.[24]

Sam's greatest exploit is his capture of the rebel leader "Gomaldo." And here Crosby's novelistic account follows the Funston episode as he had outlined it in his earlier essay "The Military Idea of Manliness":

The facts of the [Funston] case are briefly these: Funston came into possession of a letter from Aguinaldo ordering 400 men to be sent to him as reinforcements. He forged,—or caused to be forged,—an answer to this in the name of the insurgent general, Lacuna, imitating his signature and making use of his seal, which he had found. In this letter he informed Aguinaldo that pursuant to his orders, he, Lucuna, was sending him his best company. Funston then organized his expedition, composed of 78 Macabebes, of whom 20 wore insurgent uniforms and the rest were dressed as workmen. General Funston, four American officers and four ex-insurgent officers accompanied the expedition . . . the native officers announcing that they had captured the Americans and were taking them as prisoners to Aguinaldo . . . after seven days' march [they] were so enfeebled by hunger that they had to send to Aguinaldo's camp for food, which was promptly furnished them, the Filipino general giving special orders that the American prisoners should be kindly treated. When they reached Aguinaldo's headquarters . . . the Macabebes were ordered to open fire on the Filipino bodyguard, . . . Aguinaldo meanwhile was seized by one of the ex-insurgent officers and made a prisoner. General Funston took command as soon as the firing began, and assisted personally in capturing Aguinaldo. The question upon this statement of facts is whether General Funston's conduct throughout was manly and creditable.

It was Funston's treachery against the man who had supplied him with food that so outraged Mark Twain in "A Defence of General Funston." Crosby develops the incident in his novel to make the same indictment. After a struggle, during which "Gomaldo" has been captured, Sam regretfully notes that the young rebel lieutenant who had brought him food has been killed. Upon the group's return to "Havilla" with their prisoners, Sam is again hailed as a hero. To his friend, Cleary, who rushes to congratulate him, Sam says: "Is it really a great and noble act? I suppose it is, for everybody says so, but somehow it has left a bad taste in my mouth." (pp. 248-249)

The pseudo-Christian missionaries in Porsslania [China] are scathingly satirized when Crosby moves the story to that embattled country. Ostensibly the Great Powers have intervened in order to relieve the beseiged missionaries, and since, as Crosby puts it, the government in "Whoppington" felt that "it was necessary to make as good a showing in Porsslania as the other Powers," Sam, now Colonel Sam Jinks, is put in charge of a detachment and sent to represent the interests of his country. The barbaric behavior of the Great Powers is perhaps overdramatized and here perhaps Crosby's satire is flawed, but Crosby saves some of his sharpest thrusts for the missionaries. After a dinner, which includes representatives of all the allied powers, Sam is introduced to Canon Gleeb, a missionary:

"These are great days, Colonel Jinks," he said. "Great Days, indeed, for foreign missions. What would St. John have said on the island of Patmos if he could have cabled for half-a-dozen armies and half-a-dozen fleets, and got them too? He would have made short work of his jailers. As he looks down upon us to-night, how his soul must rejoice! The Master told us to go into all nations, and we are going to go if it takes a million troops to send us and keep us there." (pp. 270-271)

III

It is perhaps the dehumanizing and brutalizing aspects of militarism which excite Crosby's strongest condemnation and which most clearly reveal him as a Tolstoyan. A recent Congressional investigation into "hazing" at West Point had revealed some of the shocking details, and Crosby saw an intimate relationship between "hazing" at West Point and the behavior of the Great Powers. In 1901, he had written:

> The West Point concept of a fight, for instance, is to pick out a raw, untutored "plebe" who scarcely knows his right hand from his left, and stand him up against the best boxer in the corps, and let him take his punishment until he is knocked senseless. . . . We see in the Great Powers of the world an exemplification of the strict application of the new rule. Does any truly military nation ever tackle a nation of its size? Of course not. . . . Nations of peasants like the Boers, savages like Filipinos, may try conclusions with powers their equals or superiors in strength, but a Great Military Power? Never! They pass their time in searching the ends of the earth for little peoples to massacre and rob. . . . This is a part of the new ideal of manliness . . . .[25]

Crosby dramatizes this idea of "the new manliness" early in the novel when young Sam Jinks wins an appointment to "East Point," the army academy. Sam willingly submits to two brutal hazings—which put him in the hospital for a total of three weeks—because he is told that all the military "greats" who have preceded him at the "Point" did the same thing. Assured that Generals "German and Meriden [Sherman and Sheridan] and all the rest were hazed here," Sam tells his friend Cleary that "I wouldn't miss it for anything. It has always been done and by the greatest men, and it must be the right thing to do." (p. 24)

It is Sam's willingness to do what the military has always done which later prompts him to tell the Tutonian Emperor, when asked what he thinks of expansion, "I beg Your Majesty's pardon . . . but I do not think. I obey orders." (p. 323)

A candid evaluation of the troops of the Great Powers fighting in Porsslania is provided by Cleary, who has lost some of his awe of the military since leaving "East Point":

"Sam, it's so long since I was at East Point that I'm becoming more and more of a civilian. You army people begin to amuse me. There's always something funny about you. The Tutonians are the funniest of all. The little red-cheeked officers with their blond mustaches turned up to their eyes are too funny to live. You feel like kissing them and sending them to bed. And the airs they put on! . . . The officers jostle and brow-beat any civilian who will submit to it, and then try to get him into a duel, but I believe they're a cowardly lot at bottom. No man of real courage would bluster all over the place so." (p. 297)

Sam "admires their discipline," however, but Cleary points out that "every army is down on the others. If you believe what they say about each other they're a pretty bad lot."

Sam is furloughed home shortly after sustaining an injury, and on the night before his ship is to dock at St. Kisco, the traditional captain's banquet is held, at the end of which the martial hymns of all nations were played, ending with "Yankee Doodle." This last tune provokes laughter among the foreigners present, which displeases Sam, who storms out. On deck, he finds Cleary conversing with Chung Tu [previously identified as a Porsslanese literatus], who, when apprised of the reason for Sam's displeasure, begins a long dissertation on the essential wisdom in the song "Yankee Doodle."

"The hero came to town riding on a pony. That was a very sensible thing to do. Remember that those lines were written long before the discovery of railways or tramcars or bicycles or automobiles. . . . In riding to town on a pony, then, he was acting like a rational man. But let us read the rest of the verse:
'He stuck a feather in his cap
And called it macaroni.'
For some reason or other which is not revealed, he put a feather in his cap, and immediately he begins to act irrationally and to use language so absurd that the reading itself has become doubtful. What is the meaning of this? A man whose conduct has always been reasonable and unexceptionable, suddenly adopts the language of a lunatic. What does it mean? It is very clear to me that it is an allegory. What is the feather which he puts in his cap? It is the most conspicuous feature of the military uniform, the plume, the pompom, which marks all kinds of military dress-hats. When he speaks of his hero of having assumed the feather, he means that he has donned the uniform of a soldier. He has come to town, in other words, to enlist. Then behold the transformation! He begins at once to act irrationally. The whole epic paints in neverfading colors the disastrous effect upon the intellect of putting on soldier-clothes. . . ."[26]

Chung Tu elaborates in great detail on the absurdities of the military, but sensing the growing displeasure of his auditors, soon excuses himself:

"Pardon me, my dear sirs. Perhaps I have spoken too plainly. I mean nothing personal but when I think of these wars, I can not control my tongue. Good-night." So saying the attache gathered up his robes and went below. "Queer chap," said Sam. "He must be crazy." "We've treated them rather badly, tho," said Cleary. (pp. 344-354)

At length, Sam, now a Brigadier, lands at St. Kisco and, thanks to the press agentry of his friend Cleary, is hailed as the great "hero." Women rush to embrace him and shower him with kisses. This process is repeated in every town he visits.[27] At the same time, a popular new song sweeps the land:

> I'm Captain Jinks, of the Cubapines,
> The pink of human war-machines,
> Who teaches emperors, kings and queens,
> The way to run an army. (p. 361)

But Sam's celebrity is short-lived, for his romantic, "glory-loving" sweetheart, whom Crosby has satirized early in the novel, insists on an immediate marriage in order to stop the promiscuous kissing. This turns the public against him,[28] and Sam, broken by the shock, ends his days in an insane asylum, where he sits for hours playing with toy soldiers. "Harmless, perfectly harmless," says the keeper to Cleary, who goes to visit him. "Perfectly harmless," repeats Cleary to himself, as he gets into his carriage. "What an idea! A perfectly harmless soldier!" (p. 393)

IV

The publication of Crosby's novel did not end his attacks on militarism and imperialism, for in the same year that saw the publication of *Captain Jinks, Hero,* Crosby participated in a symposium conducted by *The Arena* in which he summarized his reasons for opposing the militarist-imperialist course of the nation.[29] All five of his reasons found expression in his novel; they coincide remarkably with some present-day critiques of American policy and clearly reflect his Tolstoyanism. *Because it is based upon physical force.* Ideas, he insists, are the real moving force in the world. Observing that the American "idea of political equality that we championed in the eighteenth century gave us for a time the right kind of leadership," he asserts that if Americans could solve the "problems of industrial democracy," we would find that the world would "follow in our train." To emphasize this relationship between ideas and leadership, he inserts an oblique reference to Theodore Roosevelt's navy mania: "to substitute a big navy for big ideas is stupid and puerile."[30] *Because expansion by force fills the world with hatred.* He finds that we have already made the Filipinos hate us as much in four years as did the Spaniards in four hundred. And no sooner did our troops enter Havana and Manila than they began calling the natives "niggers" and "monkeys." Pointing to the "two complicated race problems" we already have on our hands, which have implicated us in a "course of crime and sin," he asks if under the "pretence of uniting the world . . . are we lightly to sow the seeds of new race-hatreds [and] insure its lasting division?" *Because it is based on a false pride of race.* The American notion that they are a "chosen people," he finds, is silly and out of place in the twentieth century. Asserting that "all races have their place," he warns that the attempt to superimpose our ideas by force "must be disastrous." *Because it is steeped in cant and hypocrisy.* When one country "steals the soil from under your feet and enslaves you," while at the same time it "prates of Christianity and civilization and benevolent intentions, it turns the stomach of an honest man." While lying to the Cubans and misleading the Filipinos, he asserts, the government has conducted a war "distinguished by the most astounding cruelties," what General Miles has euphemistically called "marked severity." Yet he finds that we continue to boast of our "philanthropic work as if falsehood were bred in our bones." "Why," he asks, as he has so often asked before and will continue to ask, "Why cannot a nation behave like a gentleman?" *Because it distracts our attention and our material resources from problems that beset us at home.* He sees a fundamental contradiction in our preaching to the rest of the world while we have grave problems at home: ". . . with our slums, our lynchings, our race and labor questions—how can we decently assume the right to teach mankind." "True expansionism," he concludes, "should spring from love for neighbor and its methods would be peaceful, democratic, and transparently sincere."

Doubtless every pacifist, or non-resister in Crosby's case, has been confronted with the question of the "just war" or the "good war," as the Civil War was referred to in his day. Crosby did not shrink from the challenge, and in another of his "War and Hell" poems he answers the question and suggests that the roots of militarism and imperialism of his day are traceable to the Civil War.[31] In an essay entitled "If the South Had Been Allowed to Go," published the following year (1903), Crosby expands on the ideas expressed in this poem and suggests that slavery could have been eliminated and the Union preserved without resort to warfare.[32] Crosby's solution in this essay depends upon a continuing right of secession, but he overlooks the fact that the constitution of the Confederate States of America disallowed secession. In the concluding portion of the essay Crosby notes the consequences of the war: "the resuscitation of the spirit of war and imperialism, the laying of the foundation of the new plutocracy, and the realization that even after forty years the negro has yet to be emancipated."

In at least two subsequent articles, "Wanted, a New Patriotism" (1903) and "Militarism At Home" (1904),[33] Crosby continued his attacks on militarism. In the first, Crosby contrasts the patriotism of President Roosevelt, who upon sighting the Pacific after a trip across the country is reported to have exclaimed "What a splendid place for a big navy!" with a newer patriotism that he hoped would evolve in the land, a "new patriotism of affection and ideas, involving devotion to all that is best in our country and a determination to make her better." In the second, occasioned by the passage of the amended Militia Bill of 1904, Crosby viewed the original bill as part of a design by the War Department to build a "military empire" by "Junkerising" the state militias. Denying the need for such a centralization of military power in the War Department, he asserts that we are not only arming against ourselves (under its provisions "a Georgia regiment may be sent to put down a strike in Massachusetts"), but also "against the members of our 'set' in society—against France and Germany and Russia." Pointing to the unarmed border with Canada—"We have no navy on the Great Lakes. Why do we need one on the Atlantic?"—he asks, "if we can make a treaty with Canada to this end, why not with the other Powers?" He concludes by calling on the people to insist that the government end this military lunacy: "Let us, the people of the United States, insist on giving the world an example of national sanity, and let us beware of the complicated designs for a military empire which emanate from that storm center of military lunacy, our War Department."

In what is perhaps Crosby's last public statement on militarism (he was dead three months after its publication), he addressed a "suggestion" to the second Peace Conference called by the Tsar.[34] Pointing to the Rush-Bagot "Arrangement of 1817," which disarmed the Great Lakes and which he believed had successfully prevented armed conflict between Canada and the United States in spite of periods of ill feeling and disagreement, Crosby suggested that it might serve as a precedent for the disarming of the "Mediterranean, the Baltic, the Japan Sea," in time "the Atlantic and the Pacific"—and eventually, he hoped, "its principle could be applied to navies as a whole." By "removing, or reducing to a minimum, the instruments of strife," the treaty had eliminated the chief cause of war, and thus confirmed Victor Hugo's belief that "the chief cause of war is to be found in the armaments of nations." Consequently, Crosby urged that the American delegation carry with them this precedent of 1817, and he found it altogether fitting that Roosevelt, "the historian of the Naval War of 1812, should have a hand in applying its best lesson." Since the United States was not menaced by a mighty standing army at its doors, Crosby believed that it was, as he put it, "in a far better situation to take the initiative than any other great Power." Hoping once again that his country might serve as a model in this peaceful endeavor, Crosby's last wish was to see the American delegates "urge the extension of the principle to other international relations." The American delegates could thus take a leading part in the conference and, he concluded, "place the world under lasting obligations to them."

V

Crosby's Tolstoyan views will undoubtedly find a more widely receptive audience in America today than they did when he first expressed them. This fact is not unrelated to the American experience of the past ten years, which parallels in a remarkable manner much of that earlier American involvement about which Crosby wrote. In basing his opposition to war, militarism and imperialism on the Tolstoyan doctrine of non-resistance, Crosby was not unique, since his friend William Dean Howells also opposed war on the same grounds. Crosby was, however, the most direct, the most prolific and the most conspicuous of the public figures to be identified with Tolstoy's philosophy of non-resistance, that small minority within the anti-imperialist minority. He was unique in the wide variety of methods he employed to oppose the war and expansionism, and in that he produced the only anti-imperialist novel of merit. The satiric style that Crosby employed in *Captain Jinks, Hero* was distinctive and singularly powerful. Although Finley Peter Dunne and George Ade employed satirical styles that effectively juxtaposed American professions of altruism with contradictory actions, the effect they produced was neither so profound nor so unsettling as that produced by Crosby. That the image of the war still retains its *opera buffa* aspect is due in part to the writings of Dunne and Ade. For the impression of warfare and expansionism that emerges from their writing is a bloodless one, and in Ade's case, a passionless one. What is missing is Crosby's Tolstoyan abhorrence of war. Hence, both Dunne and Ade were tolerable to the expansionists.[35] It is not surprising, therefore, that today's reader may regard both Dunne and Ade as quaint. But the same reader may recognize in Crosby a modern mind and, consequently, a more realistic view of war. Crosby does not avoid the blood, cruelty, destruction and inhumanity we associate with war. And because he called these facts to the attention of the largely war-approving American public of his day, along with their expansionist political leaders, he was largely ignored. He should not be forgotten.

Michigan State University

notes

1. An earlier version of this paper was read at the American Studies meeting of the Michigan Academy, 1970. It has since benefited by the criticism of my colleagues Nora Landmark, Thomas Kishler, Robert Lumianski and Charles Chatfield.

I wish gratefully to acknowledge a continuing Michigan State All-University Grant which greatly aided me in my research.

2. *Addresses in memory of Ernest Howard Crosby (1856-1907) Cooper Union New York, March 7, 1907.* Ernest Howard Crosby Memorial Committee. Among the individual sponsors were such notables as Jane Addams, Felix Adler, Arthur Brisbane, William Jennings Bryan, Abraham Cahan, Bliss Carman, Clarence Darrow, Hamlin Garland, William Lloyd Garrison, Henry George, Jr., Samuel Gompers, Thomas Wentworth Higginson, Frederick C. Howe, William Dean Howells, William James, Tom L. Johnson, Edwin Markham, George Foster Peabody, Samuel Seabury, Moorfield Storey, Booker T. Washington and Erving Winslow.

3. "British Egypt: Part I," *The Arena*, 35 (1906), 582-587; Part II, *The Arena*, 36 (1906), 41-45; Part III, *The Arena*, 36 (1906), 162-168.

4. Ernest Howard Crosby, *Tolstoy and His Message* (London, 1904), 43-44.

5. Ernest Howard Crosby, "Two Days With Count Tolstoy," *The Progressive Review*, 2, (August, 1897), 407-422.

6. During the 13 years of their friendship (1894-1907), Tolstoy wrote to Crosby at least 18 times, perhaps more. In the Crosby collection are Xerox copies of 17 letters from Tolstoy to Crosby himself and one expressing condolences upon Crosby's death. There are also three letters from Countess Sophie Tolstoy. Tolstoy would often send long letters to his friends in England and America and authorize their being sent to newspapers for publication. In Crosby's "Mark Twain Scrapbook" are newspaper clippings of a number of such letters, one sent by Crosby to the New York *Tribune* (April 4, 1896). The whereabouts of the original of this letter is unknown. Since Tolstoy wrote his letters in English, and since they were rather long, Crosby doubtless merely forwarded the original letter with an introductory letter of his own. *Crosby Coll*. See note 9 below.

7. "Count Tolstoy and Non-Resistance," *The Outlook* (July 11, 1896), 52-53; "In Honor of Tolstoy," *The Critic*, 33 (Old Series), 856 (October, 1898), 282-284; "Count Tolstoy at Seventy," *The Coming Age*, 1 (February, 1899), 172-177; "Tolstoy et ses traducteurs," *L'Humanité Nouvelle*, 38 (1900), 193-200; "Count Tolstoy and His Philosophy of Life," *The Liberal Club, Buffalo: Addresses Delivered Before the Club During the Three Seasons, 1900-1903* (Buffalo, 1904), 17-58; "Count Tolstoy as Philosopher, Prophet, and Man," *The Arena*, 25, (April, 1901), 429-439; *Tolstoy and His Message* (London, 1904); *Tolstoy as a Schoolmaster* (Chicago, n.d.); *Tolstoy on Shakespeare* (New York, 1906).

8. B. O. Flower, "Ernest Howard Crosby: Prophet of Peace and Apostle of Social Righteousness," *The Arena*, 37 (March, 1907), 259-271.

9. Nor was Crosby's family sympathetic to his new career. Crosby's wife—the former Fanny Schieffelin—was the daughter of Henry M. Schieffelin, a wealthy and prominent New York importer. Both she and her mother disapproved of Crosby's reform activities. To get Crosby out of the city and thus, hopefully, to end his new career, the widow Schieffelin presented him with an estate at Rhinebeck-on-the-Hudson. The plan didn't work, for while Crosby accepted the gift, he continued his involvement in those reform and humanitarian activities which were regarded as embarrassments by his family. Crosby's behavior during the "Gorky affair" illustrates the depth of his conviction. The warm welcome that New York had given to the Russian writer and patriot cooled considerably when it was discovered that Gorky had traveled to the United States with his mistress. But while Mark Twain and William Dean Howells—two of the prominent New Yorkers who were sponsoring a gala banquet in his honor—were cowed by public opinion and backed out, Crosby remained unperturbed and boldly welcomed Gorky into his home. Needless to say, it was behavior such as this which served to exacerbate his relations with the Schieffelins. So embittered did the family become, in fact, that after Crosby's sudden death in Baltimore in 1907, his name was dropped from family discussions. Crosby's granddaughter and heiress, who visited her grandmother when she was growing up, was never told about her grandfather's career. Nor did her own father mention him, except to say that the family was afraid that "he was becoming a communist." At the same time he told her the Gorky story. Not until she had reached the age of 21, at which time she inherited the Rhinebeck estate, did she learn the full story when she discovered Crosby's books and papers in an Egyptian sarcophagus where they had been placed by the widow.

I am indebted to Mrs. Crosby Glendening for this account of her grandfather. Mrs. Glendening has graciously deposited Ernest Howard Crosby's papers and books with the Michigan State University Library. References to this as yet uncataloged collection are noted as *Crosby Coll*.

10. In an earlier article Harrington lists Crosby among those political leaders, reformers and intellectuals who supported the Anti-Imperialist League, "The Anti-Imperialist Movement in the United States, 1898-1900," *Mississippi Valley Historical Review*, 22 (September, 1935), 211-230. Merle Curti, in *Peace or War: The American Struggle* (1936), mentions Crosby only in passing, as does Peter Brock in *Pacifism in the United States: From the Colonial Era to the First World War* (1968). E. Berkeley Tompkins most recent study, *Anti-Imperialism in the United States: The Great Debate, 1890-1920* (1970) acknowledges Crosby as head of the Anti-Imperialist League of New York and quotes some of his poetry. David Healy's *United States Expansionism: The Imperialist Urge in the 1890's* (1970) mentions the Anti-Imperialist League but ignores Crosby. Robert L. Beisner's prize-winning *Twelve Against Empire: The Anti-Imperialists 1898-1900* (1968) does not mention Crosby at all. Nor is Crosby mentioned in Walter LaFeber, *The New Empire* (1963); William Appleman Williams, *The Roots of the Modern American Empire* (1969); Ernest R. May, *American Imperialism* (1969), *Imperial Democracy* (1961); Leon Wolff, *Little Brown Brother* (1961); Samuel Eliot Morison, Frederick Merk & Frank Freidel, *Dissent in Three American Wars* (1970). Nor is he mentioned in the diplomatic history texts of Alexander De Conde, Thomas A. Bailey, Richard W. Leopold, Wayne S. Cole or Robert H. Ferrell.

11. Leonard D. Abbott, *Ernest Howard Crosby: A Valuation and a Tribute* (1907).

12. Recent scholarship has revisited the economic thesis and places the origin of the imperialist impulse of 1898-1900 in earlier periods of economic depression or in factors implicit in the American capitalistic market system. More compelling, however, is Marilyn Blatt Young's conclusion that such monolithic views of American expansionism at the century's end are ill founded. See "American Expansion, 1870-1900: The Far East," *Towards a New Past: Dissenting Essays in American History*, ed. Barton J. Bernstein (1969), 176-201. Recent scholarship in American intellectual history—E. L. Tuveson's *Redeemer Nation* and Martin Marty's *Righteous Empire*, among others—points the way to a much more comprehensive interpretation of American expansion and overseas involvement, since it acknowledges the presence of powerful cultural imperatives which transcend the exaggerated economic rhetoric of a given period. Unlike the approach of the neo-economic determinists, which may be said still to be tied to 19th-century mechanistic concepts, the newer approach of the intellectual historians more closely resembles the holistic approach of the new life scientists, especially as it is revealed in the "balanced systems" approach.

13. Ernest Howard Crosby, *Swords and Plowshares* (New York, 1902), 14-15. Crosby dedicated this collection of poems "To The Noble Army of Traitors and Heretics."

14. There were remarkably few written at the time. Raymond Landon Bridgman's *Loyal Traitors* (Boston, 1903) is the only other explicitly anti-imperialist novel. It is, in fact, a virtual tract against imperialism. Gertrude Atherton's *Senator North* (New York, 1903) couples racism and elitism to oppose the war to free Cuba. See my "The Spanish-American War and the Double Paradox of the Negro American," *Phylon* (Spring, 1965), 34-49.

Two well-known humorists satirized the imperialists during this period. See Finley Peter Dunne, *Mr. Dooley in Peace and War* (Boston, 1898), and George Ade's successful musical play *The Sultan of Sulu* (New York, 1903), which satirizes McKinley's program of "Benevolent Assimilation." In a later anti-expansionist musical, *The Sho-Gun* (1904), Ade models the leading character, an expansionist, after Theodore Roosevelt.

Mark Twain produced no imaginative works of fiction about expansionism at the time. Since he originally supported the war to free Cuba—parting company with his friend Howells on that issue—he confined himself to attacks on General Funston and on the imperialism of the Great Powers. See his "To a Person Sitting in Darkness," *North American Review*, 172 (February, 1901), 161-176.

15. Ernest Howard Crosby, "The Military Idea of Manliness," *The Independent*, 53 (April 8, 1901), 873-875.

16. *North American Review*, 174 (May, 1902), 613-634.

17. "War and Hell IX," *Swords and Plowshares*, 17-18.

18. *The Absurdities of Militarism* (Boston, 1901), 11.

19. Most of Stephen Crane's stories are collected in *Wounds in the Rain* (New York, 1899). Other stories are scattered through the volumes of his collected works. Crane's Spanish-American war dispatches are collected in *The War Dispatches of Stephen Crane*, ed. R. W. Stallman and E. R. Hageman (New York, 1964).

20. See Davis' collected works for "Blood Will Tell," "A Charmed Life," "A Derelict," "On the Fever Ship," "The Man With One Talent." Davis' war dispatches are collected in *The Cuban and Porto Rican Campaigns* (1898). Both Frederic Remington and (Gen.) Charles King produced romantic stories and novels about the war: see Remington's *Men With Bark On* (New York, 1900) and King's *A Conquering Corps Badge and Other Stories of the Philippines* (Milwaukee, 1902). King also produced three novels: *Ray's Daughter* (Philadelphia, 1901), *Found in the Philippines* (New York, 1901), and *Comrades in Arms* (New York, 1904). Romantic war stories appeared in many periodicals, including *Munsey's Magazine, The Youth's Companion, Overland Monthly, The Argosy, Harper's Round Table, Scribner's Magazine* and *Cosmopolitan*. In addition, nickel and dime novels celebrating the war flooded the country. Upton Sinclair produced at least 64 such novels, all of which celebrate aspects of the war. Sinclair wrote at least 29 nickel novels for Street & Smith's "True Blue" series under the pseudonym of "Ensign Clarke Fitch"; at least 18 nickel novels for Street & Smith's "Starry Flag" series under the pseudonym of "Douglas Wells"; and at least 17 dime novels for Street & Smith's "Columbia Library" series in which he used both pseudonyms. Most of these are to be found in the Library of Congress' Dime Novel Collection.

21. William Dean Howells, "Editha," *Between the Dark and the Daylight, Romances* (New York, 1907), 124-143. The story was originally published in 1905. For confirmation of Howells' portrait, see Edith Elmer Wood, *The Spirit of the Service* (New York, 1903), wherein such a heroine is favorably depicted. See also Crosby's poem "Women and War," *Swords and Plowshares*, 43-44.

While "Editha" was the only antiwar fiction which Tolstoyan Howells produced, he was not inactive during the war years. See William M. Gibson, "Mark Twain and William Dean Howells, Anti-Imperialists," (unpublished Ph.D. dissertation, University of Chicago, 1940).

22. In the Crosby collection are a number of letters from readers of the novel. One is addressed as follows:

Ernest Crosby Esq.
The American Cervantes
% Funk & Wagnalls' Co.
New York City, N.Y.

23. See Julius W. Pratt, *Expansionists of 1898, The Acquisition of Hawaii and the Spanish Islands* (Baltimore, 1936), 279-316.

24. Material on Roosevelt's part in the Cuban campaign is voluminous. See Richard Harding Davis, *The Cuban and Porto Rican Campaigns* (1898) and *The Notes of a War Correspondent* (New York, 1911). Davis' original dispatch about the Guasimas engagement is less flattering to Roosevelt than subsequent accounts he wrote of the same incident. Compare "The Rough Riders' Fight at Guasimas," *Scribner's Magazine*, 24 (September, 1898), 259-273. See also Annie Hale Riley, *Rooseveltian Fact and Fable* (New York, 1910). Roosevelt tells his story in *The Rough Riders* (New York, 1899). See also Hermann Hagedorn's novelized treatment, *The Rough Riders* (New York, 1927).

25. "The Military Idea of Manliness."

26. Crosby knew from personal experience whereof he wrote, for he served 8 years in the National Guard of New York, attaining the rank of Major: "I used to wear a cocked hat with an ostrich feather a yard long. I know what it is to prance up and down Fifth Avenue on a riding-school nag, feeling like a composite photograph of Washington and Napoleon; and I can testify, as far as I am concerned, that there is nothing but vanity at the bottom of the whole business," *op. cit.* "The Absurdities of Militarism." Crosby developed the Chung Tu episode from some of his observations in this speech.

27. Crosby here satirizes another of the "heroes" produced by the war, "Kissing Hobson." Lt. Richmond Pearson Hobson commanded the ill-fated Merrimac in the U.S. Navy's attempt to block the entrance to Santiago harbor and thus trap Cervera's fleet inside. The scheme failed, and Hobson and his men were taken prisoner. Hobson's exploit was blown up in the popular press, and he became an instant hero. Upon his first appearance in the United States after the war, a number of impulsive young ladies and matrons rushed to kiss him. This practice became contagious, and from then on wherever Hobson went he was mobbed by women, all seeking to kiss the handsome young hero. Hobson capitalized on his fame and won a seat in Congress, where he distinguished himself in the temperance movement, and thus, as Walter Millis notes, "he managed more or less to live . . . down" his reputation as a romantic object of female affection.

As a struggling young writer at Columbia University, Upton Sinclair, using the pseudonym of "Ensign Clarke Fitch, U. S. N.," published a nickel novel concerning a similar war hero who was overwhelmed with kisses: "Hobson Junior; or, The Kissing Cadet of Annapolis Academy" (March 11, 1899). This was volume 44 of the "True Blue" weekly series Sinclair wrote for Street & Smith, Publishers. The supposed humor in Sinclair's rendering of the story hinges on a racist climax.

28. Crosby doubtless was influenced by the fate of yet another of the "heroes" produced by the war, this time Admiral Dewey. Having hailed him as the great hero of Manila Bay, New Yorkers planned an elaborate Dewey victory arch over Fifth Avenue (an honor hitherto reserved only for George Washington), and in anticipation of his visit had erected a plaster replica of the arch over the famous thoroughfare. Meanwhile, a grateful nation had subscribed to a fund for a golden victory sword—to be presented by President McKinley—and a $50,000 mansion in Washington, D.C. To the discomfort of the Republican administration, some of Dewey's more ardent admirers even began a presidential boom. Dewey's popularity plumeted, however, when the 62-year-old bachelor married a 49-year-old widow, Mildred McLean Hazen, daughter of Mrs. Washington McLean, who was more than wealthy enough to provide the newlyweds with several palatial mansions. Insult was added to injury when it was disclosed that the new Mrs. Dewey was a recent Catholic convert and that Dewey had presented the newly acquired mansion to her. With the Dewey fiasco fresh in their minds, readers of Crosby's novel in 1902 needed no further elaboration. See Margaret Leech, *In The Days of McKinley* (1959), 428-429.

29. "Why I am Opposed to Imperialism," *The Arena*, 28 (July, 1902), 10-11.

30. That the reference is to Roosevelt is confirmed in a later article which Crosby wrote on Roosevelt's intervention in the coal strike: "Mr. Roosevelt deserves the highest praise for his courageous and successful intervention. What a grand tribune of the people he would make if he could only get the idea out of his head that we can become great by taking away other peoples' liberties and that big battle-ships are more valuable to a nation than big ideas . . . . One of the greatest opportunities for strenuous life that were ever offered to man lies open before him, and it is sad to think that he will probably fail to see it." "Violence and Arbitration," *The Arena*, 29 (January, 1903), 21-25.

31. *Swords and Plowshares*, 19.

32. "If The South Had Been Allowed to Go," *North American Review*, 177 (December, 1903), 767-771.

33. "Wanted, a New Patriotism," *The Independent*, 56 (July, 1903), 1677-1679. "Militarism at Home," *The Arena*, 31 (January, 1904), 70-74.

18

34. Ernest Crosby [sic], "A Precedent for Disarmament. A Suggestion to the Peace Conference," *North American Review* (October 19, 1906), 5-6.

35. Dunne had paraphrased Henry Cabot Lodge's slogan as: "Hands acrost th' sea an' into somewan's pocket," and "Take up th' white man's burden an' hand it to th' coons." Roosevelt responded in a letter to Dunne: "As you know, I am an Expansionist, but your delicious phrase about 'take up the white man's burden and put it on the coons,' exactly hit off the weak spot in my own theory; though, mind you, I am by no means willing to give up the theory yet." Elmer Ellis, *Mr. Dooley's America: A Life of Finley Peter Dunne* (New York, 1941), 117, 147.

An Interpretation of the American Peace Movement, 1898-1914

David S. Patterson

I

The American peace movement in the two decades before the First World War grew rapidly in terms of the proliferation of peace societies, active membership and financial backing. From a tiny nucleus consisting of the American Peace Society and Universal Peace Union, both of which began long before 1898, peace work became a popular avocation in the first years of the twentieth century. Annual meetings on international arbitration at Albert Smiley's hotel resort on Lake Mohonk, New York, begun in 1895, were consistently attended by almost all the leading friends of international peace after about 1900; and beginning in 1907 many peace leaders organized biennial peace conferences in various American cities. In the decade before the outbreak of the European war advocates of peace also created many new peace and internationalist societies, most notably the American Society of International Law, the New York Peace Society, the

Now, my friends, in conclusion, the Peace Movement is no longer a little cult of cranks. Peace has at last become a practical political issue—soon *the* political issue before all the nations . . . .

It seems destined that America should lead in this movement. The U.S. is the world in miniature. The U.S. is a demonstration that all the peoples of the world can live in peace under one form of government and its chief value to civilization is the disclosure of what this form of government is . . . and when that golden period is at hand—and it cannot be very far distant—we shall have in very truth Tennyson's dream of "The Parliament of Man, The Federation of the World, and for the first time since the Prince of Peace died on Calvary, we shall have Peace on Earth and Good Will to Men."

> Hamilton Holt, The Federation of the World, unpublished manuscript [1907-1914], Hamilton Holt Papers, Mills Memorial Library, Rollins College

It is the prophets and leaders who make the changes of the world. The talk of *vox populi* is often more of a delusion than a reality. Let us make enough of preachers, teachers, editors, and particularly statesmen to see the reasonableness and inevitableness of the new order, and it can be at once established and the great changes made.

> Frederick Lynch, *The Peace Problem: The Task of the Twentieth Century* (New York, 1911), 111

American School Peace League, the Chicago Peace Society, the American Society for Judicial Settlement of International Disputes and three endowed institutions, the World Peace Foundation, the Carnegie Endowment for International Peace and the Church Peace Union. In this decade alone American friends of world peace established more than forty-five peace societies, and after 1911 the Carnegie Endowment provided the American Peace Society with an annual subvention from which it supported its affiliated peace organizations.

Yet when the European war erupted in 1914, almost all peace groups either remained aloof from the immediate issues of American neutrality or were too divided to influence the foreign policies of the Wilson Administration. As a result, some of the more active peace workers, dissatisfied with the existing peace groups, cooperated with like-minded newcomers to the movement in forming still other peace organizations to deal with the pressing problems arising out of the World War.[1]

Beneath the usual descriptions of the peace movement lie some important unanswered questions. Only a few historians have attempted more than a partial survey of the leadership of the peace movement for the years 1898 to 1914; even less have they analyzed its common and distinctive features. To what degree is it possible to generalize about these peace workers as a group? And since the growing popularity of the peace cause inevitably added to the variety of temperaments and programs in the movement, exactly what were their differences? Finally, what were the internal weaknesses of the movement which accounted for its impotence and eventual reorganization after 1914?

The answers require analysis of the backgrounds and assumptions of the thirty-six leaders who set the tone of the American peace movement between 1898 and 1914.[2] Such analysis will show that although the leaders of the peace movement were remarkably similar in social backgrounds and shared certain fundamental values, the movement failed to sustain its growing influence after the outbreak of the European war for two major reasons. First, the many divergent approaches to peace questions which existed in subdued fashion during peacetime surfaced under the pressures of a war-torn world and greatly accentuated the internal divisions in the movement. Second, despite the growing public interest in the peace movement, the strong elitism of the pre-war leadership which frustrated efforts to cultivate a mass following before the war facilitated the dissolution of the superficial support of the peace leaders after 1914.

II

It is not surprising to find considerable diversity in such a large group of peace leaders. Consider their ages. In 1909 when the movement was maturing, the age span ranged from the eighty-seven-year-old Boston minister, Edward Everett Hale, to the youthful student enthusiast at the

University of Wisconsin, Louis Lochner, only twenty-two; and there were representatives of all age groups between these extremes. Nor can it be said that the age of a peace worker had any direct relationship to his position on peace questions. About the most that can be said is that in 1909 the average and median age of the peace leadership, both between fifty-four and fifty-five, was older than the leadership of the domestic reform movements of that day.

More revealing than their ages was their length of service in the peace movement. Almost all of the peace leaders who had shown interest in the peace or anti-imperialist movements before 1900 were distinctly pacific-minded in their abhorrence of international violence. They also were more sympathetic to domestic reform movements than the later participants, most of whom tended to be conservative on domestic matters, more cautious or "practical" in their promotion of international reform, and more deferential toward political authority.[3] Of the pre-1900 recruits, few besides the Quakers—Alfred Love, head of the Universal Peace Union; Benjamin Trueblood, secretary of the American Peace Society and editor of its journal, *Advocate of Peace*; and William I. Hull, history professor at Swarthmore College—can be considered absolute pacifists in the sense that they refused to sanction any given war. But America's war with Spain and the imperialistic aftermath deeply disturbed almost all of them. If they had not been full-fledged members of the American peace movement before 1898, they actively cooperated with peace workers in the anti-imperialist movement and moved effortlessly into the peace movement once the anti-imperialist agitation subsided. For them the peace movement became in part the proper instrument for organizing American opinion against possible future imperialist ventures and against navalism which dominated American thinking on foreign affairs at the turn of the century. They opposed the use of American military force in other lands but, unlike many isolationists who shunned America's participation in world affairs, these peace workers actively urged their government's participation in movements for permanent peace. Responding to the reality of America's emergence as a major world power, they advocated treaties of international arbitration, mediation and conciliation procedures and a broad educational campaign as rational alternatives to international conflict. A few even developed general proposals for world organization. Because they all espoused pacifism or inclined in that direction and worked for international cooperation, they might best be called pacific-minded internationalists.[4]

By contrast, of the post-1900 recruits only four of the youngest—Congregationalist minister and editor of *Christian Work,* Frederick Lynch; editor of the *Independent,* Hamilton Holt; and the two college student leaders of the Cosmopolitan Club, an international friendship society, George Nasmyth and Louis Lochner—flirted with absolute pacifism, and they affirmed their love of peace more on emotional than on philosophical or religious grounds. Unlike those who had earlier entered the peace movement, nearly all these latecomers had fewer regrets concerning their nation's navalism and imperialism. They accepted America's rise to world power as largely inevitable and essentially beneficient, and they viewed the peace movement as the most useful vehicle for convincing American governmental leaders to promote a harmonious international order.

In terms of their peace ideas, these post-1900 additions to the peace movement fall roughly into three groups: generalists, world federationists and legalists. Fannie Fern Andrews, organizer of the American School Peace League; the Chicago clergyman, Charles Beals; Arthur Deerin Call, officer of the Connecticut Peace Society and American Peace Society; Samuel Train Dutton, head of Teacher's College at Columbia University; the Reverend William Short, secretary of the New York Peace Society; Lynch, Nasmyth, and Lochner most often advanced extremely broad and general proposals for the promotion of world peace. These generalists shared the positive goals of the earlier recruits in urging their government to promote international good will in its foreign policies. While they occasionally talked about the need for international organization, they rarely detailed its functions.[5]

The world federationists were more clearly internationalists. These internationalists shared the peaceful aspirations of the pacific-minded and generalists, but were unwilling to wait for the conversion of the masses to the goal of world peace or of the nations' widespread acceptance of arbitration and conciliation procedures for the resolution of international disputes. They wanted the major world powers to establish permanent international institutions which would formalize and regularize the conciliation process. They talked most often of the creation of some kind of world federation. Their proposals ranged from Andrew Carnegie's general program for a league of peace composed of the leaders of the major powers of Europe and the United States, who would agree to use economic sanctions and as a last resort an international police force against aggressor states, to more specific arrangements for the creation of an international legislature which would develop procedures for preserving the peace. Hamilton Holt, Richard Bartholdt, a Republican congressman from St. Louis, Missouri, and Raymond Bridgman, journalist and author, also urged the establishment of an international executive to apply the legislature's decisions to specific controversies.[6]

The third group composed of Nicholas Murray Butler, president of Columbia University; George Kirchwey, professor of international law at Columbia; James Brown Scott, international lawyer and frequent adviser to the State Department; and Elihu Root, Roosevelt's second Secretary of State and later Senator from New York, emphasized international law. Its members also were internationalists but they promoted only the creation of a world court. They were primarily legalists who argued that international congresses, like the two Hague Peace Conferences, could gradually formulate a code of international law, which justices of a world court could apply and further develop in their decisions between disputants.

With so many individuals involved in the peace movement, it is not surprising that there were numerous approaches to the peace question. Indeed, the differences among the peace workers were in some respects fundamental. Those individuals who inclined toward pacifism challenged reliance on armaments; but the other leaders soft-pedalled the armament question and in a few instances readily tolerated the large navy boosters in the Navy League.[7]

In addition, the legalists questioned other peace workers' faith in arbitration treaties. In their view the arbitral process might settle many controversies, but it was no panacea and contained inherent weaknesses. They pointed out that men trained in politics and diplomacy rather than well-known jurists almost always decided arbitration cases. The art of negotiation and the spirit of compromise rather than any higher concept of abstract justice were the guiding principles in these arbitrations. Compromise was also common in arbitration because of the need to harmonize different or fragmentary concepts of international law. The legalists wanted to purge the procedures of international conciliation of their haphazard, arbitral features by creating a judicial court composed of renowned judges, appointed for life and sitting in continuous session, who would rule on the "rights" of countries in accordance with the "facts" and the established law. In their view, only the correct application of accepted international law could bring true international justice, a prerequisite for any stable world order.[8]

Tensions also existed between the legalists and the world federationists. Less confident in the wisdom of nation-states to decide the rules of right conduct, the former branded schemes for an international legislature and executive as too radical. Such authoritative institutions, they pointed out, involved the surrender of national sovereignty, which nations were not yet prepared to accept. They also claimed that even if a world federation became a political reality, its use of force to preserve the peace would probably result in oppressive and unjust actions. For the legalists only renowned judges were impartial and the only acceptable sanction for their decisions was the very gradual development of "a world-wide public opinion" properly educated in the rights and duties of nations in the international community.[9]

Differences even developed within each group. Among the world federationists, for example, Hamilton Holt at times favored the establishment of some kind of international police force, but Raymond Bridgman was much more skeptical of any kind of sanctions.[10] So, too, although most of the pacific-minded members feared the possible harmful consequences of an international police force, three of the strongest opponents of national armaments—Lucia Ames Mead, Boston intellectual; Edwin Ginn, a text-book publisher; and William I. Hull—cautiously endorsed the creation of a small international police agency with limited powers to enforce the peace.[11] Furthermore, Jane Addams was developing a peculiar brand of pacifism which had little in common with that of other pacifists. Much as she wrote about peace, moreover, she often seemed more interested in domestic than international reform. This was suggested when in the presidential election of 1912 she supported Theodore Roosevelt, certainly no friend of the peace movement.[12]

Temperamental and tactical differences also threatened the fragile unity of the movement. William Jennings Bryan's erratic opposition to imperialism, his alleged radicalism and political partisanship, his flamboyant rhetoric and his deliberate avoidance of membership in peace organizations embarrassed or annoyed some peace advocates.[13] Moreover, Andrew Carnegie and Edwin Ginn were jealous of their reputations as leading philanthropists of peace and refused to cooperate in establishing their peace funds. In addition, Ginn, believing the peace movement should strive toward business efficiency, often disagreed with the directors of his own World Peace Foundation who through speeches and writings were more interested in uplifting their audiences to their high-minded aims.[14]

But all these differences paled in comparison with the fundamentally divergent views between the pacific-minded and the leaders of the Carnegie Endowment. The latter strongly disapproved of the emotional and "radical" tendencies of the peace societies. Unlike the peace societies and the World Peace Foundation, which actively disseminated their message of pacific internationalism to literate Americans, the Carnegie trustees promoted almost entirely the extremely cautious goal of international understanding among a small group of scholars and international lawyers. Compared with the Endowment's financial support of international law and other non-pacifist groups, its subsidy to the peace societies amounted to a mere pittance, and by 1913 several Carnegie trustees began to suggest the curtailment of the Endowment's subvention unless the societies abandoned their pacifistic emphasis.[15]

III

The many views and temperaments in the peace movement foreshadowed the divergent responses to the world crisis after 1914, but before that date a tenuous consensus existed among the peace forces. Indeed, a dominant note of the American peace movement before 1914 was the relative absence of overt controversy. The advocates of peace frequently appeared on the same platform at peace congresses and rarely engaged in extensive debate over their different viewpoints. When they recognized their differences, they usually assumed that they were more complementary than conflicting. Especially absent was severe public criticism of their colleagues. Edwin Mead, a vigorous anti-preparedness advocate, even convinced himself that it was "ridiculous" to believe that the Carnegie trustees did not advocate the reduction of armaments although some of them were prominent supporters of the Navy League, and the leaders of the New York Peace Society deliberately attempted to minimize differences of opinion in the movement.[16]

There are a few obvious explanations for this failure to emphasize their real differences. Perhaps most important, during these years of relative peace and isolation the pressures for defining and defending one's position on the peace question were minimal. Moreover, there existed a few areas of general agreement which helped to maintain an uneasy unity in the movement. First, all endorsed periodic international congresses for the discussion of questions of common interest. Second, they all assumed that the United States as a satiated and relatively secure power should take the lead in advancing specific proposals leading to a more harmonious international order. Third, although only the legalists were very precise in their definitions of international law, all conceded the importance of the development of "law" in establishing nations' rights and duties in the world community. Finally, none opposed the establishment of a court of arbitral justice as the next, most practical step toward instituting a new world order following the Second Hague Peace Conference's endorsement in principle of this institution.[17]

But there were also other, often deeper reasons for their cooperative behavior. One was their similar backgrounds. The social origins of almost all the thirty-six peace leaders were so remarkably alike that it was easier for them to tolerate different approaches to world peace than if their backgrounds had been more diverse. Despite their wide age-span and different lengths of service in the movement, from every other sociological perspective their social origins were virtually identical.[18] All but six—Bartholdt, Carnegie, Love, Lucia Ames Mead, Hannah Bailey (head of the peace department of the W.C.T.U.), and James Slayden (Democratic congressman from Texas)—had received college degrees, and nearly two-thirds also had earned professional certification in their chosen fields of law, education or religion. Since only relatively affluent families could usually afford to send their children to college in that day, these figures, together with other information on their parents' social standing, indicate that almost all the peace workers came from the middle or upper classes and, upon reaching maturity, formed an educated elite among the professional classes.[19]

These similarities went beyond their social class, however. Only the Chicago Unitarian minister, Jenkin Lloyd Jones, Fannie Fern Andrews, Carnegie, Scott and Bartholdt were foreign-born, and of these only Bartholdt came from a non-English-speaking nation or migrated to the

United States after early childhood. Of the native Americans all but Hull, Slayden, Short and Theodore Marburg were born east of the Mississippi and north of the Mason-Dixon line. Moreover, although many were reared in small towns, they early moved to large cities whose cultural and intellectual advantages seemed inevitably to attract men and women of education and intellect; and by 1909 nearly three-fourths of the peace workers lived in six metropolitan areas—Boston, New York, Philadelphia, Baltimore, Washington, D.C., and Chicago.[20] In addition, all were Protestants and about one-half came from strongly religious households, thought seriously of the ministry as a career or were ordained clergymen.[21]

In sum, the social characteristics of the thirty-six peace leaders were overwhelmingly urban, professional, Anglo-Saxon and Protestant. In many instances, in fact, the sociological ties were more than casual. Among the New York peace workers Frederick Lynch had been a classmate of Hamilton Holt at Yale and of William Short at Yale Theological School. Lynch married one of Samuel Dutton's daughters and introduced Short to his future wife.[22] George Kirchwey and Dutton also had received degrees from Yale and, together with James Brown Scott and Nicholas Murray Butler, became professors or administrators at Columbia University. All of these peace workers figured prominently in the formation and programs of the New York Peace Society or the Carnegie Endowment. The same close ties existed among Boston peace workers. Before moving to New York, Dutton was a school administrator in the Boston area and frequently discussed educational problems in a Boston reform organization, the Twentieth Century Club. His exposure to many Boston friends of peace in this group first introduced him to the peace movement. Furthermore, Lynch's and Call's early contacts with other Boston advocates of peace helped to foster their growing interest in the cause.[23]

IV

But of more far-reaching importance than their social backgrounds, though in large measure derived from them, were the common attitudes and values the peace workers expressed in the movement. Most important, their approach to the peace movement was distinctly elitist. The political conservatives in the movement deliberately discouraged participation by the lower classes, but even more progressive elements gave little emphasis to them. With a few exceptions, most notably Jane Addams and William Jennings Bryan, they assumed that literate gentlemen of the middle and upper classes could more easily understand and identify with the civilized quality of their movement than the unenlightened masses. Not surprisingly, they relied upon their contacts with friends in governmental circles for their influence and shunned involvement in politics and contacts with immigrant, moderate socialist or labor groups. The high-priced dinners and formal receptions of the New York Peace Society and the Carnegie Endowment, Albert Smiley's hand-picked conferences at Lake Mohonk, and the leadership of peace societies limited to educators, ministers and philanthropists exemplified this same elitism.[24]

In most instances, theirs was not deliberate snobbery. Rather, reflecting the Mugwump traditions and teachings which were common among many reformers of that era, they assumed that the man in the street was an important factor in public opinion only to the extent of his ability to absorb their own ideas. Until education could enlighten the general public, these leaders assumed that they alone were the proper custodians of the peace movement. Even progressive reformers like Lynch, Lochner and David Starr Jordan, while expressing greater faith in the populace, upheld the Mugwump emphasis on enlightened leadership and agreed that international reform would have to come from above rather than from below. Lynch, for example, assumed that "It is the prophets and leaders who make the changes of the world. The talk of *vox populi* is often more of a delusion than a reality." While they regularly expounded their views on the peace question to formal gatherings, they rarely engaged their audiences in public discussion or attempted to include them in the daily operations of the peace movement. Indeed, fascinated by great leaders of the past and present, they easily tolerated the growing involvement in the movement of influential conservatives whose participation seemed to confirm the dignity of their own peace work.[25] In consequence, the peace movement increasingly acquired an aura of gentility and respectability but at the expense of widening the gap between the peace leaders and the masses.

The peace leaders managed to maintain an uneasy consensus on other values. Above all, they shared an unquestioning belief in the reality of moral values. The acceptance of moral values as the mainspring of human behavior was deeply ingrained in the American character, as the Puritans, transcendentalists and anti-slavery reformers had earlier demonstrated; and the most pacifistic internationalists frequently referred to the humanistic values of their forebears. They also derived added inspiration for their ethical values from Christian humanists and Enlightenment philosophers throughout the Western world. Unlike American ultranationalists, who had little faith in the pervasiveness of ethical principles beyond the water's edge, these pacific-minded individuals optimistically believed that these values existed universally and already exerted a far-reaching influence on the foreign policies of nation states.[26] Other international reformers were less sanguine. They agreed that the acceptance of moral values was widespread, but they assumed that they were most obviously present in their own land and to a lesser degree in other so-called civilized or Christian nations.[27]

In the long run, the distinction between the pacifists' humanism and the other peace workers' more limited emphasis on civilized nations was crucial. The latter, more readily believing in the essential virtue of American conduct in foreign affairs, could more easily justify their nation's forceful intervention in the affairs of other states for the sake of reforming their policies along American or "civilized" lines than those inclining toward pacifism, who were profoundly skeptical about the use of force in foreign affairs. During peacetime, however, this distinction caused no difficulties.

If the peace leaders had believed only in the reality of moral values in international life, they would have had difficulty in explaining why nations had resorted to wars throughout history. But they were not Pollyannas. Admitting that man was not inherently good and might even be instinctively pugnacious, many peace workers tempered their optimism with warnings about his combative instincts. James Slayden lamented that "the spirit of the people is inclined toward war," and Holt agreed that "the great mass of men and women almost prefer war to peace."[28] Yet they stopped far short of the conclusion that mankind was therefore inevitably doomed to recurrent wars. Rather, international cooperation was still possible and worth the quest. In general, they advanced four explanations for resolving the apparent contradiction between their awareness of the persistence of international tensions and their continuing hopes for a peaceful world order.

First, the pacific-minded and a few other internationalists often blamed wars on a tiny minority of munitions makers and military men who, motivated by greed and glory, cleverly fabricated war scares and promoted wars.[29] Second, peace workers emphasized moral education. Assuming the individual had a moral sense and a capacity for reason, they stressed education as vitally important in developing these qualities. Proper education, they believed, could overcome man's ignorance, the major reason for his deviation from moral rectitude. Despite different emphases in educational philosophy, all asserted the primacy of the educator's moral function.[30] Third, they all believed that permanent international machinery would restrain man's passions and thereby reduce the chances for war. Once nations established arbitral tribunals, commissions of inquiry and especially a world court, then international controversies could be removed from the potentially wrathful populace and placed in the hands of cool-headed, impartial administrators. While promoting international agreements requiring submission of almost all kinds of controversies to the appropriate agency, in practice they accepted almost any agreement as a positive step in the long-range goal of world organization.[31]

An imposing obstacle to the implementation of permanent international institutions, however, was the reluctance of governments to relinquish their freedom of action to international agencies. Many peace advocates, especially the legalists, seemed to understand the practical difficulties, but on the whole the peace workers minimized them. Reflecting their faith in enlightened leadership, they believed that a few statesmen understood the advantages of such agencies and could establish them without waiting for the education and conversion of world public opinion. The negotiation of many arbitration and conciliation treaties as well as the nations' acceptance in principle of a court of arbitral justice seemed to suggest that many statesmen were already interested in developing peacekeeping machinery.

They further argued that there was no need to invent institutional arrangements, for the American Constitution provided the perfect model for world organization. Accepting unquestioningly the superiority of the American federal system, many peace advocates naively assumed it could function effectively on an international scale. Minimizing the differences between the cultural and political harmony of the American experience and the anarchistic condition of world politics, these advocates of peace extended the analogy of the American judiciary, legislature and executive to the international sphere.[32] The international reformers' confidence in American political institutions further underscored the limits of their internationalism. While thinking they were internationalists, their faith in the unique blessings of the American experience indicated a distinct though often unconscious nationalist loyalty as well. Instead of advancing a reasoned and full-scale critique of the excessive nationalism of their day, almost all peace workers assumed that national rivalries would be a reality until foreign leaders came to adopt American values and institutions. In this way peace workers held out vague hopes for world peace in the future without risking much, if any, of their present prestige or respectability.

The peace workers foresaw no difficulties in looking to the future for vindication of their movement because, fourth and most commonly, they always linked morality to progress. They assumed that progress was a natural force operating automatically in human affairs. While they differed in the emphasis they gave to the desirability and direction of progressive currents, they all shared this faith in moral progress. Those inclining toward pacifism believed that moral progress was at work throughout the world. As evidence of this advance, they often cited the decline of major wars among Western nations in the modern era.[33] Others, more restrained and less humanistic, stressed the slow, steady enlightenment of the great powers. Marburg, for instance, believed that only the Western nations were agents of progress. Butler was more vague but emphasized that the movement toward the organization of the world was as "sure as that of an Alpine glacier."[34]

The peace workers also explained progress in material terms. As the movement acquired a "practical" outlook, the pacifists' attacks on war as murderous and therefore immoral declined, while they increasingly joined with their friends in the peace movement in opposing war because it was destructive of material comforts and generally wasteful. They also agreed with them in deploring the high costs of war preparations, which burdened the populace with taxes and restricted the funds available for programs of human betterment. Yet they refused to accept militarism as a growing evil of modern life. Rather, they regarded it as an anachronistic survival of an earlier, unenlightened era and as incompatible with modern industrialism.[35] Citing the enormous productivity unleashed by the industrial revolution and the resulting expansion of international trade, they viewed these developments as essentially beneficient. Commercial intercourse brought the business interests closer together, hastened the development of international amity and facilitated the movement toward the federation of the world.[36] It was no accident that businessmen began to flock to peace meetings in these years, for they fully shared both the peace leaders' elitism and their faith in material progress. They warmly praised arbitration treaties as tangible manifestations of the rational, businesslike approach to international relations, and they characterized war as harmful to the material prosperity of all nations.[37]

With such a sturdy faith in moral and material progress it was inevitable that the longer world peace prevailed the stronger were the peace workers' convictions that the day of permanent peace was within their grasp. Superficial signs of progress toward their goal, especially the proliferation of international conferences and arbitration treaties, the conversion of Presidents Taft and Wilson to their high-minded aims, the reaction against the large-navy forces in Congress and the growing acceptance of the peace movement among the educated classes nourished their confidence in the future of the movement. The desire for "peace" became so infectious that even the leading boosters of the Navy League felt it advisable to proclaim their strong opposition to war.[38] Susceptible to words and gestures which provided more than a glimmer of hope for the future, a few peace leaders looked forward to the day when their movement would achieve victory.[39]

Actually, most peace workers did not think in terms of the imminent millenium, for they had frequently traveled in Europe and regularly corresponded with their trans-Atlantic counterparts on the European situation, and realized that the recurrent European crises had increased the existing tensions between the rival alliance systems to the point where a future clash between them might quickly precipitate a general war. They also recognized that the Balkan wars had led to a resurgence of the military spirit and war propaganda throughout Europe.[40] But if these peace leaders understood the immediate dangers to the European peace, only Trueblood predicted the likelihood of a major war. All the other advocates of peace, perhaps unconsciously unwilling to question their faith in inevitable progress, repressed their deeper fears about the European situation.[41]

The aftermath of Sarajevo seriously tested the superficial unity of the entire movement. For some of those most emotionally committed to the cause, the shock of war was traumatic. Carnegie, Trueblood and Edwin Mead fell seriously ill in 1915 and there is evidence that their illnesses were as much psychosomatic as physical in origin.[42] Not all the peace workers suffered so unhappily, although the World War undermined their most optimistic assumptions about world politics and forced a painful reassessment of their approaches to peace questions.

V

The American peace movement did not entirely collapse after 1914, but the pressures of the war brought to the surface its internal weaknesses. The failure of the peace workers was not their inability to prevent the European bloodbath which was beyond their control. They failed in the first place because of their optimistic and rather shallow assumptions about world politics. Surely they placed too much faith in the rationality of man, were too confident in their reliance on moral education, overestimated the applicability of American values and institutions and underestimated the importance of national self-interest and power in international relations. Moreover, in emphasizing inevitable progress, the peace workers tolerated the *status quo* in international life while still holding out hope for a gradual evolution toward a peaceful world order. Such talk tended to gloss over the real and menacing international problems of their day. In particular, while disliking excessive nationalism, they advanced neither trenchant nor persistent critiques of it. Even the few criticisms of the military and armament interests failed to probe deeply into the virulent imperial and national rivalries which fostered the armament race. Moreover, if all the peace advocates disagreed with the ultranationalists' emphasis on national power and prestige as the legitimate ends of foreign policy, they expressed a sense of mission which they could invoke to justify the forceful application of American ideals of peace, freedom and justice on an aberrant Europe. As the pressures for American involvement in the European conflict increased, only the most pacific-minded consistently resisted the temptation to approve military intervention as a prerequisite for obtaining an American version of international order.

It is important, however, to place the failure of the peace advocates in proper historical perspective. One should remember that they lived in an age far removed from the intense ideological conflicts and cataclysmic wars of post-1914 generations. Theirs was a confident era when all kinds of reform really seemed possible. Given this hopeful atmosphere in American domestic life and Americans' inexperience in world affairs, it is understandable why the peace leaders often made strained analogies between American values and institutions and international reform. Moreover, the peace advocates were not dismissed as eccentrics by the

American public but represented part of a larger cultural elite which assumed moral progress and which thought in abstract, if not idealistic terms. If one insists upon the validity of moral judgments in history, then it is better to view the peace movement within the broader context of the inadequacies of that entire culture.[43]

The elitist assumptions which the peace leaders shared with other leaders in America also account for the weaknesses of the pre-war peace movement. Although most of the earliest leaders consistently expressed a concern for human values, they reflected to a lesser extent the conscious elitism of many of the later recruits. In consequence, despite its growth the pre-war peace movement never developed meaningful contacts with movements for social and political change. Its rhetoric reflected this elitism. While it was always lofty in tone, it became less warmly humanistic and more coldly intellectual. Its idealistic message could arouse the interest of high-minded individuals in the peace movement, but because it expressed no urgent social message it could not sustain the active involvement of a reform-minded generation in the cause.

Even if the peace workers had surmounted their class biases, it is doubtful whether they would have aroused much more public commitment to the cause before 1914. During a time of peace and isolation as well as of a predominant interest in domestic reform, it would have been difficult to win over large numbers of people to the peace movement. Given the paucity of public commitment to their programs, perhaps they were wise in accepting the reality of the nation-state and in cultivating the educated elite and political leaders to their long-range goal of a peaceful world order. A unified and concerted effort among peace leaders might have converted American and perhaps European statesmen to a workable formula for world order.

But they could not agree on a formula. Beyond a tenuous agreement on general values and a common desire for world peace, they differed fundamentally on the specific details for the realization of their goal. The pacific-minded, federationists and legalists disagreed on the proper means to the idealistic end. As long as relative peace lasted, they were able to minimize their differences. But the World War intensified interest in international institutions and soon compelled the peace leaders to define more explicitly their peace proposals for the postwar world. The war especially necessitated a thorough discussion of the thorny question of sanctions in any authoritative international body. The world federationists endorsed the use of force against nations which refused to submit their international disputes to arbitration or conciliation; but the legalists insisted upon adequate rules of law, a world court and a general agreement among nations on the specific powers of the court as prerequisites to any forceful sanctions; and some inclining toward pacifism opposed all sanctions.[44]

When the peace advocates began to realize their divergent views after

1914, they gradually reorganized their movement into several autonomous organizations, each of which more clearly defined its priorities and programs. While these new groups helped to encourage President Wilson's growing interest in the principles for a new international order after the war, none had sufficient influence to convert him to a specific formula. Perhaps aware of the lack of harmony on the details of world organization, Wilson felt little compulsion to adopt any one of their plans. At the same time it is not surprising that Wilson's proposals for an international organization should fail to receive the undivided support of peace workers once they began to consider the specific features of the proposed League of Nations.[45]

Rice University

notes

1. General accounts of the movement for these years are A. C. F. Beales, *The History of Peace: A Short Account of the Organized Movements for International Peace* (New York, 1931), ch. 10; Merle Curti, *Peace or War: The American Struggle, 1636-1936* (New York, 1936), chs. 6, 7; Ruhl J. Bartlett, *The League to Enforce Peace* (Chapel Hill, 1944), ch. 1; Robert Endicott Osgood, *Ideals and Self-Interest in America's Foreign Relations: The Great Transformation of the Twentieth Century* (Chicago, 1953), ch. 5; and Barbara S. Kraft, "Peacemaking in the Progressive Era: A Prestigious and Proper Calling," *Maryland Historian*, I (Fall, 1970), 121-144. A study focusing on religious pacifists is Peter Brock, *Pacifism in the United States: From the Colonial Era to the First World War* (Princeton, 1968), chs. 21-23. Important biographical studies which also cover the World War years include Merle E. Curti, *Bryan and World Peace*, in *Smith College Studies in History*, XVI (April-July, 1931); John C. Farrell, *Beloved Lady: A History of Jane Addams' Ideas on Reform and Peace* (Baltimore, 1967); Philip C. Jessup, *Elihu Root* (2 vols., New York, 1938); and Warren F. Kuehl, *Hamilton Holt: Journalist, Internationalist, Educator* (Gainesville, Fla., 1960). Two recent studies of internationalists are Sondra R. Herman, *Eleven Against War: Studies in American Internationalist Thought, 1898-1921* (Stanford, 1969); and Warren F. Kuehl, *Seeking World Order: The United States and International Organization to 1920* (Nashville, Tenn., 1969).

2. This paper will focus almost exclusively on thirty-six leaders of the American peace movement. Admittedly, any list in such a large movement is somewhat arbitrary, and scholars' interpretations of the movement will differ considerably as long as they fail to agree on a definition of a peace worker. For instance, Michael Arnold Lutzker, "The 'Practical' Peace Advocates: An Interpretation of the American Peace Movement, 1898-1917" (unpublished Ph.D. dissertation, Rutgers University, 1969), 255-268, lists fifty-three individuals, only sixteen of whom appear in my list. Lutzker's sample differs from my own primarily because he focuses almost exclusively on the so-called practical peace workers, most of whom were tardy recruits and who managed the wealthier peace organizations, especially the Carnegie Endowment for International Peace. As Lutzker admits (p. 229), in 1910 at least "twelve trustees of the Carnegie Endowment had no prior institutional connection with the peace movement," yet he includes some of them in his sample. My main standard in selecting the thirty-six was active participation in the peace movement for most if not all of these years. Indexes for determining regularity of involvement were long-term membership in peace or internationalist organizations and/or fairly consistent participation at peace congresses in the United States. Those who participated in the peace movement only marginally or for brief periods have not been included. By these standards the thirty-six, listed alphabetically, were: Jane Addams, Fannie Fern Andrews, Hannah J. Bailey, Samuel J. Barrows, Richard Bartholdt, Charles E. Beals, Raymond L. Bridgman, William Jennings Bryan, Nicholas Murray Butler, Arthur Deerin Call, Andrew Carnegie, Samuel Train Dutton, Edwin Ginn, Edward Everett Hale, Hamilton Holt, William I. Hull, Charles E. Jefferson, Jenkin Lloyd Jones, David Starr Jordan, George W. Kirchwey, Louis P. Lochner, Belva Ann Lockwood, Alfred H. Love, Frederick Lynch, Theodore Marburg, Edwin D. Mead, Lucia Ames Mead, George W. Nasmyth, Robert Treat Paine, Elihu Root, James Brown Scott, May Wright Sewall, William H. Short, James L. Slayden, Albert K. Smiley and Benjamin F. Trueblood.

3. Twenty-one were involved in the peace and/or anti-imperialist movements before 1900: Addams, Bailey, Barrows, Bridgman, Bryan, Carnegie, Ginn, Hale, Hull, Jefferson, Jones, Jordan, Lockwood, Love, Edwin and Lucia Mead, Paine, Sewall, Slayden, Smiley and Trueblood. Only Smiley failed to question McKinley's foreign policies between 1898 and 1900.

4. For evidence of peace workers' statements opposing the Spanish-American War, imperialism and navalism see Trueblood, "Present Dangers of Territorial Acquisition," *American Friend*, V (July 7, 1898), 632-633; Love's account in *Peacemaker*, XVI (May, 1898), 206-215; Mrs. Lockwood in *ibid.*, XVII (December, 1898), 111-114; Jordan, *Imperial Democracy: A Study of the Relation of Government by the People, Equality before the Law, and Other Tenets of Democracy to the Demands of a Vigorous Foreign Policy and Other Demands of Imperial Dominion* (New York, 1899); [Edwin Mead] "Editor's Table," *New England Magazine*, XVIII, new series (May, 1898), 385-392; Bridgman, "Brute or Man—The Annexation Problem," *ibid.*, XIX, new series (September, 1898), 82-93; Isabel C. Barrows, *A Sunny Life: The Biography of Samuel June Barrows* (Boston, 1913), 151-154; Addams, "Democracy or Militarism," in Central Anti-Imperialist League, *The Chicago Liberty Meeting Held at Central Music Hall, April 30, 1899. Liberty Tract, No. 1* (Chicago, 1899), 35-39. Robert L. Beisner, *Twelve Against Empire: The Anti-Imperialists, 1898-1900* (New York, 1968), ch. 8, interprets Carnegie's opposition. Also see *Washington Wife: Journal of Ellen Maury Slayden from 1897-1919* (New York, 1963), 16; Slayden's statements, *Congressional Record*, 56th Cong., 1st sess., XXXIII (May 7, 1900), 5233-5234, and (May 15, 1900), 5549-5552; the petitions of Ginn, Bailey, and other friends of peace in *ibid.*, 55th Cong., 3rd sess., XXXII (December 12, 1898), 90.

5. Nasmyth, address, *Report of the Fifteenth Annual Meeting of the Lake Mohonk Conference on International Arbitration, May 19th, 20th, and 21st, 1909* (Albany, N.Y., 1909), 150-152. (Hereafter cited as *Lake Mohonk Conference*, with the year of the conference added.) Lochner, address, *Lake Mohonk Conference, 1910*, 185-188; Call, address, *Lake Mohonk Conference, 1914*, 34-38.

6. Carnegie, *A League of Peace: A Rectorial Address Delivered to the Students in the University of St. Andrews, 17th October, 1905* (Boston, 1906), 32-37; [Holt] "A World Legislature," *Independent*, LVII (July 7, 1904), 46-47; Bartholdt, "The Parliament of Nations," *ibid.*, LVIII (May 11, 1905), 1025-1026; Bridgman, *World Organization* (Boston, 1906), esp. 41-70.

7. For the fullest evidence of differences on military preparedness see the discussions in *Lake Mohonk Conference, 1906*, 21-38; *Lake Mohonk Conference, 1907*, 128-142; *Lake Mohonk Conference, 1908*, 150. Root was simultaneously an officer of the Navy League and president of the Carnegie Endowment, and several members of the New York Peace Society also were members of the Navy League.

8. Butler, address, *Lake Mohonk Conference, 1907*, 16-17; Kirchwey, address, *ibid.*, 181-182; Root's speeches, "The Hague Peace Conferences," April 15, 1907, and "The Importance of Judicial Settlement," December 15, 1910, *Addresses on International Subjects*, ed. Robert Bacon and James Brown Scott (Freeport, N.Y., 1969 edition), 140-142, 148-150; Scott, address, *Proceedings of International Conference, Under the Auspices of American Society for Judicial Settlement of International Disputes, December 15-17, 1910, Washington, D.C.* (Baltimore, 1911?), 3-4; Marburg, address, *Proceedings of Second National Conference, American Society for Judicial Settlement of International Disputes, Cincinnati, Ohio, November 7-8, 1911*, ed. Theodore Marburg (Baltimore, 1912?), 84-85. Cf. Lockwood, discussion, *American Society for Judicial Settlement of International Disputes, 1910*, 99-100; "Is Arbitration a Failure?" *Advocate of Peace*, LXXIII (January, 1911), 3-4; Call, "The Friendly Composition of International Disputes," *ibid.*, LXXVI (March, 1914), 61-62.

9. Kirchwey, address, *Lake Mohonk Conference, 1910*, 95-96; Marburg, address, *American Society for Judicial Settlement of International Disputes, 1911*, 81-82; Scott, "The Constructive Peace Movement," *World To-Day*, XXI (February, 1912), 1789-1792; Root, "Nobel Peace Prize Address" [1914], and "The Sanction of International Law," April 24, 1908, *Addresses on International Subjects*, 157, 25-32.

10. Bridgman, *The First Book of World Law: A Compilation of the International Conventions to Which the Principal Nations Are Signatory, With a Survey of Their Significance* (Boston, 1911), 283-284.

11. Kuehl, *Seeking World Order*, 118, 152, 166.

12. Addams, *Newer Ideals of Peace* (New York, 1907); Jones to Addams, Oct. 12, 1912, and Jordan to Addams, Nov. 25, 1912, both in the Jane Addams Papers, Swarthmore College Peace Collection, Box 4.

13. Root and Butler, both conservative Republicans, were barely able to tolerate Bryan. Also see *Autobiography of Andrew Carnegie* (New York, 1920), 364. Other peace leaders either disliked his erratic behavior on the issue of imperialism or his "radical" domestic proposals but later praised his conciliation treaties as Secretary of State. Jordan to Bryan, Feb. 7, 1900, William Jennings Bryan Papers, Manuscript Division, Library of Congress, Box 24; and Jordan to Jessie Jordan, Apr. 29, 30, 1913, David Starr Jordan Peace Correspondence, Hoover Institution on War, Revolution, and Peace, Stanford University, Box 1. Also, *Peacemaker*, XIX (November, 1900), 105; Dutton to Bryan, July 24, 1913, United States Department of State Papers, National Archives, Record Group 43, 500.A3/15; Curti, *Bryan and World Peace*, 150-152.

14. Peter Filene, "The World Peace Foundation and Progressivism, 1910-1918," *New England Quarterly*, XXXVI (December, 1963), 484-491.

15. David S. Patterson, "Andrew Carnegie's Quest for World Peace," *Proceedings of the American Philosophical Society*, CXIV (October 20, 1970), esp. 379-382.

16. For an extremely inclusive definition of the peace movement see Lynch, "The Leaders of the New Peace Movement in America," *Independent*, LXXIX (September 28, 1910), 629-638. Mead, "Peace Trustees and the Armament Craze," *Unity*, LXX (October 3, 1912), 72-74; New York Peace Society, *Year Book, 1910-1911* (n.p., n.d.), 22.

17. On periodic international congresses see the memorial of the American Peace Society presented to the Massachusetts House of Representatives, reproduced in *Lake Mohonk Conference, 1903*, 137-140; on this and other areas of agreement, see the platforms of the Lake Mohonk Conferences for the years 1901, 1904, and 1906 to 1914. Also, Kuehl, *Seeking World Order*, 104-106, 112, 114-116, 171.

18. The findings of the social backgrounds of the peace workers in the following three notes come from Allen Johnson, Dumas Malone and Richard Livingston Schuyler, eds., *Dictionary of American Biography* (22 vols., New York, 1928-1958); *Who Was Who in America* (3 vols., Chicago, 1943-1960); *The National Cyclopedia of American Biography* (62 vols., New York, 1898-1967); and biographies, memoirs and autobiographies of individual peace workers.

19. Of the twenty-three in professions, Barrows, Beals, Hale, Jefferson, Jones, Lynch and Short were ministers; Bryan, Ginn, Kirchwey, Lockwood, Marburg, Paine, Root and Scott were lawyers; and Butler, Call, Dutton, Jordan, Mead, Nasmyth, Smiley and Trueblood had obtained higher degrees in the liberal arts or education. Bridgman and Holt also attended graduate school for two years but received no degrees; both became journalists.

20. Between 1909 and 1914, the following peace workers had died: Barrows (1909), Hale (1909), Paine (1910), Smiley (1913), Love (1913) and Ginn (1914). Of the surviving thirty in 1914, only Bailey, Jordan, Sewall, Bryan, Bartholdt and Slayden did not live in one of these six cities, although the latter two as congressmen and Bryan as Secretary of State technically resided in Washington, D.C.

21. Bailey's father was a minister; Smiley, Trueblood, Hull and Nasmyth had Quaker parents; Ginn, Mead, Dutton, Addams and Bryan had thought seriously of the ministry or church service as a career; and Barrows, Beals, Hale, Jefferson, Jones, Lynch and Short became clergymen. In addition, Mrs. Lockwood's second husband was a minister.

22. Charles Herbert Levermore, *Samuel Train Dutton: A Biography* (New York, 1932), 80-83, 91, 97. Author's interview with Short's son, Frederick W. Short, February 13, 1969.

23. *The Twentieth Century Club of Boston, 1894-1904* (n.p., n.d.), 3-4, 13-16, 21; Levermore, *Dutton*, 51, 81; Lynch, *The One Great Society: A Book of Recollections* (New York, 1918), 3-5, 11-15; Edson L. Whitney, *The American Peace Society: A Centennial History* (Washington, D.C., 1928), 271.

24. Butler to Dutton, Jan. 21, 1908, New York Peace Society Papers, Swarthmore College Peace Collection, Box 2; Levermore, *Dutton*, 90-91; and Ellen Slayden, *Washington Wife*, 189-190. A few critics occasionally pointed out the elitism of the movement. Bartholdt, remarks, *Proceedings of the Second National Peace Congress, Chicago, May 2 to 5, 1909*, ed. Charles E. Beals (Chicago, 1909), 327; Lucia Mead, address, *Book of the Fourth American Peace Congress, St. Louis, May 1, 2, 3, 1913*, ed. Walter B. Stevens (St. Louis, 1913), 376-377; and John Haynes Holmes to Short, Jan. 27, 1914, New York Peace Society Papers, Box 4. For attacks by immigrants, laborers and Socialists on the peace leadership see A. M. Simon's comments, *Survey*, XXII (May 22, 1909), 279; *New York Times*, December 13, 1911, p. 1, col. 8, p. 2, col. 1; and Vincent St. John, "The Working Class and War," *International Socialist Review*, XV (August, 1914), 117.

25. Dutton, address, *Proceedings of the Third American Peace Congress Held in Baltimore, Maryland, May 3 to 6, 1911*, ed., Eugene A. Noble (Baltimore, 1911), 335; Lynch, *The Peace Problem: The Task of the Twentieth Century* (New York, 1911), 111; Mead, "The Literature of the Peace Movement," *World Peace Foundation, Pamphlet Series*, No. 7, Part IV (October, 1912), 1-14; Jordan to Ginn, Feb. 3, 1912, David Starr Jordan Papers, Supplementary Correspondence, Hoover Institution on War, Revolution, and Peace, Stanford University; Lochner, address, *Lake Mohonk Conference, 1910*, 188. The perceptive analysis of Carnegie's shameless hero worship of political leaders in Joseph Frazier Wall, *Andrew Carnegie* (New York, 1970), 914ff, can be applied to a lesser degree to all peace workers.

26. Bridgman, *The Master Idea* (Boston, 1899), 212-226; Trueblood, "The Historic Development of the Peace Idea," June, 1900, *The Development of the Peace Idea and Other Essays*, ed. Edwin D. Mead (Boston, 1932), 1-35; Mead, address, *Official Report of the Thirteenth Universal Peace Congress, Held at Boston, Massachusetts, U.S.A., October Third to Eighth, 1904*, ed., Benjamin F. Trueblood (Boston, 1904), 31-33; Holt, typescript, The Federation of the world [1907-1914], 3-4, 7, 26-27, Hamilton Holt Papers, Mills Memorial Library, Rollins College, Box 91; Hull, "The New Peace Movement: A Series of Addresses delivered in 1908-1909," *Swarthmore College Bulletin*, VII (September, 1909), 25-32; Beals, *The Higher Soldiership* (Chicago, 1912), 20, 23-29; Lucia Mead, *Swords and Ploughshares, or The Supplanting of the System of War by the System of Law* (New York, 1912), 1-12.

27. Marburg, "The Backward Nation," *Independent*, LXXII (June 20, 1912), 1365-1370; Smiley, address, *Lake Mohonk Conference, 1909*, 9-10; Butler, address, *ibid.*, 24-25; Dutton, address, *Lake Mohonk Conference, 1912*, 24-25.

28. Slayden, address, *Lake Mohonk Conference, 1906*, 60; Holt, Federation of the World, 1; Kirchwey, address, *Lake Mohonk Conference, 1908*, 73; Beals, *Higher Soldiership*, 10-11; Root, "Nobel Peace Prize Address," *Addresses on International Subjects*, 156-157.

29. "The Menace of the Navy," *Advocate of Peace*, LXVI (May, 1904), 77-78; Jefferson, "The New Navy," *Independent*, LVII (October 27, 1904), 972-974; Lucia Mead, "The Gentle Art of Making Enemies," *Advocate of Peace*, LXVIII (December, 1906), 250-251; Jones, address, *National Peace Congress, 1909*, 308-315; Mead, address, *Report of the Proceedings of the New England Arbitration and Peace Congress, Hartford and New Britain, May 8 to 11, 1910*, ed. James L. Tryon (Boston, 1910), 105-107; [Holt] "Armament Scandals," *Independent*, LXXIV (May 1, 1913), 946; Slayden, "The Traffickers in War," *Farm and Ranch*, XXXII (November 22, 1913), 4-5; Jordan, *War and Waste: A Series of Discussions of War and War Accessories* (Garden City, N.Y., 1913), 52-69; Ginn, address, *Lake Mohonk Conference, 1913*, 24.

30. Bryan, address, *Proceedings of the National Arbitration and Peace Congress, New York, April 14th to 17th, 1907*, ed. Robert Erskine Ely (New York, 1907), 393-394; Lynch, *Peace Problem*, 120-127; Lucia Mead, address, *Lake Mohonk Conference, 1902*, 64-65; Mead to Carnegie, Mar. 27, 1905, Edwin and Lucia Mead Papers, Swarthmore College Peace Collection, Box 1; Dutton, *Social Phases of Education in the School and the Home* (New York, 1900), 73-75, 140, 194-197, 236-237; *First Annual Report of the American School Peace League* (Boston, 1909), 26; Jordan and Edward Benjamin Krehbiel, *Syllabus of Lectures on International Conciliation, Given at Leland Stanford Junior University* (Boston, 1912), esp. 133-143; Hull, "New Peace Movement," 50-51; Butler, address, *Lake Mohonk Conference, 1909*, 17-18; and Ginn, address, *Lake Mohonk Conference, 1913*, 26-29. For two students' acceptance of these values see Nasmyth, "The Peace Movement in the Colleges," *Independent*, LXVIII (February 7, 1910), 362-365; Lochner, "The Cosmopolitan Club Movement," *International Conciliation*, No. 61 (December, 1912).

31. *Address of Hon. Richard Bartholdt, President of the American Group, at the XIII Conference of the Interparliamentary Union at Brussels, Aug. 29, 1905*, printed speech, Richard Bartholdt Papers, Missouri Historical Society; Scott, address, *Lake Mohonk Conference, 1910*, 71; Holt, "A World Legislature," 47.

32. Trueblood, address, *Lake Mohonk Conference, 1895*, 9; Hale, "The United States of Europe," *The Peace Crusade*, I (March 8, 1899), 5; Root, "Instructions to the American Delegates to the Hague Conference," May 31, 1907, in James Brown Scott, *The Hague Peace Conferences of 1899 and 1907* (2 vols., Baltimore, 1909), II, 191; Lucia Mead, address, *National Peace Congress, 1909*, 257; Butler, address, *Lake Mohonk Conference, 1910*, 20; Marburg, address, *ibid.*, 86-87; Holt, address, *American Peace Congress, 1911*, 7-9.

33. Jordan to Ginn, Feb. 3, 1912, Jordan Papers, Supplementary Correspondence; Bryan, address, *Lake Mohonk Conference, 1910*, 166; Mead, address, *National Peace Congress, 1909*, 306; Paine, address, *Universal Peace Congress, 1904*, 34-36; Smiley, address, *Lake Mohonk Conference, 1911*, 17-21. On the decline of wars, see Hale, address, *Lake Mohonk Conference, 1899*, 10-11; "Will War Ever Be Altogether Abolished?" *Advocate of Peace*, LXVII (May, 1905), 93; Lucia Mead, *A Primer of the Peace Movement* (Boston, 1905), [2]; Holt, "Federation of the World," 7; Mead, address, *National Peace Congress, 1909*, 41-42; Beals, address, *American Peace Congress, 1913*, 179-180.

34. Marburg, "Backward Nation," 1365-1368; Butler's addresses, *Lake Mohonk Conference, 1909*, 19, and *Lake Mohonk Conference, 1910*, 23. Also, Root, "Nobel Peace Prize Address," *Addresses on International Subjects*, 159-174.

35. "Battleships and Universities," *Advocate of Peace*, LX (August-September, 1898), 175; Hale, address, *Lake Mohonk Conference, 1899*, 12; Butler, address, *Lake Mohonk Conference, 1909*, 18-19; Slayden, "Millions Wasted for War," *Farm and Ranch*, XXXI (March 9, 1912), 1, and "What Armed Peace Costs the Nations," *ibid.*, XXXII (December 6, 1913), 5-6.

36. "Commerce a Peacemaker," *Peacemaker*, XXIV (March, 1903), 52-53; Bridgman, *First Book of World Law*, 299-300, 306-307, and *World Organization*, 82-86; Beals, *Higher Soldiership*, 20; Hull, *The New Peace Movement* (Boston, 1912), 44; Lucia Mead, *Swords and Ploughshares*, 48ff; Trueblood, "War A Thing of the Past," *Cosmopolitan Student*, I (April, 1910), 49-50.

37. See, for example, the addresses in *Lake Mohonk Conference, 1906*, 85-123; and the businessmen's bulletins, "Obligatory Arbitration and Business," and "The Business Man and International Law," *Lake Mohonk Conference, 1911*, 186, 188-189. The writings of Norman Angell, a British peace worker, bolstered the peace leaders' hopes that nationalism was declining and war was becoming outmoded. See his *The Great Illusion: A Study of the Relation of Military Power in the Nations to Their Economic and Social Advantage* (London, 1910). For the influence of Angell's views, see *After All: The Autobiography of Norman Angell* (London, 1951), 147-158; Jordan, "Bankers as Peace Guardians," *World To-Day*, XXI (February, 1912), 1786-1789; and Lucia Mead, *Swords and Ploughshares*, 139-152.

38. Harold and Margaret Sprout, *The Rise of American Naval Power, 1776-1918* (Princeton, 1939), 286-290, 308-309; David S. Patterson, "The Travail of the American Peace Movement, 1887-1914" (unpublished Ph.D. dissertation, University of California, Berkeley, 1968), 338-346. Arthur Henry Dadmun (field secretary of the Navy League), address, *American Peace Congress, 1913*, 234; and Jonathan Daniels, *The End of Innocence* (Philadelphia, 1954), 115.

39. Bryan's speech, quoted in *The Commoner*, Mar. 8, 1912, p. 3, col. 1; cf. *New York Times*, Dec. 11, 1913, p. 1, col. 6. Also, Arthur L. Weatherly, discussion, *American Peace Congress, 1913*, 150; Beals, address, *ibid.*, 194; and John Wesley Hill, address, *ibid.*, 380.

40. The International Peace Bureau Papers, United Nations Library, Geneva, and the Bertha von Suttner-Alfred Fried Correspondence, United Nations Library, Geneva, contain much correspondence between American and European peace workers. Also see Mead, "England and Germany," *Atlantic Monthly*, CI (March, 1908), 399-407; Jefferson, "The Delusion of Militarism," *ibid.*, CIII (March, 1909), 379-388; Kirchwey, address, *Lake Mohonk Conference, 1909*, 30-35; Carnegie, "A Silver Lining to War Clouds," *World To-Day*, XXI (February, 1912), 1793; Butler, address, *Lake Mohonk Conference, 1912*, 14-15; Lynch, "Peace and War in 1913," *Yale Review*, III, new series (January, 1914), 272-284; Nasmyth to Mead, Mar. 29/Apr. 11, 1913, Mead Papers, Box 1; Dutton, address, *Lake Mohonk Conference, 1914*, 80-84; and Jordan's report, "The World Peace Foundation: Work in 1914," *World Peace Foundation, Pamphlet Series*, IV, No. 7 (December, 1914), 23-24.

41. Jordan, "The Impossible War," *Independent*, LXXIV (February 27, 1913), 467-468; Addams, "Peace on Earth," *Ladies Home Journal*, XXX (December, 1913), 27; Nasmyth to Mead, Apr. 24, 1913, Mead Papers, Box 1; and Trueblood, *85th Annual Report of the Directors of the American Peace Society, 1913* (Boston, 1913), 15-16.

42. Louise Whitfield Carnegie, preface to *Autobiography of Andrew Carnegie*, v; "Secretary Trueblood's Retirement," *Advocate of Peace*, LXXVII (May, 1915), 105; Beals, *Benjamin Franklin Trueblood—Prophet of Peace* (New York, 1916), 14-15; Lucia Mead to Miss Trueblood, Aug. 2, 1915, Mead Papers, Box 1; Lucia Mead to Jordan, Aug. 24, 1918, Jordan Peace Correspondence, Box 11; and Lucia Mead to Jane Addams, July 13, 1919, Addams Papers, Box 7.

43. Henry F. May, *The End of American Innocence: A Study of the First Years of Our Own Time, 1912-1917* (New York, 1959), esp. 9-56, 396-398.

44. For a good case study of the dilemma over sanctions see Martin David Dubin, "Elihu Root and the Advocacy of a League of Nations, 1914-1917," *Western Political Quarterly*, XIX (September, 1966), 439-455; also Kuehl, *Seeking World Order*, 184-195, 205-211.

45. *Ibid.*, 213-231, 336-339. For other accounts of new groups founded after 1914 see Bartlett, *League to Enforce Peace*, 28-82; Marie Louise Degen, "The History of the Woman's Peace Party," *The Johns Hopkins University Studies in Historical and Political Science*, LVII, No. 3 (Baltimore, 1939), 11-191; and Charles Chatfield, *For Peace and Justice: Pacifism in America, 1914-1941* (Knoxville, Tenn., 1971), 15-41.

Democracy in Wartime: Antimilitarism in England and the United States, 1914-1918

Blanche Wiesen Cook

The revelations in *The Pentagon Papers* distressed many American citizens. Yet their impact on public morale far outreached their impact on national policy. Too many citizens had convinced themselves that Americans in high places would not lie to their constitutents. Despite the evidence, many Americans continue to believe that the foreign policy of the United States is propelled only by an honorable quest for international law and is rooted in democratic agreements publicly made. For other Americans, however, *The Pentagon Papers* indicated that democracy is now, and has always been, endangered by war. They have concluded that since success in war seems to require secrecy and duplicity, one of the major functions of the peace movement may be to provide the public with the truth.

> When the War was over, I saw that all I had done had been totally useless except to myself. I had not saved a single life or shortened the War by a minute. I had not succeeded in doing anything to diminish the bitterness which caused the Treaty of Versailles. But at any rate I had not been an accomplice in the crime of all the belligerent nations, and for myself I had acquired a new philosophy and a new youth. . . .
>
> Bertrand Russell, *The Autobiography of Bertrand Russell*, Vol. II (Boston, 1968), 38-39

> I believe that the people in the long run are going to do more to promote peace than any governments. Indeed, I think that people want peace so much that one of these days governments had better get out of their way and let them have it.
>
> President Dwight D. Eisenhower to Prime Minister Harold Macmillan, London, 1959

During World War I both Britain and the United States, two of the oldest and most self-congratulatory democracies, experienced periods of repression which left permanent scars on their proud heritage. But in both nations organizations emerged which sought to preserve political liberty. A survey of the goals and experiences of the American Union Against Militarism and England's Union of Democratic Control reveals not only the fragile nature of democracy in wartime, but suggests also that private citizens must prepare to fight against those forces which threaten their nation's democratic institutions.[1]

There were many parallels between the American Union Against Militarism and England's Union of Democratic Control. Not only were they similar in the vision and political attitudes of their membership, the structure of their organization and the means which they adopted to register their dissent, but also in the experiences which their members endured in wartime. These experiences served to measure the truth of that conviction which had brought the antimilitarists together in the first place—the belief that the real enemy was not Germany but war itself. They opposed war because war endangered liberty and all the political institutions which they cherished. As Jane Addams wrote, this was not a war between the forces of democracy and the forces of militarism. "War itself destroys democracy wherever it thrives . . . not only in Russia and Germany, but in the more democratic countries as well."[2] Bertrand Russell agreed with Addams' view. He wrote that what George Santayana had called "the Prussian educational-industrial-military domination" was just what the antimiltarists feared would conquer the democracies—not only by foreign imposition but internally.[3]

Both the AUAM and UDC emerged during the early months of World War I and were led by people who were convinced that the war would end all their work for progressive reform and social justice. Generally, the antimilitarists were not active in the established peace movement which flourished at the beginning of the twentieth century. They opposed World War I because they considered it the result of secret diplomacy forced on unknowing and unwilling citizens whose economic and social lives would be damaged by the war. The antimilitarists in both England and the United States were influenced by the same books and shared a common vision of democracy in which poverty would be abolished and individual freedom would thrive. Both English and American reformers were influenced by Charles Booth's monumental *Life and Labour of the People in London* and Seebolm Rowntree's first study of poverty in York, and members of both groups participated in the Settlement House Movement which was largely inspired by these studies. F. W. Pethick-Lawrence and Clifford Allen, the founder of the No-Conscription Fellowship, were identified with England's University Settlement and Toynbee Hall, whereas Jane Addams and Lillian Wald founded, respectively, Hull House and the Henry Street Settlement.

In Britain, 1906 was the year of the great Liberal election which meant to English reformers "a revolutionary swing in the direction of radicalism and social reform."[4] Many of Parliament's forty liberals were closely identified with the UDC, notably Joseph King, Richard Lambert, Arthur Ponsonby and Charles Trevelyan; J. Ramsay MacDonald was the leader of the Independent Labour Party. The other members were associated with all manner of reform activities. E. D. Morel, the UDC's secretary and most active member, was famous for his exposure of Belgian misrule in the Congo and he founded the Congo Reform Association; Helena M. Swanwick was a journalist and prominent suffragist; Charles R. Buxton, a Member of Parliament, was a leading proponent of labor reform; J. A. Hobson wrote on numerous subjects, including unemployment and the maldistribution and underconsumption of wealth; and Norman Angell through his writings inspired Angell Leagues for International Polity throughout Europe and America.

In the United States the AUAM was led by prominent reformers who worked closely with Jane Addams and Lillian Wald: Crystal Eastman, an attorney and pioneer in labor relations and fair housing legislation; her brother, Max Eastman, the editor of an exuberant magazine of protest, *The Masses;* Oswald Garrison Villard, who owned and edited *The Nation;* and Paul Kellogg, the editor of *Survey,* an important journal which focused on social problems and was directed to social workers.

In their statement of principles, entitled "Towards a Peace That Shall Last," issued in 1915, the members of the AUAM declared that their right to protest war was established by the unemployment of the waterfronts, the augmented misery of the cities, and by the financial depression "which has curtailed our school building and crippled our works of good will. War has brought low our conception of the preciousness of human life, as slavery brought low our conception of human dignity." Like Clifford Allen who wondered while in prison why England, "so famous for its love of liberty, should have never yet achieved that real liberty of the individual that can only come with the abolition of poverty,"[5] the antimilitarists on both sides of the Atlantic resented the war because it threatened to destroy their life's work. Even the Fabians who refused to join any dissident movement against the war believed that it would destroy England's rebels, feminists and Guild Socialists. Beatrice Webb, for example, feared that England might "slip into a subtle form of reaction—lose faith in democracy and gain enjoyment from the mere display of Power."[6]

The leaders of the UDC made a specific appeal to the rank and file of British labor because, as E. D. Morel noted, "British labour in the mass had never appreciated the fact that the conduct and character of its foreign relations was intimately bound up with its own internal emancipation." Morel believed that "the entire burden" of the British Empire ultimately rested "upon the shoulders of British labour."[7]

But Morel did not want the UDC specifically identified with Labour Party politics. He rejected the idea popular among some of his associates that the antimilitarists should use the occasion of the war to build momentum for a socialist revolution. Morel believed that the unjust and dangerous use of capitalism "had to be attacked from a thousand sides." However, no progress would be made so long as war could arise to "set back at any moment" the advances made by labour. Morel wanted every "people in every land . . . free to pursue their march towards emancipation." He was convinced that nothing permanent would be achieved as long as war remained a perpetually threatening force.[8]

In the UDC's first publication, "The Morrow of the War," Morel wrote that the "idea of a federalised Europe . . . involving the disappearance or substantial reduction, of standing armies and navies" was the ultimate goal. But it could not be attained until the democracies of the west realized the impossibility of having "a system of government which leaves them at the mercy of the intrigues and imbecilities of professional diplomatists and of the ambitions of military castes; helpless, too, in the face of an enormously powerful and internationalized private interest dependent for its profits upon the maintenance of that 'armed peace' which is the inevitable prelude to the carnage and futility of war. . . ."[9] According to Morel, all social progress depended on the establishment of democratic control of foreign policy.

The English antimilitarists eschewed all questions of domestic politics during wartime and worked solely for the settlement of disputes by international arbitration and a progressive and lasting peace. In the first open letter sent by the organizers of the UDC to potential members, Ramsay MacDonald, Charles Trevelyan, Norman Angell and E. D. Morel outlined the goals of the UDC: to secure real parliamentary control over foreign policy and to prevent secret diplomacy from ever again being "forced upon the country as an accomplished fact"; to establish direct negotiations with democratic parties and influences in Europe, "so as to form an International understanding depending on popular parties rather than on governments"; and to secure a peace treaty which will not, "either through the humiliation of the defeated nation or an artificial re-arrangement of frontiers," become the starting point for future wars.[10]

Like the members of the AUAM, the members of the UDC were neither absolute pacifists nor revolutionaries. Indeed, both groups worked well within the established political structure and went out of their way not to embarrass the Administrations whose military policies they abhorred. Due to hostile press reaction which followed the publication of their first open letters, the UDC issued a statement explaining that it was not "a stop the war movement."[11] Charles Trevelyan, for example, sought a reduction of armaments but, like the other members of the UDC, he was very careful to apply his demands to "all the belligerent powers" so as not to seem to be requesting the disarmament of Britain alone.[12] Trevelyan believed that it was his duty as a citizen and as an MP to vote for supplies and to avoid "hampering the conduct of the war." But he believed patriotism did not require him "to be silent about the blunders of the Government past, present, or future."[13] The UDC did not urge resistance to the war and did not "propose to take *active* steps." It was created to build an enlightened public opinion "which would take action in the Press and on the platform when the time comes. . . ."[14]

The UDC was primarily concerned with keeping liberal war aims before the public. At no time did the members of the UDC become involved in an active campaign to insure the freedoms of speech, assembly and press. But the very nature of their activities dragged them into that controversy. They asserted that the war "might have been prevented if the people had been aware of what the government was committing it to."[15] In order to counter official censorship and to make the people aware of alternatives to Britain's official policy which they believed existed, the UDC distributed pamphlets containing the early speeches of President Wilson, statements by German socialists and pacifists and, in 1916, published secret agreements made between Britain, France and Italy, along with the denials of those agreements made by Herbert Asquith and Sir Edward Grey during 1913 and 1914.[16]

The first phase of the AUAM's wartime program was almost a replica of the UDC's program. For the first three years of the European War the AUAM campaigned against preparedness and conscription and worked to maintain the neutrality of the United States. When war was declared the leaders of the AUAM announced that once the United States was in the war they would cease all opposition to it. But they still believed that America would have been in a stronger position as a neutral to bring the nations into a lasting federation for peace and that war would make "all the evils of militarism more active and virulent" and indefinitely delay "their ultimate goal of world federation and disarmament." Therefore, they demanded a clear statement of America's peace terms, the publication of all international agreements, and they promised "vigorous opposition" to compulsory military service.[17]

Several members of the AUAM wanted to move faster than did Paul Kellogg and Lillian Wald, who were particularly reluctant to oppose Wilson or embarrass the Administration. In order to maintain the support of these two prominent leaders, Crystal Eastman suggested that a statement be issued to the press clarifying the Union's position and making it clear that their's was not "a party of opposition" nor a "policy of obstruction." It was a "democracy first" movement. The declaration, when issued, also explained that the AUAM had believed that there were alternatives to war, but since "the war was a fact" it wanted "America to win." By victory the antimilitarists meant the achievement of those conditions for a negotiated peace which Wilson had called for, conditions outlined also by the UDC and by the "revolutionary government of Russia," namely, no forcible annexations, no punitive indemnities, and free development of all nationalities.[18]

After reading Wilson's June 14, 1917, Flag Day speech, however, most of the antimilitarists became more impatient and less concerned about embarrassing the Administration. Amos Pinchot wrote Crystal Eastman that Wilson had flourished "the knout over the objectors and all who would oppose the temporary little fatherhood which he is assuming in order to discourage autocracies in other climes."[19] In his address, Wilson had identified the entire peace movement with treason and called the peace people schemers who sought to insure a German victory and implant German civilization throughout Europe. The President referred to the peace movement as "the new intrigue, the intrigue for peace," and announced that the antimilitarists were "tools" of "the masters of Germany":

> The sinister intrigue is being no less actively conducted in this country than in Russia and in every country in Europe to which the agents and dupes of the Imperial German Government can get access. That Government has many spokesmen here, in places high and low. They have learned discretion. They keep within the law. It is opinion they utter now, not sedition. They proclaim the liberal purposes of their masters; declare this a foreign war which can touch America with no danger . . . ; set England at the center of the stage and talk of her ambition to assert economic dominion throughout the world; appeal to our ancient tradition of isolation . . . ; and seek to undermine the Government with false professions of loyalty to its principles.

> But they will make no headway. The false betray themselves always in every accent. . . . This is a People's War, a war for freedom and justice and self-government amongst all the nations of the world, a war to make the world safe for the people who live upon it and make it their own. . . . For us there is but one choice. . . . Woe be to the man or group of men that seeks to stand in our way in this high day of resolution when every principle we hold dearest is to be vindicated and made secure for the salvation of the nations. . . .[20]

This speech had a radicalizing effect on the antimilitarists. It served to put the repressive wartime measures sponsored by the Administration in perspective. As a result, the members of the Union pursued far more vigorously its programs devoted to the maintenance of constitutional freedoms and the rights of conscientious objectors.

From April the antimilitarists campaigned against what became, on June 15, 1917, the Espionage Act. They petitioned Wilson not to "sacrifice" the constitutional rights basic to the continuance of American democracy and objected to the comprehensive nature of the bill which included a mail censorship clause so vague that it jeopardized the freedom of every newspaper and magazine in the country. Any literature which caused "insubordination, disloyalty or mutiny" in the military, or which discouraged draft or enlistment services, or which might "embarrass or hamper the Government in conducting the war," was liable to confiscation. In their appeal the antimilitarists catalogued the meetings which already had been broken up, the instances of speakers arrested and of censorship imposed by mob violence. They urged Wilson to consider the future of America's "cherished institutions" if the "psychology of war" were permitted to "manifest itself." Lillian Wald asked if it were not "possible that the moral danger to our democracy" might become more "serious than the physical . . . losses incurred."[21]

Even before the Espionage Act passed, mail was censored and several Americans were arrested for "public criticism of the President" on the basis of a statute passed February 14, 1917, entitled "Threats Against the President Act," which covered any written or spoken word which threatened to do bodily harm or endanger the life of the president.[22] As a Canadian member of the Woman's Peace Party wrote to the American section: "Well you Americans are not going to let the Germans, Turks or Russian autocrats get ahead of you when you go in for liberty and democracy."[23]

The effectiveness of the Espionage Act was assured through the establishment, by executive order, of the Committee on Public Information (CPI). Originally the CPI was to be the Administration's news agency and was to control the press and public opinion. George Creel was chairman and the Secretaries of State, War and the Navy were members. The committee consisted of a domestic section, a foreign section and numerous divisions, including news, films, state fairs, industrial relations, civic and educational groups and a publicity establishment. Creel had been associated with the social reform movement as a crusading journalist. Indeed, as Arno Mayer pointed out, Creel's entire committee was composed of former crusaders: Arthur Bullard, Will Irwin, Ernest Poole, Louis F. Post, Ray Stannard Baker and Ida Tarbell, a veritable "roll call of the muckrackers."[24]

Creel himself noted that Wilson opposed free speech during the war and informed the antimilitarists that the President had said " 'there could be no such thing—that it was insanity.' " To allow public opposition to the war would be to permit dissenters to " 'stab our soldiers in the back.' "[25]

Shortly after the war was declared it became impossible for the antimilitarists to get an honest hearing in any newspaper anywhere in the country. Jane Addams wrote that after America "entered the war, the press throughout the country systematically undertook to misrepresent and malign pacifists as . . . a patriotic duty."[26] Most of the small magazines which reserved space for the views of the antimilitarists were either suppressed or denied access to the mails. Among the censored journals directly associated with the AUAM were *The Masses,* edited by Max Eastman, and *Four Lights,* the organ of the Woman's Peace Party of New York which was chaired by Crystal Eastman. Other suspended magazines included *The Appeal to Reason;* the *Michigan Socialist;* the *Milwaukee Leader;* the New York *Call; The Nation* (for criticizing Samuel Gompers); and The *Freeman's Journal* for reprinting Thomas Jefferson's statements which favored Irish independence; the *Irish World,* for writing that Palestine would not become a Jewish state; *The World Tomorrow,* a religious pacifist magazine edited by Norman Thomas; and a Civil Liberties Bureau pamphlet which deplored mob 'violence.[27]

The AUAM's protests against censorship and undemocratic practices were dismissed with little of the Administration's former solicitude. Amos Pinchot, for example, wrote Wilson for "an expression of opinion" regarding the numerous magazines and small papers which had been denied access to the mail. Pinchot asked Wilson if he did not think "free criticism" was of the "utmost importance in a democracy? . . . Can it be necessary, even in wartime, for the majority of a republic to throttle the voice of a sincere minority?" Pinchot concluded, "As friends of yours, and knowing how dear to you is the Anglo-Saxon tradition of intellectual freedom, we would like to feel that you do not sanction" censorship at the "bureaucratic discretion" of post office officials.[28] Wilson replied that he hesitated to make a public statement which "would undoubtedly be taken advantage of by those with whom neither you nor I have been in sympathy at all."[29]

Pinchot then went to Washington in order to request that Postmaster General Albert Burleson tell him on what basis the department suspended periodicals so that the editors might avoid suppression in the future. Burleson replied that he would not consider the question since "a remedy for the situation was amply provided for by the courts." Pinchot met with Burleson for two hours and left wondering how Wilson could "keep that elderly, village-idiot in his cabinet?" Still believing that Wilson was sympathetic to the aims of the antimilitarists, Pinchot reported his interview with Burleson to Wilson and also the rumor that Lord Northcliffe, the British War Cabinet's expert in psychological warfare, had commissioned Somerset Maugham to go to Russia to "buy up Russian newspapers" and that Northcliffe himself had organized a "vigorous campaign to persuade American newspapers to support Britain's war aims."[30] But Wilson was not sympathetic to the aims of the AUAM, and he wrote to Max Eastman that "a time of war must be regarded as wholly exceptional and that it is legitimate to regard things which would in ordinary circumstances be innocent as very dangerous to the public welfare."

In September, 1917, the AUAM itself was investigated by the Post Office Department which had decided to exclude two of the Union's pamphlets. Lillian Wald believed that both were entirely innocent and protested that all the Union's printed material had been "submitted in advance" to New York's postmaster. One of the pamphlets, written by Roger Baldwin, included a request to conscientious objectors to send letters which stated their position to the Secretary of War; the other was a reprint from the *Survey* of Norman Thomas' article, "War's Heretics."[31]

After the Department withheld the pamphlets for several weeks but refused to make a decision on their legality, Baldwin went personally to William Lamar and demanded a decision. Lamar asserted that " 'he naturally gave first attention to people whose loyalty to the government was unquestionable' " and he did not think Baldwin's organization worthy "of any particular consideration."[32] After four months the antimilitarists did go to court and the Justice Department ruled the pamphlets legal.

In October, Burleson announced his general criteria for censorship. Publications would be suspended if they implied: " 'that this Government got in the war wrong, that it is in it for wrong purposes, or anything that will impugn the motives of the Government for going into the war. They cannot say that this Government is the tool of Wall Street or the munitions makers. That kind of thing makes for insubordination in the Army and Navy and breeds a spirit of disloyalty throughout the country. . . .' " In addition, there could be "no campaign against conscription and the Draft Law. . . ."[33]

Oswald Garrison Villard believed that Wilson was unaware of what the Post Office Department was doing. When *The Nation* was suspended Villard wrote Colonel House that the President "surely cannot know what is going on."[34] Other antimilitarists were not so charitable in their estimation of Wilson's wartime behavior. James Warbasse, for example, considered Wilson's announcement that the Allies "must not be criticized," the "last blow" to democracy and wrote that "if we are not to be permitted to make the world safe for democracy we at least must continue . . . to make the world unsafe for hypocrisy."[35] Victor Berger, whose socialist *Milwaukee Leader* had been barred from the mails, believed that Wilson was "afraid of a revolution after the war" and was trying "to prevent it by putting the [radical] press out of business." Berger did not blame Wilson's advisers. He wrote to Pinchot that his criticism of Burleson was unfair. Burleson was "simply Woodrow Wilson's special delivery boy. Men of Burleson's type have no chance to become full grown men in Texas, where they . . . hold office while still very green and immature. They may get rotten . . . but they never ripen."[36]

The AUAM also protested the violence which accompanied the Administration's appeals to patriotic Americans to fight what Wilson had called the "sinister intrigue" of German dupes, and the misguided but also dangerous dissenters.[37] Some manifestations of that violence were limited to words, such as former Ambassador James Gerard's declaration that "we should hog-tie every disloyal German American, feed every pacifist raw meat, and hang every traitor to a lamp-post to insure success in this war."[38] Other forms of violence were physical. The antimilitarists were convinced that America witnessed the first victories of Prussian militarism when in Boston "thousands of peaceful citizens" who had a permit to assemble, "were attacked by lawless soldiers and sailors in uniform" as the police stood by "apparently overawed by the uniform and did nothing except to arrest the victims." The AUAM noted that this scene had already occurred in "a dozen American cities" only three months after America's entrance into the war.[39]

The greatest wartime outrage occurred in East St. Louis where scores of black people were beaten, lynched, burned and drowned, and the antimilitarists wondered at President Wilson's silence:

> Six weeks have passed since the East St. Louis riots and no public word of rebuke, no demand for the punishment of the offenders, has come from our Chief Executive. These American Negroes have died under more horrible conditions than any noncombatants who were sunk by German submarines. But to our President their death does not merit consideration.

> Our young men who don their khaki are thus taught that, as they go out to battle under the flag of the United States, they may outdo Belgian atrocities without rebuke if their enemy be of a darker race. And those who guard our land at home have learned that black men and women and little children may safely be mutilated and shot and burned while they stand idly by.[40]

It is little wonder that an English member of the Woman's Peace Party wrote: "In traveling about your country . . . it does not seem to me that you have a surplus of democracy here—certainly not enough to warrant exporting any of it."[41] The antimilitarists recognized that possibility. Crystal Eastman wrote that if America destroyed its constitutional freedoms "in the first fine frenzy of war enthusiasm, we shall not have much democracy left to take to the rest of the world." That was why the Civil Liberties Bureau was created—"to maintain something over here that will be worth coming back to when the weary war is over."[42]

The Civil Liberties Bureau was established by the AUAM after a prolonged and divisive controversy which split the Union into two groups. Paul Kellogg, for example, decided after the United States entered the war that his primary concern was no longer "the struggle to hold the fort for democracy against militarism at home," but rather to organize the world for democracy. He feared that if the Union supported conscientious objectors, the public would assume the AUAM was working for the military paralysis of America and it would lose its "influence and Power" in the postwar "drive for peace" toward a league of nations. The majority of the AUAM did not consider this a real conflict and decided to create the CLB anyway. Crystal Eastman stated that "the two go hand in hand. War is intolerable; we must get rid of war." Militarism, "which is the fruit of war," tends to destroy democracy. Therefore, Eastman asked, how could anyone work for world peace and world democracy without first guarding democracy against militarism at home?[43]

The Civil Liberties Bureau was established with offices throughout America to provide legal counsel to keep critics of the Administration out of jail and to provide advice to conscientious objectors. It was headed by Roger Baldwin, Crystal Eastman and Norman Thomas, and it was staffed by an advisory committee of lawyers who volunteered their time under the direction of attorney Harry Weinberger.

Norman Thomas was elected chairman of the AUAM committee to deal with the question of conscientious objectors, and as early as April campaigned against the proposed federal conscription bill and compulsory military training, and appealed for regular civilian trials for objectors. Jane Addams, Lillian Wald and Norman Thomas met with Newton Baker on behalf of the objectors. They requested exemptions not just on religious but on ethical grounds, since "it is a matter not of corporate but of individual conscience." They noted in their appeal to Baker that England's law was "more liberal" than the one before Congress and England had at that time 4000 objectors in prison. The AUAM believed that it was better for "some slackers to escape" than for America to "coerce men's consciences in a war for freedom."[44]

The antimilitarists were convinced that upon the issue of conscription rested the future of "the last fortress of democracy in the world," and recognized the possibility that on that issue "the greatest adventure in human history would go down in failure."[45] Consequently, after the army bill was passed Thomas wrote to congressional committees demanding its repeal. He asked how America could "wage war 'for the privilege of men everywhere to choose their way of life' while we compel the conscientious objector to war . . . ?" "Autocracies may coerce conscience in this vital matter: democracies do so at their peril."[46]

Unlike the AUAM, the Union of Democratic Control had nothing to do with the agitation against conscription and the campaign to support conscientious objectors. Some members of the UDC realized that to ignore this crucial area of repression in wartime was seriously to limit the significance of the UDC's protest. F. W. Hirst, the editor of the *Economist,* wrote to Morel that he considered the absence of a conscription program a "vital omission." He believed that the first and most important thing was to prevent a military despotism from emerging in

England, bringing with it the "substitution of martial law for trial by judge and jury." Hirst believed that if conscription was adopted self-government would be destroyed "and with it all possibility of influencing the course of events abroad" along the lines the UDC had postulated.[47] As opposed to the AUAM, the civil libertarians in the UDC were a minority, and activity in this area was rejected by E. D. Morel for much the same reasons that had led Paul Kellogg to abandon the CLB's activities.

On June 9, 1915, a group of UDC members submitted a resolution regarding conscription which would have pledged the UDC "to oppose to the utmost any attempt to impose compulsory service either for military or industrial purposes as being unnecessary for the needs of the nation" and not in England's "best interests." Morel wrote to Charles Trevelyan that the resolution was "a tremendously grave step to take." If it meant anything more than rhetoric, it meant resistance and that, concluded Morel, "would clearly bring the UDC within measurable distance of prosecution for sedition and rebellion. . . ." In addition, Morel made a distinction between compulsion for home defense and compulsion for service abroad. He personally would not resist the call for home defense, "not having reached the Quaker position. . . ." Morel also referred to what he had believed was the agreement of the UDC members: that "it was useless activity to oppose measures which would be persisted in despite opposition."[48]

While the UDC remained England's most significant coalition to end the war and promote a democratic peace, its timidity regarding the more immediate challenge of universal military conscription left a vacuum in the movement which was filled rapidly by the No-Conscription Fellowship. A. Fenner Brockway, editor of the official ILP paper, *The Labour Leader,* published a letter inviting those people not prepared to render military service under conscription to enroll their names. The response to Brockway's letter was so good that on December 3, 1914, the formation of the No-Conscription Fellowship was announced, with an initial membership of 300 men. Led by Clifford Allen, later Lord Allen of Hurtwood, the NCF became "a breathtakingly efficient conspiracy against the organized might of the state."[49]

Although the work of the No-Conscription Fellowship is beyond the scope of this paper, it is important to note that the impetus for this organization was the same as that behind the establishment of the UDC and the AUAM—the belief that war was inimical to socialism and re-form. Clifford Allen believed that men and women of commitment had "to face the only possible outcome of our Socialist faith," by which he meant non-violent resistance to militarism.[50]

During his third trial by court martial for refusing to obey military orders, Allen explained that he opposed the war because he saw "no substantial reason to prevent peace negotiations being entered upon at once. . . . I believe that the Governments of all the nations are too afraid of releasing their peoples to make peace. . . ." He added:

> I resist war because I love Liberty. Conscription is the denial of liberty.
>
> If I hold that war and militarism are evils which will only cease when men have the courage to stand apart from them, I should be false to my own belief if I avoided the dangers of military service only to accept some safe civil work as a condition of exemption from such service.
>
> This country is faced with the most insidious danger that can confront a free people on the claim of the State to dispose of a man's life against his will. . . .
>
> A war which you can only win by the compulsion of unwilling men and the persecution of those who are genuine will ultimately achieve the ruin of the very ideals for which you are fighting.[51]

The UDC's unwillingness to campaign for the conscientious objectors caused it to lose the direct support of the most prominent peace people in England. Bertrand Russell, for example, wrote that he would join the No-Conscription Fellowship because the UDC was "too mild and troubled with irrelevancies. It will be all right after the war, but not now. I wish good people were not so mild. The non-resistance people I know here are so Sunday-schooly—one feels they don't know the volcanic side of human nature, they have little humour, no intensity of will, nothing of what makes men effective. . . ."[52]

Russell's decision to support conscientious objectors led to his imprisonment because of a pamphlet he wrote for the No-Conscription Fellowship which explained that if people chose to become conscientious objectors they would be sentenced to two years at hard labor. Deemed a violation of the Defense of the Realm Act, a statute very similar to America's Espionage and Sedition Acts, Russell was tried and sentenced to sixty-one days' imprisonment or a fine of £100, which he refused to pay. During his defense, Russell summarized the convictions of the anti-militarist movement in both England and the United States. He denied that he alone was on trial:

> It is the whole tradition of British liberty which our forefathers built up with great trouble and great sacrifice. Other nations may excel us in some respects, but the tradition of liberty has been the supreme good that we in this country have cultivated. We have preserved, more than any other Power, respect for the individual conscience. . . . I think that under the stress of fear the authorities have somewhat forgotten that ancient tradition . . . and the tyranny which is resulting will be disastrous if it is not resisted. . . .[53]

The failure of the Union of Democratic Control to campaign against conscription and to support civil liberties did not prevent its members from becoming victims of the general wartime repression about which Russell spoke. Throughout the war the UDC continued to publish pamphlets and address large public meetings in order to expose diplomatic agreements and later to oppose what they considered an imperialist and reactionary treaty. In many cases they were met by riots which, according to Trevelyan, "were promoted by officers and recruiting authorities." On occasion meetings were stormed by soldiers who "were invited to break the heads of 'pro-Germans'"; these incidents were defended by the government "as spontaneous outbreaks of popular indignation." Halls were refused by local authorities at the instigation of the police, and "every kind of political pressure was exerted to prevent our obtaining places to speak in." Newspapers announced that the UDC was in the pay of Germany and later in the pay of Bolsheviks; and "threats of personal violence were constantly proffered . . . in the reactionary press." Censorship prohibited UDC literature from going to neutral countries and from being distributed to the armed services. In 1917 two of Morel's famous works, *Ten Years of Secret Diplomacy* and *Truth and the War,* were censored and prohibited from distribution in neutral and allied nations. Later, Morel was sentenced to six months in prison under the Defense of the Realm Act because he sent a pamphlet, *Tsardom's Part in the War,* not banned from circulation in Britain or France, to Romain Rolland, the French pacifist. But Rolland happened to be in neutral Switzerland at the time. By June 8, 1918, the censor refused a permit to export to any foreign destination the monthly UDC, or any of the pamphlets published by the Union.[54] As Philip Snowden noted, it became clear that the government's objective was "to suppress every opinion which is disagreeable to them."[55]

In addition to official censorship, the London police raided the UDC offices and ransacked document files and correspondence. Occasionally, the office was broken into secretly at night and papers and correspondence were taken.[56]

Trevelyan was particularly disturbed that such repression occurred under Liberal Party auspices. In a letter to Walter Runciman, the director of the Board of Trade, Trevelyan wrote that he had "never for a moment doubted that liberty of discussion would be in danger during the war. . . ." But he had hoped that the era of repression would be postponed as long as the liberals were in office. He had hoped that it would "be left to Toryism . . . to adopt a Prussian system." Moreover, Trevelyan was troubled that Tory newspapers and speakers could broadcast their views, "their creed of vengeance, and their insane policy of dismembering Germany" without repression. Only the antimilitarists who tried "to make people take saner and more Liberal views" appeared to be "silenced by police raids and confiscation of . . . literature."[57]

Like the reaction of the AUAM leaders to George Creel and his committee of former liberals, the UDC members were particularly disappointed in the attitude of the Liberals in the British government. Trevelyan wrote to John Simon, the Secretary of State for Home Affairs, reminding him that he had "remained in the Government because he had thought that it would be well to have some Liberalism left in high places." Trevelyan noted that the seizure of literature would have to lead to even greater repression because "police bullying" would not silence the dissenters who cherished England's history of liberty.[58]

The entire British propaganda department at Crewe House was remarkably similar to the structure organized by the CPI. Crewe House under Lord Northcliffe was composed of "evesdroppers, letter-openers, deciphers, telephone tappers, spies, an intercept department, a forgery department, a criminal investigation department, a propaganda department . . . , a censorship department, a ministry of education and a press bureau." Like the CPI, Crewe House, staffed by former liberals, was well equipped to mobilize patriotism for the war effort.[59]

Both the UDC and the AUAM campaigned for democratic control of foreign policy, the abolition of secret treaties, early peaceful negotiations, a declaration of war aims by belligerent governments and a non-punitive treaty on the basis of what was to become the Fourteen Points. In addition, both the AUAM and the No-Conscription Fellowship gave legal counsel to conscientious objectors and worked to protect individual conscience and political freedoms even in wartime. Still, after the war Bertrand Russell reflected that all he had done "had been totally useless" except to himself. He had "not saved a single life or shortened the war by a minute." Nor had he "succeeded in doing anything to diminish the bitterness which caused the Treaty of Versailles." But at any rate he had "not been an accomplice in the crime of all the belligerent nations," and for himself he "had acquired a new philosophy and a new youth."[60] Other antimilitarists considered their work a vital challenge to the power of the state in wartime. They had refused to recognize "the right of the Executive to put the intellect of the citizen in chains" and they had refused "to admit as tolerable the conception of a 'State'" which could extinguish freedom of thought and expression in time of war. They insisted that "the statesmanship which conceals vital facts from the nation betrays the nation. . . ."[61]

In conclusion, it should be noted that the antimilitarists judged the situation accurately. War and democracy cannot both occupy the same air space. Bertrand Russell wrote that Jane Addams had "exactly the same outlook" as he did. They both recognized that war destroyed democracy. The English in the war, Russell noted, became "daily more like the Germans. The faults one hates in them are not confined to them, but are the products of militarism."[62] No individuals were more aware of that fact than the antimilitarists. Jane Addams, for example, was followed by secret agents and otherwise victimized by those who called her traitor. John Haynes Holmes believed that he would never forget "the storm of hatred which broke over her devoted head when she denounced the [food] blockade . . . , and declared that the 'United States should not allow women and children of any nation to starve.' " In 1935, the year of her death, her name was added to a list of dangerous Reds, the enemies of America.[63]

Governments in wartime seem to fear the sovereignty of the people. Contemporary presidents have echoed Wilson's belief that the free expression of public opinion is dangerous and that to allow dissent "is to stab our soldiers in the back." As in World War I, democratic governments continue to use crude and often brutal methods to control dissent. Now, however, they also use a more sophisticated and more deceptive rhetoric in an attempt to forestall it altogether. In the United States, for example, government spokesmen now concern themselves with "peace actions" and troop withdrawal as they determinately escalate the war. But then, the more powerful and total the state becomes, the more apparent freedom it may allow its citizens. Able to transcend the limits of public opinion, the government's course need not be altered even with the publication of such revelations as were found in *The Pentagon Papers*. The vital force of a democracy can thus be threatened merely by the government's willingness to ignore the popular disapproval. As Norman Thomas wrote at the end of World War I, if "war brutalizes the individual it cannot ennoble the state."[64]

Perhaps it was such a thought which moved President Eisenhower forty years later to say during a television interview with Prime Minister Macmillan in London that "above all" he would like "to believe that the people in the long run are going to do more to promote peace than any governments." "Indeed," he added, "I think that people want peace so much that one of these days governments had getter get out of their way and let them have it."[65] The experiences of the antimilitarists of World War I and the dissonance of the contemporary peace movement have made it clear that governments will not move until large numbers of people mobilize to create genuinely public policy. If the history of the next fifty years is to be different from the history of the last fifty years, the people must recognize that the reformers and dissenters of the peace movement cannot themselves make the necessary changes in policy and democratic procedure; but that they have set the necessary example.

John Jay College
City University of New York

notes

1. For a full account of the American Union Against Militarism, see Blanche Wiesen Cook, "Woodrow Wilson and the Anti-militarists, 1914-1918" (unpublished Ph.D. dissertation, Johns Hopkins University, 1970); and for the Union of Democratic Control see Marvin Swartz, *The Union of Democratic Control in British Politics During the First World War* (New York, 1971).

2. Jane Addams, "The Revolt Against War," *Women at the Hague: The International Conference of Women and Its Results* (New York, 1915), 77.

3. Bertrand Russell, *The Autobiography of Bertrand Russell, 1914-1944* (Boston, 1968), 56.

4. Arthur Marwick, *Clifford Allen: The Open Conspirator* (Edinburgh & London, 1964), 7. Many of the UDC's leaders joined the Labour Party after the war.

5. *Ibid.*, 36.

6. Margaret I. Cole, ed., *Beatrice Webb's Diaries*, II (London, 1952), 31.

7. E. D. Morel to Mrs. Snowden, n.d., Union of Democratic Control Papers, British Library of Political and Economic Science, London School of Economics. (Hereafter cited as UDC Papers.)

8. E. D. Morel to Edward H. Driffill, August 10, 1916, UDC Papers.

9. E. D. Morel, "The Morrow of the War," UDC pamphlet #1, 14.

10. Open Letter to Potential UDC members, August, 1914, UDC Papers.

11. Helena M. Swanwick, *Builders of Peace: Ten Years History of the Union of Democratic Control* (London, 1924), 33.

12. Charles Trevelyan to E. D. Morel, September 23, 1914, E. D. Morel Papers, London School of Economics.

13. *Ibid.*, September 26, 1914.

14. Morel to Maude Royden, September 9, 1914, UDC Papers.

15. Swanwick, *Builders of Peace*, 36.

16. *Ibid.*, 63.

17. Minutes, American Union Against Militarism, April 3, 1917, American Union Against Militarism Papers, Swarthmore College Peace Collection, Swarthmore College, Pennsylvania. (Hereafter cited as AUAM Papers.)

18. Crystal Eastman to Lillian Wald, June 14, 1917, Wald Papers, New York Public Library; Crystal Eastman to Paul Kellogg, June 14, 1917, Kellogg Papers, University of Minnesota.

19. Amos Pinchot to Crystal Eastman, June 15, 1917, Amos Pinchot Papers, Library of Congress, Box 30.

20. Ray S. Baker, *Woodrow Wilson, Life and Letters: War & Peace*, I (Garden City, 1927-1937), 63-65.

21. AUAM petition to Wilson, April 16, 1917, AUAM Papers. Cf. Harry N. Scheiber, *The Wilson Administration and Civil Liberties* (Ithaca, 1960), 17-18; and Donald Johnson, *The Challenge to American Freedoms: World War I and the Rise of the American Civil Liberties Union* (Lexington, 1963), 79-84.

22. Scheiber, *Wilson Administration and Civil Liberties*, 14; for details regarding the arrests see Roger M. Baldwin to Oswald Garrison Villard, April 13, 1917, Villard Papers, Houghton Library, Harvard University.

23. Elsie Charlton to Eleanor Karsten, April 13, 1917, Woman's Peace Party Papers, Swarthmore College Peace Collection, Box 2.

24. Arno Mayer, *Political Origins of the New Diplomacy* (New Haven, 1959), 349-350.

25. George Creel quoted in Donald Johnson, *Challenge to American Freedoms*, 62.

26. Jane Addams, *Peace and Bread in Time of War* (New York, 1945), 134.

27. See Scheiber, *Wilson Administration and Civil Liberties*, 31-32; Johnson, *Challenge to American Freedoms*, 79-84.

28. Pinchot to Wilson, July 14, 1917, Pinchot Papers, Library of Congress, Box 27.

29. Wilson to Pinchot, July 18, 1917, Wilson Papers, Library of Congress, Series III, Letterbook 42.

30. Pinchot to Wilson, July 25, 1917, Pinchot Papers, Library of Congress, Box 27; for Pinchot on Burleson, cf. Pinchot to George P. West, October 15, 1917, *ibid.*

31. Lillian Wald to Joseph Tumulty, September 12, 1917, Wald Papers, New York Public Library.

32. Lamar quoted in Johnson, *Challenge to American Freedoms*, 61.

33. *Ibid.*

34. Villard to Colonel House, September 16, 1918, Villard Papers, Harvard University.

35. Warbasse to Pinchot, October 10, 1917, Pinchot Papers, Library of Congress, Box 30.

36. Berger to Pinchot, October 25, 1917, *ibid.*, Box 33.

37. For Wilson's remarks see Baker, *War and Peace*, I, 66, 129, *passim.*

38. Gerard quoted in ACLU pamphlet, "Who May Advocate Force?" 27.

39. AUAM press release by Crystal Eastman, July 2, 1917, AUAM Papers, Box 4.

40. From unsigned *Four Lights* article, August 25, 1917, XVI, Woman's Peace Party of New York Papers, Swarthmore College Peace Collection.

41. *Ibid.*, September 22, 1917. For other examples of oppression in wartime see Elizabeth Gurley Flynn Papers, State Historical Society of Wisconsin, Madison, Wisconsin.

42. Crystal Eastman to press, July 2, 1917, AUAM Papers.

43. Crystal Eastman to Lillian Wald and Paul Kellogg, June 14, 1917, AUAM Papers.

44. Jane Addams, Lillian Wald and Norman Thomas to Newton Baker, April 12, 1917, Wald Papers, Columbia University, Box 88.

45. George Nasmyth, *Four Lights*, VI, April 7, 1917.

46. Norman Thomas to congressional committees, May 1, 1917, Wald Papers, Columbia University, Box 12.

47. F. W. Hirst to E. D. Morel, August 19, 1914, UDC Papers.

48. Morel to Trevelyan, June 9, 1915, *ibid.*

49. Marwick, *Clifford Allen*, 23.

50. *Ibid.*, 22.

51. *Ibid.*, 40-41.

52. Bertrand Russell to Lady Ottoline Morrell, June 1, 1915, *The Autobiography.*

53. Russell quoted in David Boulton, *Objection Overruled* (London, 1967), 183-184.

54. Ethel Sidgwick who transported the pamphlet was not arrested and there is evidence that British officials were eager to see Morel "safely lodged in gaol." I am grateful to Professor Catherine A. Cline of Catholic University for this information. Charles Trevelyan, *The Union of Democratic Control: Its History and Its Policy* (London, 1919), 6-7; Swanwick, 89-93.

55. Philip Snowden to Morel, November 9, 1916, UDC Papers.

56. Morel to Whiskaard, August 25, 1915, Morel Papers, London School of Economics.

57. Trevelyan to Walter Runciman, August 23, 1915, UDC Papers.

58. Trevelyan to John Simon, August 12, 1915, UDC Papers.

59. Arthur Ponsonby, *Falsehood in Wartime* (New York, 1929), 12.

60. Russell, *The Autobiography*, II, 38-39.

61. E. D. Morel in foreword to Swanwick, *Builders of Peace*, 8.

62. Bertrand Russell to Jane Addams, Addams Papers, Swarthmore College Peace Collection, Box 6.

63. John Haynes Holmes, "Jane Addams Memorial," *Unity*, July 15, 1935, Wald Papers, New York Public Library.

64. Norman Thomas to Walter Mulbach, July 31, 1917, Thomas Papers, New York Public Library.

65. President Eisenhower in a TV interview, London, September 1, 1959, in UDC pamphlet "New Moves in the H Bomb Story."

Alternative Strategies in the American Peace Movement in the 1920's

Charles DeBenedetti

The principal preoccupation of the American peace movement in the 1920's was the re-definition of the nation's role in European affairs. Horrified by the destructiveness of the World War, American peace groups were determined to prevent the recurrence of violence among the advanced industrial powers who anchored the European state system. Force as an instrument of policy among the powers was demonstrably catastrophic. At the same time, American peace elements felt certain that the realization of their hope depended upon the moral and physical strength of the United States. Consciously "America-centric," postwar peace activists assumed that questions of war and peace in modern industrial civilization turned upon the decisions of the American people. It was for this reason that they debated vigorously the comparative value to American policy and world peace of the League of Na-

> It is perhaps true that the path to internationalism through small states is dangerous and uncertain; but, paradoxical as it may seem, internationalism can rest only on satisfied nationalism. The sentiment is intractable and compelling, and cannot be removed from politics unless it is recognized; peoples whose aspirations have long been thwarted will not be satisfied with anything short of self-determination. . . . International law depends for its validity upon the agreement of sovereign states, and it will continue to be weak in proportion to the number of states whose agreement is necessary.
>
> We are forced, therefore, to accept the anomaly of an increase in the number of nation states, at the same time that we are attempting, by an international league, to lay a stable basis for the federation of the world.
>
> Lindsay Rogers, "The League of Nations and the National State," in Stephen P. Duggan (ed.), *The League of Nations: The Principle and the Practice* (Boston, 1919), 86-87

tions, the World Court, arbitration treaties, collective sanctions and the outlawry of war. Yet even these issues, in the end, were no more than variants of one elemental question: how could the United States most satisfactorily introduce discipline in European politics?

Three alternative strategies arose in the postwar peace movement in response to that question. Although they are categorized here as legalist, reformist and functionalist, the strategies were by no means mutually exclusive. Proponents of one often collaborated with advocates of another. Moreover, none of the strategies was ever developed with deliberateness or articulated with precision. The premium in the post-war movement was upon action and not contemplation. Nevertheless, alternative strategies were recognizable. Each was distinguished by a unique understanding of the nature of peace. And each was animated by the mixed ideological commitments that men bring into movements.

The legalist tradition was more than an ideology or a movement. It was an *ethos* that suffused the thinking of a significant number of post-war peace leaders.[1] Organized in associations like the American Peace Society, the Carnegie Endowment for International Peace and the American Society of International Law, supporters of a legalist approach to world politics perceived peace as a state attendant upon the triumph of justice. Legalist spokesmen like Arthur Deerin Call, executive secretary of the American Peace Society, and Dr. James Brown Scott, an authority on international law and an officer of the Carnegie Endowment, held that the achievement of peace was contingent upon the extension of justice throughout international politics. The extension of justice, in turn, consisted of the codification by experts of international rules of equity, the application of these rules by an international court of justice, and final acceptance by litigants respectful of the sanction of world public opinion. Through a tightening web of procedure, substantive "legal justice" would gradually be gained and peace assured. Legalists made it clear that they did not seek the "abstract justice" of "the reformer and the idealist," but the "legal justice" of courts and codes that could be "counted upon to function with certainty" in minimizing the possibilities of future war.[2] Frightened by the antinational, class appeal of Lenin's "Mundanism," they were determined to solidify the modern state system and existing property relationships by purging the Old Order of its failings through the instruments of enlightened judicial leadership. Peace was reached through the slow, deliberate procedures of the courts and "by making the law itself its own best argument for obedience."[3] It was a trying, trial process and decidedly not one for the impatient. People must not measure "the progress of nations by the foot-rule of our short lives," warned the venerable Elihu Root. "You must think in terms of generations and centuries."[4]

Legalism essentially represented the views of a conservative elite who wielded the scepter of law against the twin dangers of international violence and social convulsion. Fearful of the alarming unpredictability of Old World politics, legalists opposed American involvement in European affairs and supported the preservation of complete freedom of action throughout the world. Any revision of America's traditional posture of "interested isolation" in world affairs was "unnecessary and unlikely."[5] Legalists reasoned that the Monroe Doctrine had irrevocably divided Europe and America into separate spheres. Its century-long success had permitted the United States to gravitate toward a polity of law while the European system had stagnated in conflict and violence.[6] In conjunction with this belief, legalists feared that embroilment in European politics would sharpen tensions among ethnic groups and unsettle social stability within the United States. David Jayne Hill stated solemnly that American intervention in Old World affairs "would result in divisions that would be deeper than they are now and involve our Government in constant domestic turmoil; for it is not realized in Europe that we have in the United States all the races, all the race affections, and all the race prejudices that exist in Europe."[7] Among legalists everywhere, there was little doubt that the risks implicit in active American participation in European politics outweighed any possible gain.

While the United States must avoid entanglement in Old World politics, it could nevertheless contribute to Europe's pacification by universalizing the principles of the American judicial system. Legalists commonly contended that the foundation of the American constitutional system lay in the power of the Supreme Court to adjudicate vital differences among sovereign states. Indeed it was in the practical validation of the principle "that when any one of the states becomes recalcitrant, it shall be coerced by law" that America had made its "supreme contribution to world peace."[8] Without physical force, the Supreme Court successfully applied the rule of law among rival states. It was the paragon of judicial order, the basis for a world founded on law and justice. The hope of peace among civilized states rode upon the internationalization of its principles and the elevation of the whole Anglo-American legal experience to world practice.[9]

Thus the purpose of legalist peace action was to urge the structuring of European politics along juridical lines inspired by the American experience. Legalist leaders supported efforts to collaborate in the codification of international law and favored American accession to the World Court. They also expressed great interest in bringing about the convocation of a Third Hague Conference. Legalists at no time, however, permitted policy preferences to lead them into support of mass action campaigns. Rather than organize popular support, they preferred to sponsor legal research and cooperate closely with government officials. "After all," Arthur Deerin Call told the directors of the American Peace Society, "the greatest peace society with which we are permitted officially to associate is the United States Government."[10] As Washington progressed in its pursuit of liberty under law, the blessings of order, peace and prosperity would spread to embrace all peoples.

While legalists identified peace with triumphant justice, other peace groups saw their goal as the simple absence of war. The social reformers who headed pacifist, church and women's organizations understood peace as the condition that followed upon the destruction of the war system. "Peace means getting rid of war," the Reverend John Haynes Holmes said firmly, "and getting rid of war means outlawing it along with piracy, the duel, and the saloon."[11] The reformist strategy was distinguished by the assumption that war was a crime, a collective sin, a hideous institution that blocked man's access to the humane, Christian life. "Each age faces one supreme moral issue," said Sherwood Eddy, a leading preacher of the Social Gospel. "For our time that issue is war. It is Caesar or Christ, man's way or God's, the appeal to force as ultimate power or to organized goodwill, war or peace."[12] Frustrated by the failure of a war to end war, reformist leaders intended to subject the monster to the grinding power of American social reform.

Reformists throughout the decade invested great faith in the progressive importance of law. Fresh from the hard-won victories of prohibition and women's suffrage, they shared the legalist confidence in the superiority of American constitutionalism. Unlike the legalists, however, reformists identified the strength of American law not in its sanction for order as much as in its capacity to liberate men's minds from prejudice and to abolish pernicious social institutions. "Making war illegal seems a long way off," the pacifist Sidney Strong told Senator William E. Borah. "So once did slavery and the saloon seem eternal, but I've seen them pass."[13] A press release from the Women's Peace Union of the Western Hemisphere expressed the same sense of reform progression, along with the sexual consciousness that actuated feminist peace leaders in the 1920's: "Women won suffrage. Women won prohibition. Now women are putting through the outlawry of war."[14]

Reformists agreed that the United States possessed the spiritual energy and material resources needed to suppress the institution of war. But they differed in their analyses of Europe's problems and in their plans for adapting America's strength to European needs. Most reformists identified Europe's postwar malaise as a spiritual exhaustion that had been compounded by social and economic dislocation. They therefore exhorted the American people to transfuse part of the country's abundant spiritual vitality to the Old World through lines of trade and law. Disclaiming any interest in the politics of foreign policy-making, the great majority of reformists worked to rouse popular sentiment behind a variety of non-entangling actions that would re-inflate Europe's confidence and "stabilize the world."[15]

In practice, the reformist strategy operated through several educational and organizational enterprises. In 1921 the Federal Council of Churches of Christ in America announced plans to lead its twenty million constituents upon a Ten-Year Crusade for a Warless World. Through its Commission on International Justice and Goodwill, the Federal Council proposed to shift modern international relations from a "war-system" to a "peace-system" by generating enlightened public opinion and by exalting juridical substitutes for war. The Church Peace Union was equally interested in changing the "state of mind that now condones war"; and it actively assisted the World Alliance for International Friendship Through the Churches in sharpening antiwar sentiment among Protestant clergymen.[16] Among secular organizations the National Council for Prevention of War took the lead in trying to activate business, labor and farm groups in a united front against war. The National Committee on the Cause and Cure of War assembled nine national women's organizations into a lobby for study and action, while pacifists gathered in the Women's International League for Peace and Freedom and the Women's Peace Union.[17] G. Sherwood Eddy and Kirby Page spread the doctrine of Christian pacifism and international cooperation across college campuses through the agency of the YMCA. The Fellowship of Reconciliation and the War Resisters League sustained those who chose to renounce forever individual participation in the war system. In meeting after meeting, pacifists, churchmen and women's groups resolved their commitment to Christian understanding, the World Court, disarmament, the outlawry of war and even (upon rigid conditions) the League of Nations.[18] Propagandizing and organizing, they hoped to calm Europe by creating in America a wave of moral unanimity that would smash the war system and uncover the foundations of lasting peace.

Several reformists dissented, however, from the majority position. Led by Bull Moose veterans like Raymond Robins, an influential reformist minority blamed Europe's discontent upon reactionary leadership and volatile class divisions. Minority spokesmen were deeply concerned with America's vulnerability to continued European wars. But they resented efforts to excite Americans into concern with Europe on the grounds that the prosecution of an active foreign policy would result in the nation's absorption in the corrupt politics of the Old Diplomacy. The philosopher John Dewey captured the progressive dilemma in these terms:

> . . . while our day of isolation is over, international affairs are still conducted upon a basis and by methods that were instituted before democracy was heard of as a political fact. Hence we engage in foreign policies only at the risk of harming even such imperfect internal democracy as we have already achieved.[19]

Distrustful of Europe and fearful of new wars, reformists like Dewey demanded that the American government lead an attack upon the legal underpinnings of the war system. Dissident progressives pressed insistently for the outlawry of the lawful institution of war and for the establishment of an international Supreme Court to settle disputes. By purging war from the body of international law, outlawry enthusiasts intended to expose war in its criminal infamy, smash the Old Diplomacy and render American-made law the prescriptive pattern of international behavior. It was a large, perhaps laughable order. But it appeared to many postwar progressives as the most effective way of purifying European politics and making the world safe for America.[20]

Despite the minority fears, the larger reformist strategy never envisioned an active American role in European politics. When they spoke of international organization and substitutes for war, reformists thought of juridical devices and developing bonds of moral sentiment. They expected the United States to assume an exhortatory, pontifical role in Europe that would bring Europe moral uplift and political tranquillity. But they regarded the total displacement of the war system as an arduous process that the American people could best promote by retaining their youth, enthusiasm and independence. As the slogan of the National Council for the Prevention of War put it, " 'America First'—In the Crusade for a Warless World."[21]

Finally, leaders of organizations like the League of Nations Non-Partisan Association, the Foreign Policy Association and the World Peace Foundation favored a functional approach to world politics. Conceiving of peace as an ongoing process, functionalists maintained that the very fragility of modern industrial civilization demanded the institutionalization of managerial controls over international affairs. Columbia University history professor James T. Shotwell believed, for example, that "peace does not mean merely the abstention from war, it means as well the maintenance of those conditions under which civilization can endure and develop."[22] Peace was a problem of management. It was a problem of rationalizing techniques which would refine European politics by excluding irresponsible violence.

The drive to rationalize the processes of European politics grew with the realization that science and technology had multiplied the scope and destructiveness of modern war by unanticipated proportions. Each new invention, each scientific advance moved industrial civilization further from human control and toward a terrifying momentum of its own. Raymond B. Fosdick, a former assistant secretary of war and a leading exponent of the League of Nations, felt that "the whole world is tottering on the edge of an abyss. Modern science has put us in a position where with another outburst of passion, . . . we can destroy all the values that have been painfully built up in the last thousand years. The race never had such weapons before, and our situation is entirely new in history."[23] Shotwell and Fosdick agreed. Without organization, without systematic direction by "creative scientific intelligence," runaway technology would "bury this thing we call civilization in a grave too deep for resurrection."[24]

Spreading along lines of industrial interdependence, modern total war promised to trap the United States and all others in its fury. Functionalists looked back upon Wilson's futile attempt at wartime neutrality as ample proof of the precariousness of the American position. They furthermore anticipated that the growing importance and complexity of international commerce would only heighten the nation's vulnerability. Certain that America could not escape the epidemic violence of modern war, functionalists demanded that Republican policy-makers cease the evasion of unilateralism and confront directly the unavoidable question: how could the United States order international relations in a way that would dampen national rivalries before they inflamed the lines of interdependence and sucked America into conflict? The nation seemed to possess little real choice. Certainly James G. McDonald, chairman of the Foreign Policy Association, thought that the matter was clear: "We may not like European entanglements, and I don't like them myself, but when forces are in operation which will inevitably create entanglements and difficulties, I prefer assuming responsibility for positive effort to avoid them rather than to assume responsibility for inaction."[25] For its independence as well as its safety, America must take the lead in rationalizing and maintaining a "definitized" world order.[26]

Functionalists placed their highest hopes for the creation of a "definitized" world order in the League of Nations and its associated agencies. For one thing, the League promised to absorb the gnawing insecurity and overcome the disorganization that together were at the bottom of Europe's discontent. By systematizing international diplomacy through continuing conferences and committees, the League apparatus would create techniques that enveloped the threat of violence in folds of investigations and reports. The League appeared as "an essentially European organization" that substituted conference, arbitration and "the ordinary processes of civilized governments" for the uncontrollable destructiveness of war.[27] In this same vein, the League represented a unique laboratory for experimentation in human and institutional cooperation. It was potentially the most attractive proving ground for the work of social engineers. And social engineers, functionalists maintained, were truly those figures who commanded the levers of future world progress. "The sword won't do the job any more," exclaimed the historian Charles A. Beard.

> The social engineer is the fellow. The old talk about sovereignty, rights of man, dictatorship of the proletariat, triumphant democracy and the like is pure bunk. It will not run trains or weave cloth or hold society together.[28]

At the same time, functionalists believed that the League served splendidly to amplify America's voice in European affairs. The United

States had no interest in strictly European affairs, they agreed, for America was more than a European power. But America did have an interest in avoiding involvement in unnecessary wars and in maintaining a prosperous international trading community. The nature of the nation's interests thus required that it assume an active advisory role in matters of international importance. Arthur M. Sweetser, a former Boston newsman and a prominent official in the League Secretariat, ably expressed the functionalist position as early as 1920. America, he declared, was "the greatest cohesive political unity in existence, the richest nation in the world, the most highly organized," and the one whose "ideals and principles" flourished best by "showing them to the whole world and urging other nations to follow them." This did not mean, however, that America must concern itself with the petty disputes of others. "I mean quite on the contrary," said Sweetser, "that she should be ever ready, in a strategic position, where, when an issue arises which is worthy of her participation, she should be able to express herself and express herself fruitfully. I cannot believe that any American wishes this country to be mute in the world's great struggle of ideas."[29] The League obviously provided the most suitable forum for America's purposes. Although a European combine, it offered a boardroom in which the United States could successfully discharge its consultative responsibility in the management of peace.

The functionalist campaign to streamline international relations by affirming America's advisory leadership took place along many fronts. The World Peace Foundation and the Foreign Policy Association sponsored programs to gather and disseminate facts which emphasized the intricate interdependence of modern international relations. The League of Nations Non-Partisan Association propagandized directly for public support of American entrance into the League. It subsidized speakers, published and distributed literature and formed local cells across the United States. In addition, pro-League leaders tried to affect national policy by staffing governmental committees of inquiry on international affairs and by influencing friendly Administration officials. Functionalists also worked to establish a network of cooperation among European peace leaders who shared their belief in the need for the rapid rationalization of international politics. The Division of Economics and History of the Carnegie Endowment supervised the formation in Europe of several national committees of scholars and industrial experts, who were charged with providing their respective governments with technical data on matters of disarmament and security. The Institute of International Education acted as a service center for the exchange among countries of scholars and students. And the International Committee on Intellectual Co-operation, first formed in 1926, facilitated the interchange of information and research through a single agency at Geneva. At every turn, functionalists strove doggedly to extend and toughen links of daily dependency throughout the modern state system.

In the end, the most striking feature of the functionalist strategy—like the legalist and reformist alternatives—was an essential modesty. Not one intended to change the independent basis of the American world role. Not one challenged the structure of decision-making within the United States.[30] On the contrary, each aimed only to modify Washington's definition of the American role in a way that would discipline European politics without jeopardizing American independence. The modesty of this ambition was the product of many factors. Intellectual uncertainty, calculations of political expediency and the hope of uniting a hodgepodge of contentious peace groups all acted to restrain the movement's ambitions and kept it from acting upon its highest expressions of principle. Yet perhaps the most powerful source of the movement's modesty was its abiding sense of nationalism. Nearly every peace activist believed that the American national experiment contained patterns of right conduct that were relevant to Europe's needs. Whether legal, spiritual or functional, the behavioral patterns at the base of the American experience seemed well designed to overcome the dangerous incalculability of Old World politics.

At bottom, the movement's confidence in the relevance of the American national experience was only part of its larger hope of founding world peace upon "a newer and higher conception of nationalism."[31] Most peace workers in the Twenties rejected the "sentimental internationalism" of the pre-war movement and disliked the exclusiveness that was inherent in Wilson's vision of national self-determination. Instead, they endeavored to create an international polity that fitted the peculiar needs of their unsettled times. Specifically, postwar peace leaders sought to institute a world order that would accommodate cultural and political diversity at the same time as it ended the raw national egoism and conflicting Great Power imperialisms that had historically produced war. Seeking a positive alternative to rank egoism and Great Power tyranny, antiwar activists struggled to build a visible Higher Nationalism from the collective experiences of those modern peoples who recognized war as their common enemy. The need of civilized man, wrote Kirby Page, was "to carry one step higher a process which has long been operating." In plain terms, the issue was "whether or not militant nationalism, greedy imperialism and international anarchy are to lead nations on to further wars, or whether an era of international peace and justice shall be ushered in by outlawing war as a crime and by creating effective social machinery through which a new conception of nationalism may find expression."[32]

With little doubt, nationalist sentiment was pervasive within American society in the 1920's. But it was not strictly a tribal affair. In the thinking of American peace leaders, nationalism expressed the reality of human diversity and the tenacity of human allegiance. Fascinated with its promise, they strove to channel its dynamism behind the functional and juridical alternatives to war that had long been vindicated by the American experience. Their hope for a Higher Nationalism was certainly grand. But it was not naive. Based upon a common interest and expanding through common institutions and common loyalties, it seemed in the Twenties to be the most humanly realistic solution to the calamity of modern total war.[33]

University of Toledo

notes

1. Judith N. Shklar, *Legalism* (Cambridge, 1965), 1-11, 104-105, 109-110, *passim*.

2. Robert Lansing, "Some Legal Questions of the Peace Conference," *The American Journal of International Law*, XIV (1920), 635-637. See also *Codification of American International Law: Addresses by Charles Evans Hughes, James Brown Scott, Elihu Root, and Antonio Sanchez De Bustamente Y Sirven* (Washington, 1926), 51; the Report of the Executive Secretary, "A Review of the Peace Movement in America," in the 96th Annual Report of the Directors, American Peace Society, 1924, Box 5, Records of the American Peace Society, Swarthmore College Peace Collection; and "Suggestions for a Plan to Promote Peace Between Nations," *The Advocate of Peace Through Justice*, LXXXV (December, 1923), 403-404.

3. Lansing, 632; David Jayne Hill, "The Janina-Corfu Affair," *The American Journal of International Law*, XVIII (1924), 98.

4. Elihu Root, "The Steps of Progress," World Peace Foundation *Pamphlets*, VII (October, 1925), 526.

5. Theodore Woolsey, "Reconstruction and International Law," *The American Journal of International Law*, XIII (1919), 187; James Brown Scott, "The Foreign Policy of the United States," *ibid.*, XV (1921), 232.

6. James Brown Scott, "America and Peace," *The Advocate of Peace Through Justice*, LXXXII (December, 1926), 667-676; unsigned editorial, "The Difference Between the United States and Europe, *ibid.*, XCI (February, 1929), 69-73.

7. David Jayne Hill, "The Third Assembly of the League of Nations," *The American Journal of International Law*, XVII (1923), 79. Also see Elihu Root to Lothrop Stoddard, June 22, 1927, Box 142, Elihu Root Papers, Manuscript Division, Library of Congress; copy of Charles Evans Hughes address at the Pilgrims Dinner, London, July 21, 1924, Box 173, Charles Evans Hughes Papers, Manuscript Division, Library of Congress. Edgar Algernon (Lord) Robert Cecil, *All the Way* (London, 1949), 178.

8. "The Difference Between the United States and Europe," 72.

9. James Brown Scott, "A Governed World," *The Advocate of Peace Through Justice*, LXXXII (January, 1920), 2; Arthur Deerin Call, "Three Facts in American Foreign Policy," *ibid.*, LXXXIII (April, 1921), 140-145.

10. Call, "A Review of the Peace Movement in America"; Call, "The Churches Can Promote International Peace," *The Advocate of Peace Through Justice*, LXXV (February, 1923), 47-49; "Our Country's Greatest Peace Society, *ibid.*, XC (February, 1928), 78-80.

11. *Unity*, XCVII (July 12, 1926), 307.

12. Sherwood Eddy and Kirby Page, *The Abolition of War: The Case Against War and Questions and Answers Concerning War* (New York, 1924), 66.

13. Sidney Strong to William E. Borah, February, 1928, attached to Sidney Strong to Elinor Byrns, February 2, 1928, Box 20, Records of the Women's Peace Union of the Western Hemisphere, Swarthmore College Peace Collection.

14. *Ibid.*, press release, Box 3.

15. Frederick Libby, "Why an American Peace Movement," National Council for the Prevention of War *News Bulletin*, VII (July 1, 1928), 1.

16. Report of the General Secretary of the 13th Annual Meeting of the Board of Trustees, December, 1926, p. 5, Box 1, Records of the Church Peace Union, Swarthmore College Peace Collection.

17. The National Committee on the Cause and Cure of War, the more conservative of feminist peace organizations, was formed in 1924 by the suffragette leader Carrie Chapman Catt and "a large number of women who are not in the least satisfied with the situation they find themselves in and that is, carrying out the orders of the men managers of the different peace societies." Finding the movement's male leadership "both timid and incompetent," Mrs. Catt and her sympathizers moved to unite national women's organizations like the League of

Women Voters and the Women's World Court Committee behind a feminist drive for peace. Carrie Chapman Catt to Lucia Ames Mead, January 9, 1924, Box 6, Lucia Ames Mead Papers, Swarthmore College Peace Collection.

18. The Women's International League for Peace and Freedom, for example, was willing by 1927 to support American accession to the League, "providing only that it does so with the understanding that the United States is exempt from any obligation to supply military forces, or to join in exerting military pressure in any case." The WIL also hoped that the American government, in applying for League membership, "would not only secure acceptance of this position, but would express its earnest desire to see the League renounce, or at least abstain from, all use of military sanctions." Emily Greene Balch to WIL members, April, 1927, Correspondence Box 5, Records of the Women's International League for Peace and Freedom—U.S. Section, Swarthmore College Peace Collection.

19. John Dewey, "Our National Dilemma," *The New Republic*, XXII (March 24, 1920), 118.

20. For the fullest statement of the Outlawry position, see Charles Clayton Morrison, *The Outlawry of War: A Constructive Policy for World Peace* (Chicago, 1927).

21. National Council for the Prevention of War, *New Bulletin*, IV (July 25, 1925), 1.

22. James T. Shotwell, "An American Locarno: Outlawing War As an Instrument of Policy," *The Rotarian*, XXXI (December, 1927), 7.

23. Raymond B. Fosdick to Felix Frankfurter, November 27, 1923, Raymond B. Fosdick Papers, Firestone Library, Princeton University. For the same idea expressed at length, see Raymond B. Fosdick, *The Old Savage in the New Civilization* (Garden City, 1928).

24. James T. Shotwell, "Preliminary Memorandum on the Organization to Prepare for a Disarmament Conference," September 15, 1925, Box 269, Tasker H. Bliss Papers, Manuscript Division, Library of Congress. Raymond B. Fosdick to Wallace Buttrick, April 11, 1924, Fosdick Papers. Or James T. Shotwell, "Are We at a Turning Point in the History of the World?," in The Report of the Division of Economics and History, Carnegie Endowment for International Peace, *Yearbook*, No. 16 (Washington, 1927).

25. James G. McDonald to Ivy Lee, ca. November, 1922, Box 1: General 1, James G. McDonald Papers, Herbert Lehman Collection, Columbia University.

26. Raymond B. Fosdick to Sir Eric Drummond, April 9, 1920, in Raymond Fosdick, *Letters from the League of Nations, From the Files of Raymond Blaine Fosdick* (Princeton, 1966), 123.

27. James G. McDonald, "Seven Roads to Peace," *The Survey*, LII (August 1, 1924), 497; James T. Shotwell, in *Report* of the Third Conference on the Cause and Cure of War, January, 1928, Box 1, Records of the National Committee on the Cause and Cure of War, Swarthmore College Peace Collection.

28. Charles Beard to Raymond Fosdick, May 20, 1922, Fosdick Papers.

29. Arthur M. Sweetser, Jr., to William Hamlin Childs, n.d., but ca. January, 1920, Box 13, Arthur M. Sweetser, Jr., Papers, Manuscript Division, Library of Congress.

30. Kirby Page was one of the few peace leaders to express an opinion on this subject, declaring that he saw "little hope of an intelligent foreign policy until there are drastic changes in personnel in Washington." But even he was contented that "such changes will take place within the very near future" through the normal rotation of electoral politics. Kirby Page to A. Barr Comstock, March 12, 1924, Box 2, Kirby Page Papers, Southern California School of Theology, Claremont, California.

31. Kirby Page, "Working Toward a Warless World," *The Christian-Evangelist*, LXII (June 11, 1925), 745. Esther Everett Lape, ed., *The Ways to Peace: Twenty Plans Selected from the Most Representative of Those Submitted to the American Peace Award for the Best Practicable Plan by Which the United States May Cooperate with Other Nations to Achieve and Preserve the Peace of the World* (New York, 1924), 44-46. Dr. Sidney Gulick, chairman of the Commission on International Justice and Goodwill of the Federal Council, referred to this objective as "the higher patriotism" or "Christian patriotism." Gulick, *The Christian Crusade for a Warless World* (New York, 1922), 45-47.

32. Kirby Page, *Imperialism and Nationalism: A Study of Conflict in the Near East and of the Territorial and Economic Expansion of the United States* (New York, 1925), 90-91.

33. Each of those components is vital to modern nationalism. See David M. Potter, "The Historian's Use of Nationalism and Vice Versa," *American Historical Review*, LXVII (July, 1962), 931-938.

Alternative Antiwar Strategies of the Thirties

Charles Chatfield

The 1930's opened with an omen of the pressures that would intensify attempts to form an effective antiwar coalition and at the same time would wedge irreconcilable differences of view between the factions of the peace movement. Japanese troops drove into Manchuria in September, 1931, and Toyohiko Kagawa wrote:

Again I have become a child of an aching heart,
Carrying the burden of Japan's crime,
Begging the pardon of China and of the world,
With a shattered soul;
I have become a child of sadness.[1]

The American State Department countered the Japanese attack on China with the

This crusade is being launched because of the serious possibility that within the near future a general war will break out in Europe and Asia. The signs of the times are more disquieting than during the years preceding the outbreak of the World War.

* * * * *

In such a world governments have little confidence in treaties and are sceptical concerning the effectiveness of pacific agencies of justice. As an instrument of war prevention, the League of Nations is weak. And this fact constitutes one of the most ominous aspects of the present world situation. International anarchy produces war.

* * * * *

The peace sentiment of the nation must be adequately organized if peace legislation is to be adhered to during the hysteria of crisis. Mass pressure from citizens is required both for the enactment and maintenance of a pacific foreign policy.

No-Foreign-War Crusade (1937)

Stimson Doctrine that it would not recognize any settlement that impaired the territorial or political sovereignty of China. The League of Nations vacillated, formed a commission to investigate, and finally condemned Japan, while trying to leave the way open for a negotiated peace in the Far East. About eighteen months after her attack, Japan withdrew from the League.

The Manchurian crisis pre-empted the attention of the American peace movement, which had focused on fairly remote considerations of world organization, international law and moral regeneration. Even the program of arms reduction by international agreement, a political objective upon which the movement was united, was disrupted by the crisis.

In April, 1932, leaders of major peace groups formed an Interorganization Council on Disarmament (ICD) in order to coordinate activities designed to promote the success of the international disarmament conference in Geneva.[2] The member groups fell into at least two broad wings. One consisted of traditional internationalists who, whether committed to international law or organization, were oriented to informational programs. They sought to educate the public; and, because their leaders were influential men, they also hoped to influence policy-makers informally. These were groups such as the Carnegie Endowment for International Peace and the World Peace Foundation, which antedated World War I, or the League of Nations Association and the Foreign Policy Association, which had their origins in the Great Crusade.[3]

The other wing of the ICD consisted of groups whose leadership was largely, if not exclusively, pacifist—men and women who not only worked for peace but repudiated any given war. They, too, sought to inform the public on international affairs, but there were differences. For one thing, throughout the Twenties they had cultivated a moral opposition to war itself. For another, they were issue-oriented and had in fact considerable staff experience in organizing various segments of public opinion. The liberal pacifist groups were without exception formed during or immediately after World War I, and they combined a traditional pacifist repudiation of war *per se* with a progressive emphasis on social-political reform and transnational humanism. They included the Fellowship of Reconciliation, the Women's International League for Peace and Freedom and the National Council for Prevention of War.[4]

Ironically, in view of their later alignment against collective security, liberal pacifists were most militant in response to the Manchurian incursion. Not all pacifists agreed, but the major pacifist groups supported collective sanctions against Japan, and they were a driving force within the ICD for collaboration with the League. James G. McDonald, chairman of the Foreign Policy Association and the ICD, was "shocked and horrified by the willingness of so-called radicals and pacifists to jump into the use of sanctions almost without thinking."[5] Nonetheless, the ICD itself was converted temporarily from a conference site into a pressure group, as an aroused peace movement tried to pull together in response to the Far Eastern crisis.

Unanimity did not last. The council divided over what programs it should urge upon policy-makers the following winter and spring. By autumn, 1932, the council had returned to its original design as an organization for educating and conferring. Six months later it dissolved, thus ending a major attempt to coordinate the whole peace movement and paving the way for fresh coalitions.

The fleeting Interorganization Council for Disarmament contributed little to antiwar work and could be dismissed outright, except that it conveniently illustrates the pressures that determined the configuration of the peace movement in the Thirties.

At that time the cause of peace required a political response to the threat of real war and totalitarianism. Peace advocates of almost all persuasions accepted the validity of political activity—influencing decision-makers through personal contact or public groups—and political action required coalitions of peace societies to build and sustain antiwar public pressure. The consequence was a politically articulate, aggressive antiwar movement, aligning and realigning in search of bases for effective coalition. That was one axis (as it were) of antiwar strategy in the Thirties, and it represented continuity with coalition efforts in the previous decade.

The impact of war and totalitarianism also heightened latent differences of approach within the peace movement. These differences underlay and disrupted coalition efforts on behalf of arms limitation, neutrality legislation, an international conference for economic redistribution and neutral mediation. The ICD floundered in 1932 because the campaign for arms limitation had largely failed. (The Geneva conference accomplished nothing. It adjourned in July, 1932, resumed discussion from the following February to July, adjourned again and lingered on from October, 1933, until spring.) Disarmament, like defense, always had been an instrument of national policy; and in the Thirties peace advocates divided and realigned over basic, prior policy questions. The consequences were that traditional internationalists became increasingly political in their support of collective security, and that those liberal pacifists who in the Twenties had related to every internationalist approach became isolated from the broad peace movement in their pursuit of neutrality. That was the other axis of antiwar strategy in the Thirties—an ever sharper cleavage between pacifists and traditional internationalists—and this represented discontinuity from the Twenties.

Following the Manchurian crisis some traditional internationalists tried to develop an energetic program. Their efforts were given a fresh impetus when on January 29, 1935, the Senate failed to carry adherence to the World Court. Raymond Rich, general secretary of the World Peace Foundation, complained, "The peace forces, having for the most part disregarded the popular, are losing the populace."[6] After a series of meetings, leaders in the League of Nations Association devised a political program and an organizational base which largely reflected the thinking of James T. Shotwell and Newton D. Baker. Their political program coupled issues then quite popular—control of arms traffic, war profits and disarmament—with the traditionalist objectives of world economic cooperation and close American association with the League. Their organizational base envisioned a new coalition with the politically experienced pacifist wing, which itself was drafting a coordinated program through the fledgling National Peace Conference. Shotwell wanted the pacifists, their organizational apparatus and their constituency, but not their distinctive programs. He believed that it would be possible to give "recognition" to the National Peace Conference "while subordinating it to the broader plan" of traditional internationalists by naming the leadership and providing the funds.[7]

Quite to the contrary, when the new coalition was organized, late in 1935, it was coopted by the liberal pacifists. There were at least three reasons for this. First, Shotwell and Baker were unable to get the fifty thousand dollars they had budgeted, whereas the pacifists were able to raise that much or more on their own.[8] Second, although the traditionalists were able to name the chairman, Walter Van Kirk, the pacifists won numerical balance on the steering committee and, with their prior involvement in politics, they obtained considerable initiative there.[9] Third, the liberal pacifists already had designed a "broader plan" of their own to which the National Peace Conference itself was subordinated—a half million dollar Emergency Peace Campaign "to keep the United States from going to war," to promote such political and economic changes as "are essential to a just and peaceable world order," and to enlist pacifist organizations and individuals in this common cause.[10] The Peace Campaign was fashioned and operated largely by leaders in the American Friends Service Committee and the Fellowship of Reconciliation.

FOR leaders especially looked to the political center for an antiwar coalition as the pressures of war and totalitarianism mounted. They found no effective base on the Left, with which they had frequently associated in the cause of social justice. Some of them had been attracted to the united front American League Against War and Fascism, organized in September, 1933, in response to a similar coalition in Europe. Other pacifists opposed cooperation with Communists in any case, and even those who initially were sympathetic soon were repelled when Communists coopted the League and manipulated it for their own purposes. The Socialist Party was riddled with factionalism in the mid-Thirties, and soon was placed in an awkward position on foreign affairs by the Spanish Civil War; Norman Thomas lobbied for strict neutrality legislation at the same time that he tried to defend his Party's legal right to intervene in the Spanish Civil War through the "Debs Column" of socialist volunteers.[11] The Emergency Peace Campaign was aimed, therefore, at the political center.

It purported to represent a broad coalition of pacifists and non-pacifist civic groups, but actual decision-making was in the hands of a nucleus of pacifists who wielded large financial and staff resources. Special departments were set up to reach youth, labor, church and civic groups respectively. A coordinated lobby swung into action in Washington. News releases and pamphlet literature flowed from a publicity department. Well-known speakers (including Admiral Richard Byrd) were shuttled around the country. The campaign proceeded in a series of programs designed to stress the international crisis, to develop a "No-Foreign-War-Crusade" and to popularize world economic cooperation. Public events were numbered by the thousand; literature was distributed by the hundreds of thousand. The liberal pacifist leaders were able to focus public attention on specific issues, particularly neutrality; and traditional internationalists became increasingly restive in the coalition, which they feared was building isolationist sentiment.[12]

Their cooperation was based on the fact that there were many areas on which the peace movement agreed, that the pressure of a deteriorating international scene was clear, and that their own foreign-policy programs were not yet clear. Under the varied rhetoric and diverse programs of the Emergency Peace Campaign there was a dual emphasis: neutrality and world economic cooperation. During the course of the campaign the alternative premises underlying both neutrality and international economic reconstruction became increasingly clear and divisive.

Pacifist leaders clarified their views on neutrality earlier than did traditional internationalists or the Administration. Early in the decade they lost hope in the League of Nations as an agency of either maintaining international order or negotiating changes in it; and as they watched the rise of totalitarian states they became convinced that peaceful change was necessary in order to maintain order.[13] Their neutralism was thus grounded in their perceptions of events in Europe, although it was popularized by a moralistic rhetoric that obscured the analysis of a small coterie of leading pacifists—notably Socialist leader Norman Thomas, Socialist author and journalist Devere Allen, influential speaker and author Kirby Page, and Socialist Scott Nearing. Frederick Libby, of the National Council for Prevention of War; Dorothy Detzer, the lobbyist and political organizer for the Women's International League for Peace and Freedom; John Nevin Sayre and Harold Fey of the Fellowship of Reconciliation; A. J. Muste, FOR leader and an early radical organizer; and C. C. Morrison, editor of the *Christian Century,* also were influential as was Reinhold Niebuhr until the mid-Thirties.[14]

Briefly, then, according to pacifist political theory, Germany, Italy and Japan faced serious internal weaknesses, and the means by which their rulers dealt with their problems increased the danger of war. Authority there rested superficially on military power, but actually it was based on an insecure and temporary acquiescence of the people. In order to secure control, therefore, dictators not only developed extraordinary economic measures, but also identified themselves with militant nationalistic creeds which they fashioned into elements of state cohesion and party loyalty.[15]

Moreover, these inherently belligerent states were the have-not nations of the industrial world.

The western democracies had divided up the markets, resources and underdeveloped territories of the world, explained Kirby Page. These nations had won and maintained their holdings through economic imperialism and military might. Then they had piously agreed that imperialist acquisition should be brought to an end. The most-favored nations thus perpetuated the status quo which benefitted them and which they alone could change peaceably.[16]

Their analysis of the threat to world peace apparently posed by both the internal instability and the international disadvantage of totalitarian states led some pacifists to react to fascist aggression in terms of two principles: to strengthen democracy in non-fascist countries (such as Spain), and to alleviate the differences between have and have-not nations through peaceful means. They shared this analysis and these goals with many non-pacifists, including especially Socialists.

At this point they concluded that the crux of the peace problem was not totalitarianism *per se* but, rather, the inflexibility of political and economic arrangements. They differed from traditional internationalists principally in their belief that collective security as interpreted by the great European powers in their own economic and territorial interests contributed to the very rigidity in international affairs that made war likely. Pacifists who had advocated collective sanctions against Japan quickly lost hope in the League and abandoned collective security. Years later, when Nazi warplanes multiplied Shanghai's horror in Warsaw, Charles Clayton Morrison recalled that the principle had broken down in Manchuria. In the absence of a working international system, he said, a discriminatory embargo was clearly an alliance for war.[17] The great powers would act only in their own interests to freeze the status quo. The League was an international instrument, but not an agency of internationalism. Pacifist leaders interpreted neutrality as a strategy for a flexible foreign policy which might be used in order to strengthen internationalism.

Neither the State Department nor the traditional internationalists had formulated a firm neutrality policy by 1935. The situation was ripe for aggressive congressional initiative at just the time that pacifist-led groups became virtually unanimous in pressing for neutrality legislation that would be impartial and apply to all belligerents, and mandatory in regard to the President. They operated through the National Council for Prevention of War, the Women's International League for Peace and Freedom and the isolationist bloc in the Senate. They were instrumental in securing the Neutrality Act of 1935 which abandoned the traditional neutral rights to trade and required an impartial embargo of all belligerents, which was extended with few changes to May 1, 1937.[18]

Accordingly, when the traditional internationalists joined pacifists in a political coalition in 1935-1936, they joined a movement already geared for impartial neutrality designed to keep America out of war. This did not seem to be a serious obstacle at the time.

The traditionalists had expected to dominate the coalition, of course. But, in any case, they still regarded collective security as consonant with a neutral embargo. That was the minimal commitment to collectivism that Norman Davis had pledged at the Geneva Disarmament Conference in 1933: the United States would promise *not to obstruct* collective sanctions applied against an aggressor state. This "negative declaration" seems to have been assumed adequate in 1935-1936 by the leaders of the League of Nations Association, although it was thrown into serious question in the Ethiopian crisis. An American embargo on all belligerents would act unilaterally but in concert with any international embargo applied to an aggressor. It would be the best of all possible worlds.

Not the impartiality of the embargo, but rather the question of whether it should be mandatory upon the President seems to have pre-cipitated the split in peace forces. In negotiating the Neutrality Acts of 1935, 1936 and 1937 the Administration had jealously guarded its dis-cretionary ability to determine when a state of war might exist and when, therefore, an embargo should be applied. Anything less permissive than that would jeopardize the power of the Executive to conduct the foreign relations of the United States, in the view of the State Depart-ment. Pacifists were not satisfied with the way the Administration ex-ercised its discretion, however; they pressed for the invocation of an im-partial embargo in the China war, in Ethiopia and—with Socialists—in the Spanish Civil War.[19] When, in the fall of 1937, they received the impression from Roosevelt's "Quarantine Speech" that the President might pursue a policy of applying sanctions selectively in alliance with other great powers, they resumed their attack upon his discretionary powers in foreign policy. They campaigned actively for the Ludlow constitutional amendment requiring a national referendum on involve-ment in any foreign war; and consideration of it was narrowly defeated in the House on January 10, 1938.[20]

The Ludlow Amendment campaign precipitated the political or-ganization of traditional internationalists and helped them to define the neutrality issue. Convinced that so-called impartial neutrality legisla-tion was operating to isolate American policy and that the neutrality campaigns were generating isolationism, Clark Eichelberger and his League of Nations Association staff began to mobilize traditional inter-nationalists on behalf of discretionary embargoes against aggressor states. In effect, they began to promote actively that very concept of collective security which the pacifists had feared. They solicited support for a "Statement on Behalf of Concerted Peace Efforts" and opposition to the Ludlow Amendment. The significance of their efforts was not lost on James T. Shotwell, who himself had tried to create a peace coalition without securing adequate political leverage within it. "Good generalship in the strategy of the peace movement," he now said, was represented by the aggressive director of the League of Nations Association [Eichelberger] who, with his staff, would organize a series of committees to make successive assaults on American neutrality.[21] The controversy generated alternative organizations for political influence within the peace coalition and the public.

Meanwhile, the liberal pacifists and traditional internationalists were still working together in the Emergency Campaign, now promoting world economic cooperation. This was not a new idea. It had been sponsored by League of Nations bodies since at least 1922; and in the winter of 1936 George Lansbury, leader of the British Labour Party, had sought in vain to secure a resolution committing England to call a world conference to negotiate equilization of the resources of discontented nations.[22] Lansbury was the featured speaker opening the Emergency Peace Campaign program in April, and he not only dwelt on an international conference in his speeches, but also discussed it with President Roosevelt before leaving the country. The President was cautious, saying he would need some solid "peg" upon which to hang a meeting of such magnitude.[23]

Lansbury got his peg with the help of the International Fellowship of Reconciliation, with headquarters in England, which created an Embassies of Reconciliation in order to take the cause of peace directly to national leaders. Private citizens were designated as informal ambassadors in order to confer with government officials and establish some basis for negotiating peace before fighting should break out. Lansbury was the first citizen-ambassador appointed. In the spring of 1937 he conferred with the prime ministers of France, Belgium, Denmark, Norway and Sweden, and with Hitler in Berlin. Subsequently he interviewed Mussolini and traveled with other representatives of the private group to the capitals of southeastern Europe, and to Prague, Warsaw and Vienna. The most important conversation was, of course, that with Hitler who assured Lansbury that Germany would cooperate in a united effort if Roosevelt would take the lead in calling an economic conference.[24]

Peace leaders of all political persuasions were imploring Roosevelt to take the lead, and their project got unimpeachable support in January, 1938, from an exhaustive report on international economic conditions by a former Belgian prime minister, Paul Van Zeeland (with whom Lansbury had met). Van Zeeland urged the great powers to collaborate on specific items which would "impart to the world the impetus which it is awaiting in order to recover confidence in the pacific destiny of nations."[25]

Roosevelt was already, and unhappily, familiar with the idea of a world conference, for the British had spurned the notion when it was broached early in 1938.[26] Preliminary negotiations had been initiated in January for a comprehensive peace conference emphasizing economic problems and treaty revision, but the plan was rejected by Neville Chamberlain. The President had realized then that a conference to redress international grievances was not a realistic alternative to European war because such a conference could not be convened. Peace advocates learned this after September, 1939; but even in the process of promoting an economic conference they had divided over its meaning.

The Emergency Peace Campaign convened its own Conference on World Economic Cooperation at the end of March, and the traditional internationalists were dominant. Their experts supported Cordell Hull's reciprocal-trade-agreements program and also some aspects of the Van Zeeland report, but they argued, too, that any revisions of the Neutrality Law should be made flexible enough to distinguish between aggressors and victims.[27] Their report fixed the division among internationalists between those who supported a strategy of collective action to contain aggression on the grounds that political order was a prerequisite for economic cooperation, and those pacifists who opposed the further alignment of the world into armed ideological camps on the grounds that basic economic change was a prerequisite for international order.

The project for a world economic conference, like those for disarmament, neutrality and the Emergency Peace Campaign itself, yielded division. There was no alternative to separation. About a week after the disruptive conference on economic affairs, Eichelberger resigned as director of the Campaign for World Economic Cooperation, organizing instead what Shotwell called a series of assaults on neutrality. During the next three years, under the pressure of fascist war abroad, his search for a coalition in support of collective sanctions against aggressors aligned him and his committees with those who urged outright intervention on behalf of the democracies.

That is to say, the pressure of war and totalitarianism still operated to engender political coalitions even as it divided the internationalists.

Pacifists felt this pressure acutely after the defeat of the Ludlow Amendment and the debacle of world economic cooperation. By the spring of 1938 they had formed a coalition with Socialists under the leadership of Norman Thomas, the Keep America Out of War Congress. Thoroughly alarmed by the organization of collective security advocates, pacifists cemented their alliance with Thomas early in February and launched it with a public meeting in New York on March 6.[28] This was still the only national antiwar coalition opposed to collective security when the German troops rolled out across the low countries two years later. There were serious weaknesses in it. Pacifist organizations, particularly the Fellowship of Reconciliation and the Friends Service Committee, were shifting their resources away from political lines in order to provide for their relief work and their religious- and conscientious-objector constituencies in the event of war. The Socialist Party was divided over foreign policy, among other issues, and Communists still exerted a disruptive and unpredictable influence. Moreover, the initial void on the political right was quickly filled by the America First Committee, organized in the summer of 1940 in reaction to Eichelberger's efforts for collective security.

By January, 1941, the America First Committee was obtaining public and financial support that the Keep America Out of War Congress could not tap. Reluctantly, the antiwar Left associated with America First in an effort to build antiwar public pressure, but in doing so it associated with the fortress America concept. The conservative and isolationist drift of the coalition resulted in the loss of most pacifist support by the spring of 1941. Increasingly, it was dominated by antiwar Socialists. By fall the Keep America Out of War Congress was a bankrupt, paper organization.[29]

World War II seemed to hit the American people with the suddenness of the waves of planes that unleashed destruction over Pearl Harbor. But it came as something of an anticlimax in the travail of those who had advocated a strategy of neutrality in the cause of peace, because they already had suffered defeat in their essential political goals. The President had extended American military and economic goods to the Allies, had accepted naval commitments in the Atlantic and had revised neutrality legislation. Whether or not the country would have taken additional steps into the European war had it not been attacked in the Pacific, the President had sufficient executive power to conduct limited intervention. That, and not the war itself, was the essential political defeat for the neutralists.

For those neutralists who also were internationalists there was a more profound, subtler defeat. Faced with the impact of real war and totalitarianism, they had organized brilliantly for political effectiveness. They had formed a strong coalition with traditional internationalists whose commitment to peace through international organization and justice they shared. Conceiving of neutralism as a flexible instrument for internationalism and viewing collective security as a way of making lines of national conflict more rigid, a few pacifists had bent every effort to commit the public to strict and adamant neutrality. They had tried to press even the peace coalition into this service, and they had seen it break apart.

Equally serious, tactically, was their inability to maintain an independent, transnational and political organizational base once the coalition of the Center had been shattered. Besides, to a great extent they elevated specific political objectives above their own perceptions of international affairs, and they stressed the moral imperative of keeping out of war over their own political analysis of international conflict. Consequently, neutralism was unalterably—if not, indeed, logically—associated only with isolationism. The very pressures of war and totalitarianism that had led to the formation of a great coalition symbolized by the Emergency Peace

Campaign had heightened the differences of outlook that broke it; and they ultimately weakened the force of the international vision claimed by those opposed to the strategy of collective security.

There was neither an ideological nor an organizational base for a broadly progressive antiwar coalition just prior to World War II or during it (as there had been in World War I). Internationalism was identified with collective security and then with wartime alliance. Neutralism was identified with isolationism. A premise of Cold War analysis—that international, liberal values are best served by being unconditionally committed to one side in a polarized world—was laid late in the Thirties. Or, rather, alternative world views were deprived then of a significant organizational base, at least until the nation would become the child of an aching heart, carrying the burden of crime, begging the pardon of Viet Nam and of the world:

> "With a shattered soul;
> I have become a child of sadness."

Wittenberg University

notes

1. "Child of an Aching Heart," *The World Tomorrow*, XV (April, 1932), 112.

2. The Interorganization Council on Disarmament was designed as a clearinghouse, but it soon became a lobbying and publicizing agency, even sending a delegation to Secretary of State Henry Stimson on November 14, 1931. A preliminary meeting took place on March 30, 1931, and the organization was operational in April, although its name was not formally adopted until September 29, 1931. James G. McDonald, chairman of the Foreign Policy Association, was the first chairman, and he was succeeded by Walter Van Kirk in the fall of 1932 in the wake of disagreements over the role of the council. Particularly active were McDonald, Van Kirk, Philip Nash, Roswell Barnes, Dorothy Detzer, Frederick Libby, Tucker P. Smith and John Nevin Sayre. Minutes of the ICD, Swarthmore College Peace Collection (SCPC), 1931-1933.

3. The interwar peace movement has been characterized systematically in John Masland, "The Peace Groups Join Battle," *Public Opinion Quarterly*, IV (December, 1940), 36-73; Elton Atwater, *Organized Efforts in the United States Toward Peace* (Washington, D.C., 1936), and "Organizing American Public Opinion for Peace," *Public Opinion Quarterly*, I (April, 1937), 112-121; and Allan Kuusisto, "The Influence of the National Council for Prevention of War on United States Foreign Policy, 1935-39" (unpublished Ph.D. dissertation, Harvard University, 1950), 24-25. Only the latter is based on research in primary materials and its focus is limited. The groups representing traditional internationalists were often related through Carnegie Endowment funding.

4. The National Council for Prevention of War (NCPW) was not a pacifist organization, but its dynamic leader, Frederick J. Libby, was a Quaker pacifist and its staff, except for Mrs. Laura Puffer Morgan, was thoroughly committed to strict neutrality. See Libby, *To End War* (Nyack, N.Y., 1969), NCPW Papers (SCPC), and Libby's diaries (in possession of Mrs. Libby).

Some of the liberal pacifist groups were, like the Fellowship of Reconciliation (FOR) and denominational peace groups, religious; others, such as the Women's International League for Peace and Freedom (WILPF) were secular, civic societies. The records and minutes for nearly all of them are in the SCPC.

5. McDonald, address before the Seventh Congress of the Committee on the Cause and Cure of War, quoted in Justus Docnecke, "American Public Opinion and the Manchurian Crisis, 1931-33" (unpublished Ph.D. dissertation, Princeton University, 1966), 94.

6. Report of the general secretary to the trustees of the World Peace Foundation, February 13, 1935, Newton D. Baker Papers, Library of Congress, Box 241.

7. James T. Shotwell to Newton D. Baker, October 22, 1935, Baker Papers, Box 242. The committee was composed of James Shotwell, Roland Morris (a Philadelphia lawyer), and Senator John Pope. George Blakeslee (president of the World Peace Foundation) and John Clarke (former Supreme Court Justice and a founder of the League of Nations Non-Partisan

Association) also were involved in the consultations of the committee, and the primary draft was Baker's. See corr. April 20-May 11, 1935, Baker Papers, Box 242.

8. Baker had thought in terms of a $50,000 budget as he developed a program, and he approached Van Kirk on that basis, thinking he was "authorized" to do so. Henry Haskill to Nicholas Murray Butler, with attachment, November 19, 1935, Carnegie Endowment Archives, IV A141. The Carnegie Endowment granted $7,500 until June 30, 1936, with the possibility of renewal; the Carnegie Corporation granted a similar amount for 1936.

9. Van Kirk was its director. John Nevin Sayre (FOR) became president and chairman of the steering committee. The minutes show that the most active persons in the National Peace Conference (NPC) during 1937 were Van Kirk, John Nevin Sayre, Clark Eichelberger, Dorothy Detzer (WILPF), Frederick Libby, and Jessie MacKnight (NCPW).

10. "Buck Hills Falls," notes of the organizing conference of the Emergency Peace Campaign (EPC), by Miriam and E. Raymond Wilson, December 4, 1935, EPC Papers, Box 1, SCPC.

11. Thomas sought at first to exempt the Spanish Civil War from the provisions of the neutrality law, since it worked a particular hardship on the loyalists, by supporting a neutral embargo against all belligerents *except* in the case of armed rebellion against *"democratically elected government."* Thomas to the Hon. Sam McReynolds, February 20, 1937, Norman Thomas Papers, New York Public Library. When the embargo was retained, he urged that it be applied also against Italy and Germany, which were supplying Franco with arms.

12. The full records of the EPC are held at the SCPC, and include the Minutes. See also Devere Allen's publication, *World Events*, for coverage in this period, and the parallel files of the NCPW, FOR and WILPF.

13. It must be emphasized that this analysis was not confined to pacifists, but that elements of it can be found in the writings of traditional internationalists—in the work of James Shotwell, for example, and in the *Memoirs* of Cordell Hull. Perhaps the best example of a similar but non-pacifist evaluation is John Foster Dulles, *War, Peace and Change* (New York, 1939). Dulles wrote his approval of Kirby Page's *Must We Go to War?* (New York, 1937) insofar as its analysis of the international situation was concerned.

14. Their point of view was developed in detail in *The World Tomorrow* and was scattered throughout organizational minutes and resolutions. It was not shared systematically by the great body of pacifists or the public, but these leaders largely defined the issues for their constituents.

15. Liberal pacifists were in close touch with pacifist friends in the totalitarian countries and, in the cases of Norman Thomas and Devere Allen particularly, with Socialists there. They knew personally exiles such as Paul Tillich. John Nevin Sayre and his friends received extensive and astute commentary throughout the Manchurian crisis from a pacifist missionary in Japan. The German situation was followed closely and intelligently in the pages of *The World Tomorrow*.

16. As Kirby Page put it, a conflict between the democracies and the totalitarian states would be a struggle between "the self-righteousness of the surfeited with the self-assertion of the frustrated." *Must We Go to War?*, 25. See also Norman Thomas, *Socialism on the Defensive* (New York, 1938), 11-12, 187.

17. Morrison, "The Shattered Fabric of World Peace," *The Christian Century*, LIV (September 15, 1939), 1128-1129.

18. Pacifist groups had supported discretionary neutrality legislation in 1929, 1931, 1932 and 1933, so that their shift in the wake of the Manchurian crisis was all the more significant. The NCPW and WILPF provided extensive lobbying services, gathering material, writing speeches and radio talks for neutralist senators, providing the press with news releases, scheduling public meetings and mobilizing civic contacts built up in years of disarmament campaigns, as well as working in the capitol itself. Regarding the 1935 legislation see Department of State, Peace and War: *United States Foreign Policy, 1931-1941* (Washington, D.C., 1943), 266-271; for detailed treatment of the 1936 legislation see Robert A. Divine, *Illusion of Neutrality* (Chicago, 1962), 122-159.

19. The FOR, WILPE and NCPW urged the invocation of neutrality legislation with regard to Ethiopia, and asked that it be extended to subsidiary exports as well as arms. Spain was more difficult. Some urged outright repeal in order that Spanish Loyalists might receive aid, but most urged that the neutrality laws be applied and, in fact, extended to Germany and Italy. In any case, the prevalent feeling was expressed by Devere Allen that American pseudoneutrality actually benefitted the Nationalists, that the Western democracies had elevated their own national interests and called them principles.

20. The Ludlow Amendment was introduced in the House of Representatives in 1935, 1937 and 1938. Similar measures had been introduced in every Congress since 1922. The NCPW helped to organize a hearing on the bill in 1935, and its whole staff worked on the project in 1937.

21. James T. Shotwell to Mrs. Emmons Blaine, January 4, 1938, Shotwell Papers, League of Nations Records, Columbia University.

22. New York *Times*, March 5, 1936. Previous international conferences included the Genoa Conference, April 10-May 19, 1922, called to consider Russian relations and world economic problems; the International Economic Conference at Geneva, May 4-23, 1927; and the International Economic Conference, June 12-July 27, 1933, at London.

23. Lansbury to Roosevelt, May 26, 1936, FDR Papers, OF 394, Box 1 (Hyde Park); and Lansbury, *My Pilgrimage for Peace* (New York, 1938), 61-63.

24. The joint statement by Hitler and Lansbury was forwarded immediately to Hull by Ambassador William E. Dodd. It occasioned great interest because the State Department had been sounding out various nations that spring regarding a conference on economic cooperation and arms limitation with previously ambivalent to negative responses from Germany. New York *Times*, February 23, 1937; U.S. Department of State, *Foreign Relations*, 1937, Vol. I (Washington, D.C., 1954), 638-651; Hull, *Memoirs* (New York, 1948), Vol. 1, 549.

25. See New York *Times*, January 28, 1938, for the text of the report, and see also Percy W. Bartlett, *The Economic Approach to Peace, with a Summary of the Van Zeeland Report* (London, n.d.).

26. See William L. Langer and S. Everett Gleason, *The Challenge to Isolation: The World Crisis of 1937-1940 and American Foreign Policy* (New York, 1952), Vol. 1, 23-32; and Arnold A. Offner, *American Appeasement: United States Foreign Policy and Germany, 1933-1938* (Cambridge, 1969), 217-225.

27. *Report of the Committee of Experts to the Conference on World Economic Cooperation* (New York, 1938), and New York *Times*, March 24, 25, 26 and 27, 1938.

28. Originally called the Keep America Out of War Committee, the name was changed to Congress at a large meeting in Washington that spring. Frederick J. Libby Diary, January 17, 18, 22 and 26, 1938; "Keep America Out of War Committee; An Outline of Its Origin, Program, and Plan," n.d. [1938], Kirby Page Papers (Claremont, Calif.); Minutes of the Keep America Out of War Committee, February 7, 1938, Norman Thomas Papers, Box 27.

29. Minutes of the Keep America Out of War Congress, especially September 30, 1941.

A. J. Muste and Ways to Peace

Jo Ann Robinson

Time magazine, with its penchant for fastening indelible labels upon historical phenomena, made its contribution to the peace movement in 1939 when it laid upon A. J. Muste the mantle of "the Number One U.S. Pacifist."[1] Among many nonviolent activists of today Muste's right to that title is still accepted. Whatever modifications the designation may undergo when placed in historical perspective, Muste's role as a leading organizer of pacifist efforts, from the late Thirties to his death in 1967, is hard to ignore. Key organizations—the Fellowship of Reconciliation, the War Resisters League, the Committee for Nonviolent Action— valued his leadership. Recent studies show how substan-

> When the typical reformer or revolutionist proclaims the new order, he goes on to urge men to organize, agitate, get out the vote, fight. Jesus also proclaimed The Kingdom of God [i.e., the revolution] is at hand; but immediately added in true prophetic fashion, Repent. That is to say, if we are to have a new world, we must have new men; if you want a revolution, you must be revolutionized. A world of peace will not be achieved by men who in their own souls are torn with strife and eagerness to assert themselves. In the degree that the anti-war or pacifist movement is composed of individuals who have not themselves, to use Aldous Huxley's phrase, achieved detachment, who have not undergone an inner revolution, it too will experience the same failure to achieve self-discipline, integrity, true fellowship among its own members which has afflicted other movements for social change.
>
> A. J. Muste, *Non-Violence in an Aggressive World* (New York, 1940), 175-176

tially their history was affected by it.[2] His writings pervade the pacifist press and he was a founder and editor of its outstanding organ, *Liberation*. For draft resisters from the World War II generation symbolized in David Dellinger to the draft-card burners of the Vietnam era, Muste served as a chief mentor. Martin Luther King, Jr., James Farmer and

Bayard Rustin are only the most prominent among the civil rights workers who have acknowledged his influence on their development.[3]

The magnetism which A. J. Muste exerted over these men and movements was rooted in passionate religious conviction. Muste's closer associates have perceived the importance of this faith. David McReynolds (WRL) wrote that Muste's "Christianity was so central to him that his life cannot be understood without realizing that he was, even at his most political moments, acting out his religious convictions." Labor-radical Sidney Lens devoted several paragraphs in his commemorative article at Muste's death to the theme that "for Muste the term 'religion' and the term 'revolution' were totally synonymous." And one of the pacifist's oldest and dearest friends, John Nevin Sayre (FOR), has said with certainty that religion was his colleague's "motivating force . . . right up to the end of his life."[4] But more commonly peace-movement commentators and the public press have neglected this central force in their portraits of the man. The causes which he espoused were, on their face, purely political and for a few years carried Marxist overtones. Muste's public image accordingly took on these entirely materialist traits. That image requires revision. The spiritual quality of his motives is the key to A. J. Muste's biography.

I

Abraham John Muste was not prepared to assume the role of America's number one pacifist until he was fifty-one years old. He was born January, 1885; he achieved the psychological equilibrium upon which his pacifist leadership rested July, 1936. In the intervening years his immigrant cultural experience and Calvinist religious heritage were gradually harmonized with intellectual integrity and a growing political consciousness.

The Dutch Reformed community in Michigan where Muste was raised had been established in the 1840's by men who were set upon creating "the truly orthodox kingdom of Calvinism."[5] It was characterized by a theology that could deaden the mind and a politically stultifying patriotism. A gripping sense of the imminence of God permeated the entire setting. Young Abraham, possessing an introspective and poetic temperament, absorbed the community's religiosity. He also drank in its love for America. Possessing equally a keen, ever-inquiring mind he strained against his elders' restrictive world view. He rebelled against their political quietism, turned to the past of the Dutch Reformed Church and found there a crusading tradition which stirred the germinal activist in himself. He rebelled also against his elders' theology. But on this score church history did not help. It held no theme to counter their rigid orthodoxy.[6]

After five years (1909-1914) as an ordained minister of the Dutch Reformed Church, Muste underwent what he later described as an " 'agonizing reappraisal' of the beliefs in which I had been reared." He ceased professing them and sought "a freer denomination." Congregationalism provided a new measure of intellectual freedom when the young pastor was called to the pulpit of Central Congregational Church in Newton-ville, Massachusetts.[7] But soon, in the face of World War I, Muste was seeking to express his faith in a manner which he described to his parishoners in 1917 as "to do something that costs and hurts, something for humanity and God."

His search led him to a study of the writings of Quaker scholar Rufus Jones on "spiritual religion." In this strain of the Judaeo-Christian tradition Muste found the link between religion and social action which he had sought. In the lives of Belgian mystic John Ruysbruck, Quaker founder George Fox, and Quaker saint John Woolman, he perceived how faith and moral conviction could inspire what Jones described as "great reforms and movements of great moment to humanity."[8]

Muste affiliated with the Christian pacifist movement in 1916 and became a Quaker in 1918. This earliest phase of his pacifist career was marked, however, by ambivalence. In the first days of United States entry into the war A. J. Muste's boyhood conditioning—his parents' eagerness to be loyal citizens, his school studies of "the Man Without a Country," his infatuation with Lincoln mythology, the entire patriotic ethos of the "heartland of America"[9]—was more in evidence than his year-and-a-half-old membership in the Fellowship of Reconciliation and recent public avowals of pacifism. One finds him in April, 1917, eulogiz-ing the stars and stripes as "the best flag in the world" and calling for national prohibition to conserve "the food supply of the nation" and protect "the moral and physical well being of our soldiers."

By summer, his thinking had crystallized into an antiwar commit-ment which was at least clear enough to create friction between him and his non-pacifist congregation. But, contrary to the standard story of his departure from Central Congregational Church, the record shows that the Rev. Muste resigned his pulpit, March 31, 1918, only after consider-able vacillation and that his final decision to leave in order to pursue full-time antiwar activities was his own, not that of the parishoners or their officers.[10]

Ambivalence also characterized the early work which Muste under-took on behalf of conscientious objectors. In describing a group of con-scientious objectors held at Ft. Devens, Massachusetts, whom he had been permitted to visit as a counselor, the inexperienced and experimenting opponent of war could praise only "some . . . at least" of the draft resisters and allowed that all of them might be "mistaken." He commended for sympathy only those with "beautiful trust in God" and an absolute desire to "do the will of Christ," and empathized with army officials who feared that lenient treatment of war resisters would encourage "slackers" to "de-velop consciences overnight."[11]

Further experience in pacifist circles gradually increased the firmness of the positions which the Quaker convert took. At the end of the First World War Muste became the leading figure in the Fellowship of Reconciliation in Boston. Beginning in 1919 and through the early 1920's he demonstrated a solid commitment to Christian pacifism in his application of it to labor organizing.[12] Until about 1930 Muste remained convinced that the struggle for social justice was essentially a religious undertaking. He pictured labor unions as embodiments of salvation. "Am I writing as if the Labor Union of the Future, the developing labor movement were the Messiah for our modern world?" he asked in 1923, and answered, "Quite so." He assured political activists that they could best arrive at sound policy decisions by regular and devout prayer. And he was wont to declare that the yearning of radicals and progressives toward a new social order was tantamount to issuing in "The Kingdom."[13]

In the later years of his labor career these assumptions were altered. Muste's comments on churchdom became biting and sarcastic. His interest in probing the spiritual implications of political action disappeared from view. He espoused a Marxist-Leninist philosophy and for a year and seven months (December, 1934, to July, 1936) was actively affiliated with the Trotskyist Workers Party of the United States.[14] This period of alienation from the religious habits and attitudes of a lifetime was one of great stress. Bitter factional fights undermined the organizer's efforts to create a truly American labor party. Duplicity on the part of Trotskyist colleagues reduced the leadership position which he theoretically held in the WP-USA to a sham.[15] Friends anxiously observed the physical and emotional toll which these developments were taking. In 1936 a campaign was begun to raise funds for a vacation for the tired Trotskyist and his equally weary wife. The sum collected provided them with a two-month trip to Europe. On a June day in 1936 they boarded a ship at Hoboken pier. As the ship pulled out to sea the friends who had gathered to say farewell saw A. J. Muste raise "his skinny arm in the clenched fist salute of the bloody revolution."[16]

Less than a month later, while resting in a Parisian Catholic church, the Marxist was overcome by a sense of not belonging among secular revolutionaries. In courting their favor, he felt, he had been denying some fundamental prompting within himself. "I must lead a religious life," he declared.[17] It is impossible to exaggerate the importance of this moment in the life of Abraham John Muste. It is the point toward which all the forces of his formative years had pushed him and the point from which all activities in the remaining thirty-one years of his life would emanate. A psychologist might interpret the event of this July day as the climax of a series of identity crises. Earlier mystical experiences had first brought to intense consciousness the religious passion within him, when he sought full church membership at the age of fourteen, had freed his mind from the dogmatism of his native church when he moved to Newtonville in 1914, and later had liberated his social conscience from the unquestioning patriotism of his immigrant upbringing during World War I.[18] In this final moment of truth the demands of the passion, of the mind and of the conscience were reconciled. The fifty-one-year-old man achieved emotional integration and equilibrium.

For all these years he had been seeking to improve, if not to replace, the provincial and often simplistic values upon which he had been raised. Now he found that the essence of those values—their religious nature—had so permeated what he called his "innermost being" that it could not be eluded. His Trotskyist colleague, James Cannon, had been correct in fearing that "the terrible background of the church" had marred Muste for life.[19]

In achieving his newly integrated being Muste apprehended what he called "the essential nature, the heart of the universe in which we live." He declared "comradeship" to be "the law of human existence," because "God . . . Love, is the basic reality," and concluded from this that violence in any form—injustice, deception, greed, oppression, all-out war—flies in the face of reality. He rejected his former arguments that labor violence in the face of capitalist provocation was sanctionable, and declared the need to evangelize among the working classes on behalf of "the Christian spirit" and "the method of nonviolence." In one sense he retained his earlier belief in labor as "the messiah of the future." He theorized that physically powerless workers were far more capable than the *status quo* of adopting spiritual instruments of force. The task remained to develop that capability.

Muste's critique of working class movements in general was accompanied by an analytical rejection of Marxist-Leninist organizations in particular. Their reliance on "armed insurrection, civil war and terrorism" was reactionary, he argued. Far from being able to destroy exploitative political and economic systems, violence perpetuated them and was their foundation. As long as advocates of a new social order accepted that same foundation as their own, their every effort was doomed.

Unmistakable signs of the onset of World War II, which the Mustes had noted throughout their European travels, were for the reconverted Christian the final proof of the futility of violent means. He concluded that in the implementation of non-violence lay mankind's only hope for averting war and the tragedies that would follow in its wake.[20]

II

For the rest of his life A. J. Muste labored to persuade others of the validity and critical importance of his revelation and to formulate strategies of peace action in its light. He was constantly faced with what he once described as "the eternal problem of the religious man, of every man who lives the moral life, namely how you are going to put your vision to work in the actual situation."[21] As he worked on that problem across the next thirty-one years, he relied primarily upon three theoretically distinct but practically overlapping strategies.

First, on occasion, A. J. Muste assumed the stance of a biblical prophet exhorting men to ready themselves for the total shock of a certain miracle. Second, and more regularly, he followed the tactic of organizing on the principle of what we might loosely call "geometric progression"—bringing together into "cells" individuals who were both affiliated with a key social institution and committed to the way of love, helping these cells convert their institutions to the way of love; then mobilizing the institutions, in turn, to convert the power centers to which they related. Muste looked to the church, the scientific establishment and academe for manpower to implement this plan. Implicit in the strategy is the assumption that vast numbers of recruits must be added to the peace movement and that a spiritual minority could not hope to directly and immediately influence the strongholds of political authority.

Third, Muste approached the problem of established authority from a different angle. He developed the notion of a spiritual power center to be offered to men and women as an alternative to the hopelessly polarized and incredibly violent power blocs that were vying for their allegiance. Sometimes Muste described the spiritual center as developing a mighty enough attraction to drain off all loyalties from the loci of violence. He seemed to suggest that the established powers had done the movement's recruiting for it and that disaffected peoples needed only to be organized into a third camp, where they could develop the non-violent instrumentalities to sustain and build their moral strength. The seeds of future civil-disobedience campaigns were planted in this suggestion. At other times, he referred to the nonviolent third camp in the scriptural context of "the saving remnant." In this context the power center had strength enough to survive morally and physically while old structures collapsed around it. But it did not directly compete with those structures.

In none of his strategies was there the slightest inclination to work through the accepted channels, or follow the "proper procedures" or strive for recognition within the American political system. The governing concept behind all his plans of action was one of persistent nonconformity. Unlike peace-movement leaders of the Thirties, whose acceptance of established institutions as legitimate has been described by Charles Chatfield, Muste believed that all ruling bodies rested upon violence.[22] Thus any cooperation with them amounted to acquiescing to an insidious force. Violence is totalitarian, he warned: obey one of its wishes and before you know it you are completely in its grips.[23] As we briefly look at some of the workings and outcomes of Muste's strategies, then, we might bear in mind Paul Goodman's remark that all of A. J. Muste's "serious actions are shoestring operations," because "he is too sane to be able to withdraw from the front page world and too sound to be corrupted by it."[24]

Anticipation of a miracle is a recurrent theme in the thought of A. J. Muste. He had experienced divine intervention and was certain that it could occur in the lives of others and could transform society. In the period 1936-1940 he believed that the entire American Left was verging on conversion, similar to the experience he had undergone.[25] In the same period he entertained the notion that either Germany—out of the depths of suffering—or the United States—out of richness and might—could perceive the futility of a second world war and, as he put it, come by "the sublime horse-sense, the divine foolishness to break the evil spell that is on mankind [and] lay down [their] arms."[26] When the war came instead of the miracle and ended with the 1945 atomic bombings of Hiroshima and Nagasaki, Muste declared that now "man in his extremity must turn to God." He suggested that by repentance and unilateral disarmament the United States could act out the historical possibility which theologian Paul Tillich had once described. "A people can become the church," Tillich said, "if in an unexpected historical moment it is seized as a whole by the transcendental idea and for its sake renounces power."[27]

In ascribing such a role to the United States Muste was perhaps partaking of some of that nationalism which Charles DeBenedetti has described as so characteristic of peace advocates a quarter of a century earlier and which had been so much a part of Muste's own upbringing.[28] In the wake of World War II Muste could still expound upon the "American Dream . . . of equality, of freedom, of brotherhood, of peace." Americans had never taken the dream seriously, he said. "But now we have come to the final crisis . . . [We] have to be deadly serious about it. And we have to share it with all the world." He envisioned Americans dismantling their armed might and sending their armies on great missions of mercy around the globe. However, he did not pin his hopes on America alone. Other nations sometimes appear in his writings as carriers of redemption, most frequently, in the post-World War II period, Germany. The German people, he argued, "after having twice experienced the material and moral catastrophe of being involved in a major war," could lead the way in seeking alternatives to rearmament and international power politics. When it later became evident that Germany would not move in this direction Muste not only criticized the leadership of Konrad Adenauer but—in a clear departure from hopeful nationalism—bitterly assailed the "criminal prodding from the U.S. State Department and the Pentagon" which, he charged, had urged Adenauer on.[29]

Neither increased American armament nor German rearmament eradicated Muste's faith in a possible miracle. In 1959 he prayed, during the Eisenhower-Khrushchev talks of that year, that the two leaders would experience "a moment of truth" and end the arms race.[30] In the final great campaign of his career—the struggle against the war in Southeast Asia—A. J. Muste again looked toward a miracle. He argued that the nation which had been first with the physical atomic bomb was now called to cease "shooting at people and . . . roasting them with napalm," to unilaterally disarm and "make the changes in its own social structure which this entails." The effect of such a policy, he predicted, could be likened to a spiritual atomic bomb.[31]

But America's number one pacifist was never content to proclaim the coming of a miracle and then wait for the trumpets to sound. He always hedged his millenarian bets with other plans and programs of action.

Muste consistently worked *to leaven academic, scientific and religious institutions with pacifist values.* His approach was to organize what he sometimes called "cells" in these institutions.[32] Academic and scientific personnel proved only slightly responsive to this strategy. After years of communication with individual educators and intellectuals, Muste finally saw in 1960 the establishment of a small committee of academics dedicated to persuading "the intellectual community that the concept of stockpiling arms as a deterrent to war must be radically reappraised." This Council for Correspondence, which attracted some attention among writers and theorists in the early Sixties, was not long lived.[33] It might be argued, of course, that Muste's influence on individual scholars (the names of Noam Chomsky and Staughton Lynd come most readily to mind) transcends the limited success of organizing efforts such as that which culminated in the Council. The response of scientists to Muste's overtures was similarly not overwhelming, but was productive of some results. His pleas to Albert Einstein at the end of World War II, that the great physicist take the lead in extricating science *completely* from military involvement, fell on deaf ears. A few other scientists were receptive. Dr. Victor Paschkis derived from Muste part of the motivation that went into his founding of the Society for Social Responsibility in the Sciences in 1949. The Society is still functioning today.[34]

The main target for Muste's "cell" strategy, until the 1960's, was the church. It was the natural target for one who possessed his upbringing and experience. Immediately after his 1936 revelation Muste began to push the idea of pacifist cells within Christian churches.[35] But very soon, events surrounding the Second World War drained the manpower supply for such a program. Young war resisters, such as the Union Theological Seminary students who refused their deferments and went to prison, became disillusioned with religious pacifism and especially with the organizations that cooperated in the National Service Board for Religious Objectors. These included the Fellowship of Reconciliation of which Muste was executive director.[36] The rising tide of "crisis theology" swept others out of the pacifist movement and into a widening circle whose center was Reinhold Niebuhr.[37] Muste labored feverishly in these years to keep young conscientious objectors from going off in the direction from which he had just returned in 1936, and to demonstrate to former pacifist war supporters that the "proximate justice" which Niebuhrians would substitute for absolute love was fatally unrealistic and not defensible on Christian grounds.

By the end of the 1940's spiritual comradeship among war resisters had survived the upheavals of the war years. The advent of the atomic age had put crisis theologians—at least as Muste apprehended their position—on the defensive. Then, in 1948, the World Council of Churches acknowledged pacifism as one of the positions which Christians might embrace. "In other words," Muste interpreted, "pacifists belong in the main body of the church, not outside as sects."[38] He lost little time in capitalizing upon this recognition. By 1950 the Church Peace Mission—a coalition of denominational pacifist groups, religious pacifist organizations and traditional peace churches—was functioning under his direction. Through conferences, colloquies, sermon competitions, petition circulation and literature distribution, the CPM proselytized churchmen and seminarians throughout the United States and made some incursions into the thorny area of separation between western Christianity and churches in Eastern Europe and the Soviet Union.[39]

The effect upon the Christian establishment was hardly commensurate with the hours and energy which Muste poured into CPM work. Pacifists may have been embraced by the church in 1948, but they were expected to "stay in their place." CPM recruitment efforts were not welcomed. A revival of the concept of "vocational pacifism" hindered them considerably. This notion held that a certain minority of Christians must pay homage to Jesus' antiwar teaching in order to remind the majority—as they prepare for war—to be appropriately penitent.[40] Even churchmen who took the pacifist position more seriously shunned the complete program of Mustean pacifism. John C. Bennett of Union Theological Seminary urged Muste in 1959 to support "more moderate emphases"—the scaling-down of armaments rather than unilateral disarmament. "For the first time," Bennett wrote, "I agree with you that if the USA did take the initiative [in unilaterally disarming] this would probably be a better policy in terms of prudence as well as in terms of ethical sensitivity." But, Bennett added, "I am still hung up by the realization that the USA will not do this."[41]

Paul Tillich, whose concept of a nation becoming the church had assumed a central position in Muste's thought, shared Bennett's reservation. He wrote to the pacifist leader in 1963, "the idea [of a people renouncing their power] still has much attraction for me. But my doubts have increased."[42] Muste's own doubts increased about the feasibility of expecting church people to initiate the beloved community. In 1962 he left the CPM.[43] In 1966 he warned that expecting the church to live up to its teachings and its prophetic function "might lead to great disappointment."[44]

The Christian radical's disappointment with the church increased the attention which he gave to his third main strategy—the *creation of a non-violent third way*, either a magnet depowering centers of violence or at least a remnant to survive their destruction. During the Second World War Muste had envisioned the religious pacifist movement assuming at the war's end a magnetic position between the exhausted enemy camps.[45] But war-weariness gave way so quickly to the taking of sides in the Cold War that Muste could not even begin to put his theory into practice. Instead, he started to experiment with the moral tools— tax resistance, civil disobedience, non-violent direct action, fasts, etc.— upon which a spiritual power center would rely if ever it came into existence.[46] Simultaneously he struggled against factionalism among those who were the most likely candidates for the third force. The principle guiding his campaign against this constant bedevilment is unique in the annals of leftist history. He had declared it emphatically in 1944: "I am done forever," he said, ". . . with political sectarianism." Forever after, he poured endless patience into resolving personal conflicts and heading off power-politicking among peace workers in the American organizations to which he belonged. He consistently counselled, with regard to national and international organizing, that "it is seldom wise to spend time in fighting other organizations. Let people give themselves wholeheartedly to what they do believe in, and let each concede the other that right."[47]

In the 1950's Muste's hopes for the third way soared when civil rights leaders—including men who had looked to him for guidance and support—began demonstrating a pacifist alternative to white racism and black despair. Though thrilled by indications of the alternative's potential, Muste was ever aware of its imperfections. In 1964 he warned that, in the black movement, "the concept of nonviolence has fallen upon hard times."[48] Expectations which he had entertained in the 1950's for the emergence of an international third force of uncommitted peoples were also dampened by the mid-Sixties.

These expectations had risen during the Bandung Conference of Asian and African nations in 1955. The proceedings of that conference had carried the message, as Muste read it, that "great multitudes are coming to the conclusion that for them the most important cleavage is not that between . . . Russia and America, but between . . . atomically armed Russia and America on the one hand, and the rest of the world on the other." Just as Negroes in the United States were beginning to envision a special non-violent destiny born of powerlessness, so the Asian-African nations were coming to a new sense of vocation, "precisely because," Muste argued, "they lacked physical force and were therefore driven to generate a different kind of power." First by promoting the Third Way International Movement and later (in the early Sixties) by helping to establish the World Peace Brigade, Muste attempted to encourage and enhance what he deemed the real "strength of the peoples-in-between," i.e., "their ability to say No" and the consequent "slowing down and perhaps drying up of recruiting by the big powers for atomic war." In 1964 he conceded that these efforts, at least for the time being, had failed. He observed that the uncommitted peoples had fallen victim to the same illusion that had briefly trapped him in the Thirties and that posed for the radical pacifist and non-violent revolutionary a recurrent "psychological and spiritual problem"—the illusion that violence alone is realistic.[49]

As his life neared its end, A. J. Muste's prospects for finding some institution to convert to pacifism or some group to shape into a pacifist power center were dwindling. In his last years he placed great faith in activist youth. But he knew that they, too, could be frustrated into violence and could fall prey to factionalism.[50] America's leading pacifist did not speak often in his final days of issuing in the beloved community. He acknowledged, indeed, that a wasteland could be in the offing. If so, he pleaded three months before his death, at least let there be "Voices crying in the wilderness."[51]

His plea was not an utterance of despair. "To acquiesce, to go along, to create the impression that there is no 'real' opposition" to the forces of death—that, Muste said, was despair. For even one individual "to pit himself in Holy Disobedience against the war-making and conscripting State"—that was hope.[52] The meager successes yielded by Muste's strategies never became tokens of defeat for him. In the first place, he made no claim to being a strategist. Professional scholars and theoreticians should and could assume that role he believed. In the second place, his vision that "the essential nature, the heart of the universe is love" had immunized him from defeat forever.[53]

A. J. Muste became "Number One U.S. Pacifist" by virtue of his keen insight into the nature of violence and his unquenchable faith in the power of love. His reputation for political acuity and non-conformist activism revolved around his insight. But the prime and sustaining factor was his faith. It lent his political predictions the power of prophetic warning, enriched his pragmatic analyses of society with timeless wisdom about the human condition, and transformed bold confrontations with the state into "holy disobedience." In his writings the peace movement has inherited a body of thought that brilliantly pinpoints the flaws in strategies of violence. In the religious conviction behind those writings his successors have the principle that Muste believed must govern the antiwar and non-violent strategies which they seek: "There is no way to peace; peace is the way."[54]

Morgan State College

notes

1. *Time*, July 10, 1939, 37.
2. Charles Chatfield, *For Peace and Justice, Pacifism in America, 1914-1917* (Knoxville, 1971), *passim*; Lawrence S. Wittner, *Rebels Against War* (New York, 1969), *passim*.

3. David Lewis, *King, A Critical Biography* (New York, 1970), 35, 36, 72, 106, 359; James Finn, ed., *Protest: Pacifism and Politics* (New York, 1967), 331. James Farmer to A. J. Muste, February 17, 1961, A. J. Muste Papers at Swarthmore College Peace Collection, Swarthmore, Pennsylvania, Box 8 (hereinafter cited as AJM:SCPC).

4. David McReynolds in "A. J. Muste Memorial Issue," *Win*, February 24, 1967, 9; Sidney Lens, "Humanistic Revolutionary," *Liberation*, September/October, 1967, 7; John Nevin Sayre, "Fighting Reconciler: A. J. Muste as I Knew Him," *Fellowship*, March, 1967, 11.

5. Albert Hyma, *Albertus C. Van Raalte and His Dutch Settlement in the United States* (Michigan, 1947), 237.

6. Muste immigrated with his parents and three siblings from the Netherlands in 1891. The Grand Rapids, Michigan, community in which they settled is examined in my study of Muste which was completed as a doctoral thesis at the Johns Hopkins University in January, 1972. Other topics raised in the first part of this article, relating to his life before 1940, are also examined in the thesis.

For a glimpse of Muste's early rebellion see "The Problem of Discontent," *The Essays of A. J. Muste*, ed. Nat Hentoff (New York, 1967), 175-179 (hereinafter cited as *The Essays*).

7. Muste, "Sketches for an Autobiography," *The Essays*, 43, 44 (hereinafter cited as "Sketches"); Muste, Oral History Memoir #589, Columbia University Office of Oral History, New York, the early 1950's, 221 (hereinafter cited as Oral Memoir).

8. Muste, "The Opportunity of Lent," *The Congregationalist*, April 13, 1916, 501-503; Rufus Jones, *Studies in Mystical Religion* (New York, 1909), xiv-xv. Muste was influenced directly by Jones's writings. See "Sketches," 47 and Oral Memoir, 269.

9. "Sketches," 21; Oral Memoir, 74.

10. "Gift of Flags," clipping, April 15, 1917, in Central Congregational Church record book, Newtonville, Massachusetts, 530. Muste's call for prohibition in same record book, 531-532. Details of his resignation may be found in: clipping from *The Newton Graphic*, Friday, January 4, 1918; Muste, "To Whom It May Concern," December 12, 1917; Muste to Wallace Boyden, December 12, 1917; Muste to Wallace Boyden, March 31, 1918, all in Central Church files. In the record book see pp. 546-554, 583-584, 585, 587-588, 593-595.

The standard story of Muste's departure from Newtonville holds that the congregation was essentially responsible for his resignation. This version has been repeated several times. See Devere Allen, *Adventurous Americans* (New York, 1932), 99-117; Milton Mayer, "The Christer," *Fellowship*, January, 1952, 1-10; Nat Hentoff, *Peace Agitator* (New York, 1963), and Muste, "Sketches for an Autobiography," in *The Essays*.

11. Muste, "The Present Status of Conscientious Objectors," *The Congregationalist and Advance*, January 10, 1918, 49-50.

12. An introductory summary of Muste's activities in this period may be found in Hentoff, *Peace Agitator*, 47-72.

13. Muste, "The Union of the Future," *The World Tomorrow*, February, 1923; Muste, "Contradictions the Rebel Faces," *The World Tomorrow*, May, 1924.

14. Muste's increasing sarcasm toward the church is illustrated in Muste, "The Christian Employer," *Labor Age*, July, 1930; and Muste, "Capitalism in the Raw," *Common Sense*, December 5, 1932. His thinking as a Marxist-Leninist may be sampled in Muste, "An American Revolutionary Party," *Modern Quarterly*, January, 1934, 713-719, and as a spokesman for the Trotskyists in Muste, "Which Party for the American Worker?" (New York, 1935).

15. The two most bitter factional disputes were that which separated Muste from Brookwood Labor College in 1933 and the "French Turn" controversy which contributed to his resignation from the Trotskyists. On the Brookwood affair see "Muste Quits In Rift Over CPLA," *The Brookwood Review*, May, 1933, and "Whither Brookwood," *Labor Age*, February-March, 1933, 14-15. On the French Turn see "Sketches," 163-167; Max Schactman, Oral Memoir at Columbia University, 254; George Novack, "A. J. and American Trotskyism," *Liberation*, September/October, 1967, 22; Sidney Lens, *Left Right and Center* (Hinsdale, Illinois, 1949), 262.

16. Cara Cook and Doris Prenner to Dear . . . April . . . 1936 in Elizabeth Glendower Evans Papers, Schlesinger Library, Radcliffe College; Cara Cook Ms. in AJM:SCPC, Box 1a; Milton Mayer, "The Christer," *Fellowship*, January, 1952, 7.

17. This revelation is described in Muste, "Fragment of Autobiography," undated Ms. (probably 1939), AJM:SCPC, Box 2. Quotation is from the statement which Muste reportedly wrote immediately after the revelation, undated Ms. (July, 1936?), AJM:SCPC, Box 3a, 15.

18. This series of religious experiences was reported by Muste in the "Fragment of Autobiography," *op. cit., passim*. Corroboration for this report exists for the 1914 event in "Pastor Yields to Heavenly Vision," clipping from *Sunday New York Herald*, n.d. (Spring, 1914), in Newtonville Central Congregational Church files, and for the 1917 experience in Central Congregational Church record book, 546-554.

19. James P. Cannon, *History of American Trotskyism* (New York, 1944), quotation from 171.

20. Muste's statement after his revelation, 15.

21. Muste, lecture notes for address at New Brunswick Theological Seminary, February 16, 1944, AJM:SCPC, Box 2.

22. Charles Chatfield, "Alternative Antiwar Strategies in the Thirties," *American Studies*, 13 (Spring, 1972).

23. In "Of Holy Disobedience," Pendle Hill Pamphlet #64 (Wallingford, Pennsylvania, 1952), Muste spelled out this position.

24. Paul Goodman, "On A. J. Muste," *The New York Review of Books*, October, 1963, 14.

25. The position which Muste took based upon this belief has been described in Jo Ann Robinson, "Pharos of the East Side: Labor Temple Under the Direction of A. J. Muste, 1937-1940," *Journal of Presbyterian History*, Spring, 1970, 25-27.

26. See, for example, "The Problem of German Rearmament," undated Ms. (1936) for "Pastor Niemoller and Other Peace Workers in Germany," AJM:SCPC, Box 4 and a letter to President Roosevelt from "The Annual Meeting of the American International Church of Labor Temple, Monday, May 20, 1940," AJM:SCPC, Box 1, as well as Muste, *Nonviolence in an Aggressive World* (New York, 1940), *passim*. Quotation is from 157.

27. See Muste, *Not By Might* (New York, 1947), *passim*. Muste is quoted from 37. His quotation from Paul Tillich's *Interpretation of History* is on 106-107.

28. Charles DeBenedetti, "Alternative Peace Strategies in the Twenties," *American Studies*, 13 (Spring, 1972).

29. *Not By Might*, 131 on the "American Dream"; 112 on U.S. missions of mercy; Muste, "Trends in Peace Movements Abroad," 1960?, Ms. AJM:SCPC; remarks on early hopes for Germany and later Adenauer policy, 3-6 (quotation, 6).

30. Muste, "Meditation on Khrushechev-Eisenhower Talks," September, 1959, and Muste to Hon. Dwight D. Eisenhower, September 24, 1959, AJM:SCPC, Box 1a.

31. "Who Has the Spiritual Atom Bomb?" *The Essays*, 479-502 (quotations, 500-501).

32. Discussions of the "cell" idea are numerous in Muste's papers. See, for example, AJM to Rev. Ralph N. Mould, September 14, 1937, AJM: Labor Temple Collection, Presbyterian Historical Society, Philadelphia, Pennsylvania (hereinafter cited as LT:PHS), Box 1; untitled Ms. on cells and discipline, dated July 29, 1944, AJM:SCPC, Box 3a; Minutes of the National Council meeting of the FOR, May 29-31, 1947, FOR:SCPC, minutes on microfilm; Muste, "One World Groups—Draft of Manifesto," January 15, 1948, AJM:SCPC, Box 5; Muste, "Wednesday Evening Lectures on the Peace Testimony, Lecture # 5" Pendle Hill, April 28, 1954, AJM:SCPC, Box 2. See also Muste, *Not By Might*, 215.

33. A fulsome file on the Council of Correspondence (at first called the Committee of Correspondence) is in AJM:SCPC, Box 9. See also Hentoff, *Peace Agitator*, 183. The last edition of the Committee's newsletter (#35) appeared in the fall of 1965.

34. Muste, "Open Letter to Dr. Einstein, II," September, 1947 and "An Open Letter to Atomic Scientists and Others," March 12, 1946 in an unsorted box of papers at the Fellowship of Reconciliation, Nyack, New York. Also see Hentoff, *Peace Agitator*, 184-185.

35. Regarding cells in churches, see note 32 above.

36. For the objectors' side of this story see Lawrence Wittner, *Rebels Against War*, 70-84. For Muste's point of view see Muste to David Dellinger and other conscientious objectors in Lewisburg Prison, April 21, 1944; Muste to Don Smucker, June 2, 1944; Muste to Norman Whitney, June 6, 1944, all in FOR:SCPC, Box 19. One might also consult the minutes of the National Council Meeting of the FOR, September 22 and 24, 1944, FOR microfilm at SCPC.

37. Jo Ann Ooiman [Robinson], "Essays on Pacifism," unpublished undergraduate honors thesis, Knox College, June, 1964, SCPC, examines the Niebuhrian position and Muste's response to it. For an introduction to Muste's position see "Theology of Despair," 302-307, and "Pacifism and Perfectionism," 308-321 in *The Essays*.

38. See World Council of Churches, *Findings and Decisions, First Assembly*, Amsterdam, Holland, August 22-September 4, 1948 (New York, World Council of Churches, n.d.), 54, *passim*. Muste discusses these developments in "Christian Pacifism Yesterday and Today," n.d. ca. 1963, AJM:SCPC.

39. Materials on the CPM were scattered throughout Muste's papers at SCPC, the heaviest concentration was in Box 18 and 19. A helpful introduction to the group is J. Harold Sherk and Muste, "Summary of CPM Activities 1950-1962," at SCPC.

40. Muste, "Christian Pacifism Yesterday and Today," *op. cit.*; for discussion of "vocational pacifism" see Edward Leroy Long, Jr., *War and Conscience in America* (Philadelphia, 1968).

41. John C. Bennett to A. J. Muste, March 29, 1959, AJM:SCPC.

42. Paul Tillich to Muste, August 23, 1963, AJM:SCPC, Box 16.

43. Muste explained his departure from the CPM on grounds of ill-health. But the fact that health did not restrain his extremely active participation in other peace groups raises a question as to the validity of that explanation. See Muste to Harold Row and others, May 2, 1962, AJM:SCPC, Box 18. One of his CPM colleagues has suggested that Muste turned from the organization because of a "growing sense that what was called for in the CPM format of conversation was a different kind of organizational gift of investment of organizational effort than he was interested in. To do this kind of careful prodding would have been for him a burden in time and nervous energy. . . . The activities he gave his time to later were just as

demanding in his time and energy but were more compatible with the kind of energy he had and the irregular or flexible ways of working." Letter to the author, February 11, 1969.

But one still suspects that the burden had become so heavy for Muste because the results of CPM efforts had been so meagre. As Ralph Potter has pointed out, "Throughout the nuclear era, virtually every major American denomination has issued statements or pronouncements pertaining to the use of armed violence in specific instances or to more general questions of the role of force in international relations. . . . It cannot be said that any of these materials made a fresh contribution to ethical reflection upon the dilemmas surrounding the use of violence. They seldom exhibit a profound appreciation or even awareness of the ethical tradition of the Christian churches." Ralph B. Potter, *War and Moral Discourse* (Richmond, Va., 1969), 112-113.

44. Muste, "Cleveland and After," *The Mobilizer*, December 19, 1966.

45. See for example, Muste, "Pacifism—After the War," pamphlet, Fellowship publications, 1943.

46. For a sketch of Muste's activities along these lines see Hentoff, *Peace Agitator, passim.*

47. Muste to David Dellinger and others in Lewisburg Prison, April 21, 1944, FOR:SCPC, Box 19, for quotation about "political sectarianism." For quotation beginning "It's seldom wise . . ." see untitled Ms. at SCPC regarding conference at Somerville in 1963, p. 4. For one example of Muste's role as mediator and faction-dissolver within peace movement ranks see the correspondence regarding controversy over CNVA's Cheyenne Project in August, 1958, in Box 7, AJM:SCPC.

48. Muste, "Problems of the Radical Peace Movement," mimeographed essay, New York, September 10, 1964, SCPC, 9.

49. Muste, "The Peoples Between" (1954); "The non-Communist World—Where Are We?" (1954); "Neutralism or Third Force" (1955?), all typed Ms., AJM:SCPC. Quotations regarding the significance of Bandung come from the last, 6 and 13. Muste's admission of failure can be seen in "Problems of the Radical Peace Movement," mimeographed essay, New York, September 10, 1964, SCPC, 9.

50. See Muste to Larry Gara, April 19, 1960, AJM:SCPC, Box 12; Muste to Miss Margaret Leonard, March 1, 1961, AJM:SCPC, Box 16; Muste, "A Strategy for the Peace Movement," *Liberation*, June, 1962 (Ms. in Box 4a, AJM:SCPC); Muste to Gordon Christiansen, June 18, 1963, AJM:SCPC, Box 21; "New Haven," Muste lecture notes, October 12, 1965, AJM: SCPC, Box 2; Muste, "Problems of the Radical Peace Movement," *op. cit., passim.*

51. Muste, "Cleveland and After," *The Mobilizer*.

52. Muste, "Of Holy Disobedience."

53. His son John touched upon Muste's immunization from defeat when he told Nat Hentoff, "the basic thing about my father is that . . . he's always at peace with himself. He's the *happiest* man I've ever known. I can't believe a man can *be* that happy. But *he* is, he really is." Quoted in *Peace Agitator*, 148.

Regarding his reliance on professional scholars and theoreticians for strategies note how Muste's essays and speeches in the 1960's are studded with references to the experts whose work he believed was laying the necessary foundation—Herbert Marcuse, Joan Bondurant, Hannah Arendt, C. Wright Mills. See also his correspondence with such figures as David Riesman and Erich Fromm in AJM:SCPC, Box 9. Even Herman Kahn and other officials of Hudson Institute struck Muste as potential aids in formulating strategy. He became a "public member" of the Institute himself in 1962, to be in a position to encourage the thinkers there to consider his goals. J. Robinson, personal interview with Muste, Lake Villa, Illinois, April 12, 1964; "Hudson Institute, Inc. List of Members," July 1, 1962. See also D. G. Benner (of Hudson Institute) to Muste, November 3, 1965, AJM:SCPC, Box 30, temporary.

54. It has been claimed that the late Mrs. Caroline S. Urie of Yellow Springs, Ohio, is the originator of this quotation widely attributed to and often used by A. J. Muste. See *Fellowship*, January, 1968.

The United World Federalists: Liberals for Law and Order

Jon A. Yoder

I

"The question inevitably arises, 'How is it that nations composed of people who don't want war are continually fighting?' The answer is that opinion against war has been without adequate institutions to give it effect. . . . The important thing is to get the right kind of an institution started, even though it be in the most rudimentary form."[1] Idealistic attempts to construct an institutional answer to the question Elihu Root posed have a history approaching the lengthy record of war.[2] But for recent peace advocates of a legalistic orientation, the continuing presence of international disorder results from the absence of enforceable international law. They contend that although few people acknowledge the

> The fundamental problem of peace is the problem of sovereignty. The welfare, the happiness, the very existence of a miner in Pennsylvania, Wales, Lorraine or the Don Basin, a farmer in the Ukraine, the Argentine, the American Middle West or the Chinese rice fields—the very existence of every individual or family in every country of the five continents depends upon the correct interpretation and application of sovereignty. This is not a theoretical debate but a question more vital than wages, prices, taxes, food or any other major issue of immediate interest to the common man everywhere, because in the final analysis, the solution to all the everyday problems of two thousand million human beings depends upon the solution of the central problem of war. And whether we are to have war or peace and progress depends upon whether we can create proper institutions to insure the security of the peoples.
>
> Emery Reves, *The Anatomy of Peace* (New York, 1946), 126

sanity or legitimacy of a "might makes right" philosophy, force often becomes the eventual arbiter of international disputes because there is no supranational governmental authority capable of imposing its will upon the disputants. Thus they argue vigorously and coherently for the calm construction of an international sovereign.

Thrust forward by the energy displayed at Hiroshima and Nagasaki, this point of view attained unprecedented strength in the United States in the late 1940's and early 1950's; it found its most developed expression in the United World Federalists (UWF), a movement which fully intended to actualize its motto, "world peace through world law." The story of the dramatic rise and fall of this movement, now almost forgotten, is the sad account of how easily idealism regarding the rational handling of international affairs dissolved in the acidic and hysterical nationalism usually called McCarthyism.

It is my contention that the failure of the UWF to retain its vigor as a political pressure group, much less achieve its goal, is partially attributable to a characteristic weakness on the part of American liberals, a weakness which the present peace movement might keep in mind. For although Louis Hartz has argued convincingly that dominant American values are (and always have been) liberal, it is equally useful to take note of the argument of Arthur Ekirch, Jr., a historian who finds in the same history a chronicle of continual decline in liberalism. Reading both analyses, it is impossible not to notice that Hartz supports his case primarily with references to what our Jeffersons, Lincolns, Wilsons and Roosevelts believed while Ekirch refers to accounts of how they behaved when under extreme pressure. Both have given valid half-portraits. For the American liberal's dilemma, as defined in this analysis, involves an inability to put into practice what he sincerely preaches—concurrently believing in what he is doing while he actively negates principles he would not consider denying.[3]

Thus the American liberal accepts Locke's contentions regarding the individual's claim to what has been guaranteed by the Bill of Rights. But he also values what he chooses to call pragmatism. And this value, in the opinion of this liberal, often comes into direct conflict with all the others, a clash usually discussed in terms of idealism versus realism. Representing a significant weakness in the liberal mentality, the belief that liberal values cannot stand up under stress becomes a self-fulfilling prophecy. This handicaps liberal ideology during long periods of continual crisis—a state of affairs which the United States entered after World War II.

It is significant, I think, that current criticism of American liberalism from those who call themselves radical is based on a rejection of recent liberal behavior rather than a new set of ideals or goals. Noticing a marked discrepancy between stated belief and observable action, radicals are contending that liberals are hypocrites or cynics. Self-induced paralytics, I believe, would be a more accurate description. For this diagnosis makes the illness psychosomatic, arguing that a dying mentality could yet recover if it changed its mind about itself, accepted the revolutionary implications of its own ideology and decided that stressful periods of rapid social change are times in which liberalism can be practical.

The history of the UWF, then, becomes a case study in the traditional way American ideals are suspended "for the duration" of periods demanding "realism." After arguing that the American experiment in self-government could now be given universal application, after having based a case for world federalism upon the demonstrable failure of the nation-state, the UWF responded to a nationalistic attack from those who would conserve rather than extend the "American Way of Life" by diluting its argument into a plea for support of the United Nations, based on the contention that it was the best tool available to a United States wishing to restrain an aggressive, atheistic, conspiratorial and communistic Soviet Union.

According to UWF analysis, the basic threat to humanity was nationalism. Thus nationalists—whether Stalinists or Sons and Daughters of the American Revolution—could have been attacked ideologically, using the armaments of recent history to destroy an archaic concept of patriotism. Instead, the UWF indulged in the "More American Than Thou" battle which it waged skillfully enough to keep itself off lists of subversive organizations. But the taint of having been accused remained, and in the very waging of the battle the UWF conceded defeat in the war for the minds of men which were to be purged of the poison of nationalism. The ideal, which was originally *intended* to subvert an entrenched national patriotism, was sold by the organization for a conservative mess of containment during a period which, according to that organization, demanded political leaps across ideological chasms—and all in the name of pragmatism.

II

This war had been fought before and very largely on the same grounds. Assuming that the nation-state had been created to protect its citizenry from internal chaos and external attack, pressures which culminated in World War I were sufficient to convince many political theorists that nation-states could no longer fulfill their function. Americans, tending to look back into their own history for organizational solutions, saw their Constitution as a transformation of a struggling confederacy into a vigorous federation, a modification of a political institution which geared it toward survival. In 1910 Theodore Roosevelt advised the Nobel Committee that the United States Constitution was a useful model for "a species of world federation for international peace and justice."[4] Typically, Americans during this period began to organize themselves into "action" groups intent upon bringing this ideal into existence—just as had been done in 1787.

Two years before Roosevelt's pronouncement, the American School Peace League started circulating literature aimed at teaching school children to view peace efforts as something more than antiwar reaction. Rational construction of a world legislature was to be seen as an aspect of these children's future which they would accept as they began to see themselves as citizens of a world republic. Another educational organization, the Peace and Arbitration League, was formed the same year. With Roosevelt as honorary chairman, it attempted to work toward the same goals through state congresses.[5]

The UWF would later repeat both of these approaches, but in tactical terms its primary predecessor was the New York Peace Society, an organization formed in 1906 and headed by Andrew Carnegie. This group was soon completely oriented toward internationalism, forming subsidiary organizations such as the World-Federation League (1910) and the League to Enforce Peace (1914). As Warren F. Kuehl, the historian of these movements, describes the World-Federation League, he also anticipates the later position of the UWF. For it too "sought, not to change existing nations or to intrude upon their domestic concerns, but 'only to lessen the occasions of war' and to hasten 'the day of establishment of *some* form of central government empowered to keep the peace.' "[6]

Having faded in importance, the World-Federation League was replaced by the League to Enforce Peace, an organization which anticipated the problems of later federalists by being plagued with splintering differences of opinion.[7] For its concept of a world government involved the potential use of military sanctions against a national offender, a prospect offending many pacifistic supporters of world law who consequently favored the more gentle and evolutionary aspirations of the World's Court League.[8] By the time the war was over, internationalists began to see their dream of federation as at least temporarily utopian.[9] But with the decision to accept a confederation, The League to Enforce Peace split on whether or not to accept a League of Nations "with reservations." William Howard Taft accepted the reservation on Article 10, but his position was rejected by the rest of an Executive Committee which wanted to retain him as its president.[10] At this point, the World's Court League merged with the New York Peace Society to form the League of Nations Union, a group which supported Woodrow Wilson.[11]

Many other organizational attempts preceded the UWF commitment to internationalization of the American mentality. Efforts by the Woodrow Wilson Foundation, the Foreign Policy Association, the Council on Foreign Relations, the Carnegie Endowment for International Peace, the American Union for Concerted Peace Efforts and the Commission to Study the Organization of Peace are all cited by Robert A. Divine as contributing to "The Triumph of Internationalism in America During World War II."[12] More specifically, the last group listed, chaired by James T. Shotwell, represented a preview of UWF arguments by declaring in 1941 that "the present conflict has taught us that something at once stronger and more adjustable than the League of 1919 is necessary. National sovereignty must yield more and more to the community of nations. The world must evolve from League to federation."[13]

However, instead of evolving into a federation, the League of Nations became merely the United Nations. Instead of shaping world opinion into a perspective which saw clearly the insanity of modern warfare, these groups only reflected tendencies toward social disorganization. Kuehl concludes that the participants in the earlier movements may have "believed so strongly in the inevitability of their success that they thought it unnecessary to combine in more than a temporary movement."[14]

III

The UWF may have learned something from previous failures, because it did represent an attempted coalition of likeminded movements. But it too believed success to be inevitable and largely for the reasons argued by its predecessors. Federalists had traditionally argued that their ideas had to be possible because all other options seemed to be closed or closing. Shocked by the incapacity of the League of Nations to prevent a second world war, Denna F. Fleming articulated most of the later UWF arguments for world federation in a speech given in 1943 which concluded: "We are moving towards World Federation because untold millions of people are learning that the Nation State can no longer protect them."[15]

These millions included political leaders, members of the intellectual community and the common citizenry. In 1946 fifty-three of the sixty-five candidates for the Eightieth Congress who answered a questionnaire approved of changing the United Nations into a world federation with majority-rule legislation. Two more approved with qualifications, while seven disapproved and three were undecided.[16] And in his annual message to Congress, President Truman chose that year to say: "The United Nations Organization now being established represents a minimal essential beginning. It must be developed rapidly and steadily . . . . Our ultimate security requires more than a process of consultation and compromise. It requires that we begin now to develop the United Nations organization as the representative of the world as one society."[17]

Similarly, a poll conducted by Arthur Kornhauser of the Columbia University Bureau of Applied Social Research reported that not one person of all the editors, historians, political scientists and church leaders deemed expert on international affairs "suggested that America should turn its back on the world and keep out of global organizations, as it did after the last war."[18] According to this poll, informed debate concerned only how soon international sovereignty could be achieved, with eleven percent thinking it could come within five years.

Perhaps more surprisingly, a Gallup poll taken in 1946 indicated that the man in the street was not far behind his leaders. It noted that in stark contrast to the isolationist mood which followed World War I, fifty-two percent of the American public favored United States participation in the liquidation of national armed forces, with an international police force to be given the responsibility of keeping the peace. Only twenty-four percent were opposed to this, with twenty-two percent still undecided.[19]

Riding this groundswell of public opinion, five of the groups dedicated to world government convened in February, 1947, in North Carolina and combined to form the United World Federalists For World Government With Limited Powers Adequate To Prevent War. Further identifying their mutual aim as "to mobilize popular opinion and action toward world government so that the local and national representatives of the people will be impelled to world federation by an irresistible political force,"[20] these groups—Americans United for World Government, World Federalists, Massachusetts Committee for World Federation, Student Federalists and World Citizens of Georgia—announced the following credo:

> We believe that peace is not merely the absence of war but the presence of justice, of law, of order—in short, of government and the institutions of government; that world peace can be created and maintained only under world law, universal and strong enough to prevent armed conflict between nations.[21]

The growth of the new organization was immediate and striking. By November of 1948, Cord Meyer, Jr., the President of the UWF during its early years, was able to announce the expenditure of $550,000 in an expansion program involving the development of the already existing six hundred chapters in the United States toward the goal of one chapter in every community.[22] Earlier that year, in a letter to the editor of the *New York Times,* Meyer was eager to cite a new poll conducted by Roper which showed an increase in public support to sixty-three percent for the UWF proposal that the United States initiate action to change a weak United Nations confederation into a strong federation.[23]

By 1948, Robert Lee Humber, a North Carolina attorney who operated as a one-man UWF lobby on the state government level, had succeeded in persuading sixteen state legislatures to pass resolutions asking the federal government to officially support world federalization.[24] And that fall the voters of Connecticut approved the UWF position in a referendum attached to the Presidential election by a vote of 130,548 to 11,467—thus exceeding the nine-to-one margin which had endorsed the UWF in an earlier referendum in Massachusetts.[25]

The total membership of the constituent groups at the time of the formation of the UWF was approximately 18,000.[26] But by 1949 there were forty-five thousand members paying three dollars' annual dues in 720 local chapters.[27] In June of that year, eight thousand people came to Madison Square Garden for a UWF rally in support of a Congressional resolution which advocated the official announcement by the State Department that the goal of American foreign policy involved the development of the United Nations into a world federation.[28] The chief speaker of the evening was Supreme Court Justice William O. Douglas, followed by Cord Meyer, Jr., and Senator Charles W. Tobey, the man who joined with twenty-one others to sponsor the resolution in the Senate and who was supported by over one hundred committed sponsors in the House of Representatives.[29]

What happened? Two decades later, Americans are still living in the United States; the United Nations is neither universal nor capable of keeping its members from fighting each other; and the planet seems to be no closer to planetary government than it was two world wars ago. If the UWF failed, was this failure based on inadequate theory, tactical error or events outside its control?

These questions cannot be conclusively answered, especially with respect to events outside the control of the UWF (such as Soviet behavior), because how history might have been cannot be documented. However, with the acknowledged benefit of hindsight, both tactical and theoretical weaknesses can be identified which now seem to have precluded any possibility of success; and these weaknesses have a direct bearing on how the U.S.S.R. could reasonably have been expected to react to the prospect of world federation.

World federalists could never quite believe they were right. They argued that a world federation was absolutely and immediately possible and that anything less was suicidal; but, they decided in the meantime they would support the United Nations. The liberal's inability to believe his own rhetoric is closely associated, I contend, with his suspicion that his ideals are not built to withstand stress. This ambivalence in theory leads to tactical cowardice, a combination which makes short range relief look like a pragmatic purchase of time. The effect can be seen in the general haplessness of American liberalism after World War II and in the more specific decline of the UWF as a viable political group. This virtual disappearance of the UWF from the political scene is symbolized quite graphically in capsule form by the career of Cord Meyer, Jr.—a sad parable of the All-American Boy who tried to live to the liberal hilt the American Way of Life in the 1940's and 1950's.

Meyer, who graduated from Yale (Phi Beta Kappa, goalie on the hockey team) in 1942, joined the Marines, lost an eye on Guam, returned in 1945 to wed Mary E. Pinchot (daughter of Amos, niece of Gifford) and to be Harold Stassen's aide at the founding of the United Nations. In 1947 he wrote *Peace or Anarchy* and founded the UWF. In 1951 the UWF publication, *The Federalist,* announced: "Because he has undertaken a U. S. Government post, Cord Meyer, Jr. is unable to continue as honorary president of UWF or as a member of UWF's Executive Council."[30] Personifying the way the UWF had begun to support rather than castigate the American variety of nationalism, Meyer had joined the CIA. Sheltered from the heat of McCarthyism by Allen Dulles, he became the agent who slipped subsidies to the National Student Association and other left-liberal organizations.[31]

He served for sixteen years an organization which has a world-government orientation differing significantly from that of the UWF; and it is now possible to consider the Soviet evaluation of Meyer when he was launching the UWF remarkably prescient and atypically humorous. For in 1949 Meyer had said: "Moscow radio has spent some time attacking us, and it attacked me personally not so long ago as the fig leaf of American imperialism; I think that was the nice phrase used."[32]

IV

The unhappy ending of Meyer's story was not, I think, implicit in its beginning. The ideas of post-World War II federalists, presented by Meyer in sketchy fashion in *Peace or Anarchy,* were too benevolent to be imperialistic and too obvious to benefit from fig leaves. As indicated above, these ideas had been advanced before, but they seemed to make a lot more sense to many Americans in the late Forties. The title of Meyer's books stated the alternatives, and since international anarchy was widely assumed to imply the impending extinction of the human race, the base from which world federalists built their case was the conviction that there was really no other choice. According to Meyer, the immediate future was going to entail either world government or total chaos via atomic warfare; the world was obviously not unified enough for a unitary form of government, so only federalism seemed to represent a viable system which could both assert power in its limited realm (prevention of international war) and acknowledge the cultural and economic differences of member states.[33]

It is almost impossible to exaggerate the importance of the feeling that there were no alternatives to federalism. As early as 1943, Norman Cousins had editorialized that "one of the greatest obstacles to world citizenship today is the lack of a world consciousness that the ideal is not only possible but mandatory if we are not to slide into a long period of retrogression."[34] But the driving force behind the sentiment that world federalism was "the only visible alternative to mass suicide" was clearly the bombing of Japan, an event which suddenly made the UWF seem less utopian than earlier federalists.[35] Witness Henry Stimson and Vernon Nash: "Now, with the release of atomic energy, man's ability to destroy himself is very nearly complete. The bombs dropped on Hiroshima and Nagasaki ended a war. They also made it wholly clear that we must never have another war. This is the lesson men and leaders everywhere must learn, and I believe that when they learn it they will find a way to lasting peace. There is no other choice."[36] "There is now no other choice possible; it is either the utopia of world government or the cataclysm of an atom-germ-poisons third world war."[37]

Within the negative thrust of this "no other choice" stance, moreover, is the concurrent belief that world federalist recommendations are, indeed, viable options. Reflecting a faith in man's ability to change his institutions when necessary, Meyer contended that the current emphasis on "preparedness," while mandatory because of the absence of law in governing international relations, was bound to lead to the sort of totalitarian state America was supposedly insuring itself against. "Preparedness in foreign policy means the subordination of economic considerations to political and military goals. The implementation of such a policy seems to necessitate the strictest governmental regulation of foreign trade and the use of tariffs and quotas as weapons. The effect must be further centralization of power within the United States. . . ."[38]

Ironically, Meyer sharply cirticized the sort of government which needed to hide its activities from its own citizens: "To Americans, the existence of the Russian secret police is the most damning indictment against the Soviet state."[39] However, this is not to argue that Meyer was an early Cold Warrior. In an interpretation which would shortly appear seditious and which has only recently been extensively accepted, Meyer refused to make a bogey of the Soviet Union, saying that the increasing hostilities were the fault of both countries and chiefly the result of nationalism.[40]

The other central propagator of UWF ideas, and the man who became *the* spokesman for the movement when Meyer dropped out of sight, was Norman Cousins. Using his editorial page as a useful podium, Cousins wrote many defenses of federalist positions in the *Saturday Review of Literature,* often giving other advocates such as Clement Attlee, Joseph S. Clark and Oscar Hammerstein II a chance for guest editorials.[41] Associated with federalist movements long before the creation of the UWF, Cousins wrote in 1945: "For the last five years, the editors of *The Saturday Review* have dedicated this page to the principles of world citizenship. We have no intention of abandoning that fight—now or at any other time."[42]

Indeed, Cousins did not abandon the fight. It seems fair to say that his value to the movement was not (and is not) in developing new and fresh ideas, but in the dogged effort to keep the issue before the public, trying to arouse that irresistible movement which was to sweep the world toward sanity.

But resistance was forthcoming, for Cousins and Meyer were not universally convincing when they attempted to project the concepts of *The Federalist Papers* onto the twentieth-century situation. Arthur Schlesinger, Jr., believed that our "national unity results less from the Constitution than from Civil War."[43] Harold Bradley argued that a sense of community is necessary before any sort of federalism is feasible, and that this sense was present in post-revolutionary America but almost totally absent on a world scale after World War II.[44] In a more recent analysis, John W. Spanier summed up this position with the conclusion that the world federalists never had a theoretical chance:

> In short, world government is not acceptable even as a *theoretical* answer to the problem of our time—and cannot be until a global consensus exists. Only then can the conflicts among national interests be resolved more peacefully. Only then will a world government acquire the legitimacy necessary for the obedience of its laws—laws that are the product of political rather than judicial decisions. It is precisely the absence of such consensus today that explains the survival of sovereign states and the high expectation of violence.[45]

In the Forties and Fifties, people of this persuasion were very much attracted to the ideas of Clarence K. Streit, a man who argued for *Union Now: A Proposal for a Federal Union of the Democracies of the North Atlantic.* The Atlantic Union movement, which grew out of Streit's work and which claimed that federation of likeminded democracies was immediately possible, had appreciable support in Congress (from Senator Kefauver and Representative Judd).[46] It had support as well in the general public.[47] This group, which became the chief federalist competition of the UWF, essentially responded to the contention that no other choice was possible by negating the possibility of world federalism: "To dismiss regionalism in favor of an abstract idea of a world government would be to ignore realities and engage in search of perfect solutions in an imperfect world."[48] It would be, in short, idealistic instead of realistic.

But advocacy of regional alignment had disastrous overtones for those who were hoping to avoid the sort of perpetual war between blocs which Orwell envisioned in *1984*. F. L. Schuman contended that federalism of this sort would be more likely to cause conflict than to prevent or ameliorate it. And as Chester Bowles saw it: "The purpose of world government is not to bring Russia and America together; *the purpose of the world government is to keep them apart. . . .* In the absence of a superior force, each seeks the security that can be obtained only at the expense of what the other regards as its own security. . . ."[49] Alan Cranston, speaking as President of the UWF in 1950, cautioned against those who conceive of government as feasible only "over likeminded peoples. This, I submit, is a common misconception of the whole purpose of government. In my simple definition, government (which nobody likes) is only instituted by people who have to live together and find it difficult to do so peacefully."[50]

Since both regional and world federalists ultimately desired the same sort of world order, the debate over whether government must precede or follow a sense of community was reduced to a difference in tactics—immediate universalism versus gradualism. Einstein contended that "the trouble about taking little steps, one at a time, in the hope of reaching that ultimate goal is that while they are being taken, we continue to keep the bomb secret without making our reason convincing to those who do not have the secret."[51] And in the most picturesque portrayal of the inefficiency of gradualism, F. L. Schuman quoted Lloyd George to the effect that "nothing is more dangerous than to try to leap a chasm in two jumps."[52] Therefore, in its first General Assembly, the UWF proclaimed its opposition to the Union Now point of view: "We dissociate ourselves most explicitly from those who would exclude the Soviet Union or who would welcome her unwillingness to join [a world federation]."[53]

However, when confronted with an organization which presented itself as a body which *might* eventually develop into real world government, the UWF was in a quandry regarding whether or not to believe what it had been saying about gradualism. On the one hand, its statement of beliefs included an endorsement of "the efforts of the United Nations to bring about a world community favorable to peace."[54] And Chester Bowles maintained that the work of the UWF was to give "blood and bones" to U.N. efforts.[55] Yet, in *Peace or Anarchy*, Meyer indicated agreement with Emery Reves's powerful polemic against the nation-state, *The Anatomy of Peace*, in which a case was made that the U.N., if a half step at all, was in the wrong direction. According to Reves, the sovereignty of member nations was only emphasized in the way the General Assembly was constructed, with organizational ineffectiveness guaranteed by giving members of the security council the power to veto decisions.[56] Along the same lines, E. B. White, who had long argued the federalist cause within the *New Yorker*, "ridiculed the proposed world organization as the 'Fifty Sovereign Nations of the World Solemnly Sworn to Prevent Each Other from Committing Aggression.' "[57]

This theoretical dispute among federalists was not resolved by federalists; it was overwhelmed by nationalistic opposition to the whole concept of yielding national sovereignty to any supranational organization. Unfortunately for the public-relations campaign directed by Meyer and Cousins, the mood in America changed drastically during the Fifties; and theoretical considerations once again took second place during a period when good tactics seemed to involve back-pedalling for one's organizational life. In 1951 the UWF had an income of over $180,000—obtained from about forty thousand members; but within five years these figures had shrunk to about $65,000 and 17,000 respectively.[58] A closer examination of the UWF reaction to the attack launched by nationalists leads to the conclusion that instead of opting for the politics of "pragmatism" the group would have been well advised to remain idealistic. As Norman Cousins has more recently concluded, the UWF "was strongest when its message was purest."[59] In evaluating reasons for its present condition, then, it becomes important to note that UWF salesmen were responsible for the adulteration of the product.

In 1950 the Senate Foreign Relations Committee heard testimony branding the UWF as subversive from witnesses representing societies such as: Women's Patriotic Council on National Defense, National Society of New England Women, National Society of Women Descendants of the Ancient and Honorable Artillery Company, Dames of the Loyal Legion of the United States of America, The American Coalition, The Veterans of Foreign Wars, and the Society of the War of 1812.[60]

Also in 1950, the prolific Joseph P. Kamp published a book with the caustic title: *We Must Abolish These United States.*[61] Asserting that this was the essential message of the UWF, he provided lists of those in Congress who had traitorously supported UWF proposals in the past. One by one, the state legislatures began to pass memorials remanding their earlier endorsements. In the reconsidered opinion of the Senate of the Virginia General Assembly, "it appeared world government 'would entail the surrender of national sovereignty.' "[62] By 1952 the Senate Appropriations Committee, under the leadership of Pat McCarran, approved a bill banning funds from any organizations which "directly or indirectly promoted one world government or world citizenship."[63] This particular attack was directed against UNESCO, but the UWF received its full share of special attention. Thus, when a Methodist minister, guilty of forming a UWF chapter, was accused of aiding the Communist cause, the charge was vigorously refuted by *The Federalist.*[64] Cranston, as President, found it necessary to deny that the UWF "stinks of Communist Government" and went so far as to maintain that they were barred from membership.[65]

The Fifth General Assembly (June, 1951) found students splitting off from the UWF to form their own organization. However, rather than rejecting their elders' consuming concern with Communist infiltration, these dissidents were interested in a larger share of the funds. So the credo which the younger universalists issued reflected rather than corrected the conflict between theory and behavior being acted out by older idealists. Those who were forced to live in a world full of Communists proposed to expel them from an organization devoted to world unity—in the name of American liberalism:

> As Americans, as student federalists and as citizens of the world, we believe . . . that we must displace from any leadership in this movement for freedom the communists whose methods would destroy freedom; that we must preserve and expand freedom at home, combatting tendencies to limit traditional liberties in times of crisis.[66]

The close connection between panicky tactics and dilution of theory is demonstrated by the fact that although the 1950 General Assembly had reaffirmed the UWF belief in universalism, the convention in 1951 adopted an endorsement of partial federation in case the U.S.S.R. could not or would not participate in a world federation.[67]

It is possible to criticize the UWF for its feeble defensiveness. Doubtless, better tactics would have involved reacting as vigorously as did Truman when he was criticized by the VFW for appointing federalist T. K. Finletter as Secretary of the Air Force. Truman's response was a healthy defense of his own personal choice, but it also indicated something of the shrinking status of the UWF: "All this howl about organizations a fellow belongs to gives me a pain in the neck. I'd be willing to bet my right eye that you yourself and I have joined some organizations that we wish we hadn't. It hasn't hurt me any and I don't think it has hurt you any . . . ."[68]

Norman Cousins, outraged at the effectiveness of the red-baiting, was perceptive enough to be self-critical under pressure: "There is a tendency to deny every charge just because a charge is made, rather than affirming our own beliefs and carrying the fight to the open arena where public opinion can be rallied behind us."[69] But Cousins, who became President of the UWF in 1952, responded to an attack upon his own position from the right by conceding that the principal charge within that attack had validity; he too saw the ultimate threat to American liberalism coming from the fanatics on the left: "There could be no more ghastly irony than is presented today by those who in the name of Americanism are actually helping to prepare this country for the eventual triumph of Communism."[70]

Hagerstown, Maryland, provided the setting for a dramatic presentation of the way the UWF under Cousins responded to charges of subversive activity. Although the Junior Chamber of Commerce had agreed to co-sponsor a play entitled "The Myth," it was responsive to pressures from the American Legion and the UWF was forced to present the play without the support of other local organizations. At the close of the performance, Daniel Burkhardt, the American Legion Adjutant for the State of Maryland, asked for and received permission to present his views. According to *The Federalist:*

> Norman Cousins came to the stage and in answering Burkhardt's statements said, 'My real flag is the U.S. flag, but there must come a day when there is a banner to represent the human race.' Mr. Burkhardt then referred to the charge from the Un-American Activities Committee report that Cousins had spoken at a meeting of the Scientific and Cultural Conference for World Peace, a Communist-front meeting, in New York in 1949. Cousins replied that he had done so at the request of the State Department in order to present the United States' anti-Communist views, had been roundly booed and hissed and had needed police escort to leave the hall.[71]

This can be read in a way not intended by the UWF publication. For it reveals that in 1949, *before* McCarthy, a leading founder of the

UWF was busy giving anti-Communist speeches for the State Department of the nation into which he happened to have been born. Although he was the spokesman for a movement based on the theoretical ability of hostile people to live in peace, he flaunted as patriotic credentials the fact that he could not communicate with Communists—a quality which might have produced mortification. One is forced to conclude that if Cousins' "real flag" was the United States flag, he was not buying what the UWF was selling.

Perhaps more important, because of the dramatic curtain call, little attention was paid to the message of the play itself. The incident received national publicity, but interest in the event was limited to the alleged subversiveness of the UWF. Thus "The Myth," the idea of world government, got lost in a dialogue which was essentially beside the point in much the same way as the original ideals of the UWF disappeared into the righteous rhetoric of the early Fifties.

Defensive, rather than aggressively subversive, *The Federalist* cheered when a California high school teacher who had been called a Communist over the radio because of her UWF affiliations received over $50,000 damages in 1953.[72] That same year Rev. Donald Harrington used the same publication to consider the possibility of a change in the U.S.S.R. with the death of Stalin. He concluded: "Are the Soviets ready for peace? Only to the degree that it may serve the long range objective of world conquest which they have set forth."[73] In 1956 Harrington became President of the UWF. That year the General Assembly passed a platform which supported both "Self-Determination of Peoples" and "Halting Communist Expansion."[74] Like the State Department they supported so consistently, the federalists of the Fifties could not imagine that these two principles might contradict each other, even though their own paper had reported that a vote in Vietnam would be "overwhelmingly" for Communism.[75]

The Federalist during the early Sixties reads much the same way. In 1961 a $50,000 gift from Cousins made possible the hiring of a professional public relations firm "to aid in the visibility program."[76] The following year the organization attracted 3000 new members but lost 2000 through non-renewal.[77] That was the year in which the UWF President, Paul W. Walter (a former campaign manager for Robert A. Taft), sent three telegrams to President Kennedy congratulating him on his handling of the Cuban missile crisis.[78] The most interesting unification project discussed from September, 1963, through June, 1965, was a proposed merger with SANE. Although this represented an appreciable scaling down of earlier goals, most members felt it would be invigorating. But a committee set up to work out the details regarding each group's loss of individual identity was unable to do so.[79] A letter from a member of both groups explains part of the problem involved: "I have noticed that UWF always, or almost always, stops short of criticism of a national administration (whether Republican or Democratic). SANE does not restrain itself in this manner."[80] In 1964 the UWF gave a "Federalist Founders Award" to Everett Dirksen; in 1966 another went to Robert McNamara.[81]

But by this time the membership was restive. McNamara's award was most bitterly disputed.[82] Although the UWF was still red-baited occasionally, the war in Vietnam was making open opposition to the United States government by American citizens much more popular. Thus in 1966 President C. M. Stanley began asking for a change in American foreign policy. He argued that merely containing Communism was not enough; it was time for the United States (and the UWF) to begin moving positively again.[83] The General Assembly of 1967 identified the American government as the primary problem in Southeast Asia, and the UWF became part of Negotiation Now![84] Its student branch, not to be outdone, displayed a President and Vice President who had turned in draft cards and held conventions featuring speakers such as Benjamin Spock, Joan Baez, David Harris and Herbert Marcuse.[85] But having arrived with too little after most of the people were already there, the world federalists have been little noticed in the current peace movement.

During recent years the UWF newsletter, *The Federalist,* has tended to consist largely of photographs of UWF dignitaries shaking hands with government dignitaries, photographs of UWF delegates congratulating each other at banquets, and reproductions of telegrams sent by the UWF to encourage support of the United Nations. In 1970 it was decided to cease the publication of this newsletter as a separate entity. What had been called the United World Federalists (UWF) is now labeled the World Federalists of the United States of America (WFUSA). But these do not represent particularly meaningful motions within the recently stagnant peace movement.[86]

VI

The nice phrase Cord Meyer, Jr., had used to describe the early UWF involved seeing the organization as the vanguard of an "irresistible political force." This force having been easily resisted by a diversionary offensive on the part of nationalists, federalist liberals have retreated from the realm of activist movements to the security of academic impact and influence. In 1958 the first edition of Grenville Clark's and Louis B. Sohn's *World Peace Through World Law* was published, with later revisions appearing in 1960 and 1966. This book, called the "bible" for world federalists, amounts to a detailed restructuring of the United Nations from a useless confederation into a viable federation.[87] Among later federalist efforts, most notable is a series of volumes entitled *The Strategy of World Order,* edited by Richard A. Falk and Saul H. Mendlovitz. But although many positive things could be said about these publications, there is no doubt that they represent a lowering of the aspirations and a tempering of the optimism of the earlier UWF efforts. Instead of hastily organizing the avoidance of cataclysm, the UWF currently limits its activism to a lobbyist in Washington, with its primary emphasis now involving the more leisurely process of educating the children of those who missed a chance for world peace through world law after World War II. If this is wiser, it is also sadder. According to a UWF chapter head, D. M. H. Cowden, "Many believed—in the euphoria of the post-war period—that world government was imminent. Age has altered our ideology over the years."[88]

This would appear to be accurate, if understated. From an organization which once had 60,000 members (according to Cowden) to one with only 15,000 during the depths of the Fifties, the UWF has managed to recoup its losses only minimally, counting now about 20,000 paying adherents. So the history of the aspirations and accomplishments of the UWF, in a world far from federalized, has to be considered an account of failure. Official UWF publications do not concede this.[89] Rev. G. G. Grant, S.J., has contended recently that whereas the early concerns of the group involved *only* the prevention of war via world government, by 1965, "over and above the need for the elimination of war, there was recognized a parallel need for the development of those agencies that could alleviate hunger, disease and ignorance—the seeds of war."[90]

Here is no more talk about leaps and chasms; having capitulated to the gradualists, the emphasis of the movement is upon "development" and "alleviation." If it is conceded that this falls far short of original goals, it is possible to conclude that federalist liberals degenerated as a vigorous political force because they failed to sterilize one of the seeds of their own destruction, an inability to believe what they heard themselves saying.

Already in 1946 Sumner Welles had red-baited Einstein's argument for world government by contending that the United States and England should never agree to join a "World Union of Soviet Socialist Republics," and thus "abolish all those cherished principles of individual liberty which are sacred to the Anglo-Saxon peoples."[91] However, the Soviet Union had never endorsed the movement for world federation, and two years later a liberal journal in the United States could still give a liberal explanation of that sad fact by noting that Russia's suspicions of yet another capitalist plot were not merely reflections of paranoia. After all, argued the editor of the *Christian Century*, the U.S.S.R. had been excluded, then admitted and then expelled from the League of Nations; and with the current structure of the United Nations, it *was* possible to see any attempt to deprive the Soviet Union of its veto as a step by the United States toward the possible legitimization of the use of atomic weapons against Russia by means of a vote within a General Assembly in which America controlled many more votes than the Communist bloc could muster.[92]

From the very beginnings of the movement, however, publications which wished to give favorable accounts of the federalists did so by merely denying Communist participation rather than by inquiring (with frustration and disappointment) why this was so. *Newsweek,* which noted contentedly that Norman Thomas represented the left edge of world-government advocates, stated:

> The Communist fellow-traveling fringe, with one or two lonely exceptions, has kept aloof, obviously, because the official Communist party line frowns on the idea of world government as a 'reactionary utopia.' It insists, in accordance with current Soviet policy, on the inviolability of national sovereignty. This means that for the time being, at least, the world-government movement is one of the few political currents of our time in which liberals can participate without getting tangled up in Communist party intrigues and 'front' maneuvers.[93]

The logic of this is amazing. Communists, including the feeble American variety, are given the capability of destroying a "political current" merely by joining it, and yet the driving force of that current consists in its contention that we are all in the world together, until death does us part.

According to the liberal mentality, if liberalism (being good) is not likely to do well during periods of extreme stress, Communism (being evil) then approaches omnipotence. This seed of hysteria, cultivated by those concurrently claiming that there was no longer any choice but for disparate groups to trust each other, grew to the extent that when Mrs. Anita McCormick Blaine established the Foundation for World Government the fact that someone as far to the left as Henry Wallace was expected to be one of the trustees was enough to impel other organizations dedicated to unity to dissociate themselves. Ely Culbertson spoke for the Citizens Committee for United Nations Reform: "As far as our organization is concerned, anything Wallace is associated with is a red herring—doubled and redoubled."[94]

Thus guilt by association was not the invention of the less than mediocre public servant who needed an issue on which to justify his own re-election. In fact, McCarthy could have discovered from the leadership of the UWF that "Soviet aggressive expansionism is the major problem in the world today."[95] This spokesman made distinctions between the Soviet army and Communism as a religion, but such subtleties were soon to be dropped as McCarthy became a fire-breathing symbol of much that liberals had conceded. By 1950 the same Truman Administration which had nodded in the direction of world government in 1946 was issuing official proclamations which could just as well have been written by McCarthy himself:

> For if there is one thing that is clear, it is that the Soviet Union does not have, and has never had, the slightest in-

tention of joining in any plan of world federation in any sense that would be acceptable to any believer in democracy. In fact, it is precisely because the Soviet Union has its own unbending ideas of how the entire world should be organized that the tensions exist today . . . . It is difficult to see how there can be a 'general agreement' with anyone whose single-minded objective is to extinguish you . . . . The objective of the free world is to erect a stone wall against aggression.[96]

When the professional articulators of diplomacy begin to depend on the imagery of stone walls, it is easily seen that the federalists had failed to sterilize all the seeds of war. For this particular seed, a paralyzing preoccupation with Communism, germinated in the liberal's lack of faith in his own ideology. It was then nourished by the tears shed in the pathetic liberal's lament that he was unfairly charged with Communist sympathies; it grew into the rhetorical jungle of the Cold War. As liberal rejection of revolutionary change slid over into a defense of the status quo, all efforts toward change were given the label of revolutionary fungus and liberals broke out the defoliants. Tragically paralleling the larger movement in which American liberals became conservatives during a period demanding rapid social change, a well-financed, intelligent, internationalist peace movement succumbed to an obsolete and ignorant nationalism by sacrificing its ideals "for the duration" upon the altar of expediency, committing organizational suicide in the name of American pragmatism.

Idaho State University

notes

1. Quoted by Raymond B. Fosdick in *Pioneers in World Order*, ed. (New York, 1944), *Harriet E. Davis*, v.

2. In *The City of Man* (Baltimore, 1967), Warren Wagar traces ideas about world government and the universal brotherhood of mankind back through Dante to the Greek Stoics. See, especially, 27, 38-39.

3. See Louis Hartz, *The Liberal Tradition in America* (New York, 1955), and Arthur Ekirch, Jr., *The Decline of American Liberalism* (New York, 1967).

4. Quoted by Warren F. Kuehl, *Seeking World Order* (Nashville, 1969), 127.

5. *Ibid.*, 109, 111.

6. *Ibid.*, 108, 125. For this reason the UWF was called a "minimalist" organization. It desired universal participation in a very limited world government.

7. See Ruhl J. Bartlett, *The League to Enforce Peace* (Chapel Hill, 1944), 208-209.

8. Kuehl, *Seeking World Order*, 208. For a full display of the hawkish characteristics of the League to Enforce Peace, see *Win the War For Permanent Peace* (New York: League to Enforce Peace, n.d.), especially the keynote address by its president, William Howard Taft. This book, made up primarily of speeches made at the 1918 convention, "breathes the crusaders' spirit that animates a great people engaged in a Holy War and determined to let no sacrifices stand in the way of victory" (p. 7).

9. Kuehl, *Seeking World Order*, 340.

10. Robert A. Divine, *Second Chance* (New York, 1967), 6-9.

11. Kuehl, *Seeking World Order*, 306.

12. This is the subtitle of Divine's book, *Second Chance.*

13. *Commission to Study the Organization of Peace: Preliminary Report and Monographs* (New York: Commission to Study the Organization of Peace, [1942]), 6. Members of the commission signing this statement included John Foster Dulles, Denna F. Fleming, Owen Lattimore, Max Lerner, Daniel A. Poling, Clarence Streit, William Allen White and Quincy Wright.

14. Kuehl, *Seeking World Order*, 345.

15. "America and the World Crisis," *Vital Speeches*, X (October 15, 1943), 7.

16. *New York Times*, November 1, 1946, p. 16, col. 1.

17. *New York Times*, January 22, 1946, p. 16, col. 2.

18. "Is World Government Possible?," *American Magazine*, XCLI (April, 1946), 52.

19. *Newsweek*, XXVIII (October 14, 1946), 44.

20. *New York Times*, February 24, 1947, p. 3, col. 7. The new UWF Executive Council included Mark Van Doren, Raymond Gram Swing, Norman Cousins, T. K. Finletter, Edgar Ansel Mowrer and Helen Ball.

21. *New York Times*, February 23, 1947, p. 25, col. 4. This account also lists World Republic as one of the organizations which merged into the UWF, a version of its formation erroneously repeated by Frederick L. Schuman in *The Commonwealth of Man* (New York, 1952), 436. According to the *New York Times*, the students making up World Republic (formerly Students for Federal World Government) were persuaded to join the UWF by the conciliatory efforts of Norman Cousins. Actually, although both UWF and World Republic were American affiliates of the World Movement for World Federal Government, World Republic—the very organization responsible for setting up the meeting of "likeminded" groups in order to facilitate a merger—retained a separate identity. See Harrison Brown, "The World Government Movement in the United States," *Bulletin of the Atomic Scientists*, III (June, 1947), 156; George A. Bernstein, "World Government—A Progress Report," *Nation*, CLXI (December 22, 1945), 712-715; Lawrence S. Wittner, *Rebels Against War* (New York, 1969), 171. For a discussion of World Republic, made up mostly of young people from the Chicago area who dropped out of school to work for world government, see Dorothea Kahn, "Design for Peace," *Christian Science Monitor Magazine*, March 1, 1947, 6. Unlike those groups which became the UWF, World Republic was oriented toward a "people's convention" rather than trying to transform the United Nations into a federation.

22. *New York Times*, November 15, 1948, p. 17, col. 6.

23. *New York Times*, April 4, 1948, Sec. IV, p. 8, col. 6.

24. See Bernstein, "World Government—Progress Report," 628; and "Proposals for Now Revising the United Nations into a Federal World Government," *Congressional Digest*, XXVII (August-September, 1948), 195. Humber had begun this sort of work years before, having successfully persuaded his own state's legislature to pass such a resolution in 1941. See Divine, *Second Chance*, 58.

25. J. R. Lyford, "Vote For World Government," *New Republic*, CXIX (December 27, 1948), 16-18.

26. *New York Times*, February 23, 1947, p. 25, col. 4.

27. Mary Hornaday, "Nations Move To Free Union," *Christian Science Monitor Magazine*, August 27, 1949, 2.

28. *New York Times*, June 10, 1949, p. 3, col. 6.

29. Hornaday, "Nations Move To Free Union," 2.

30. November, 1951, p. 6.

31. *New York Times*, March 30, 1967, p. 30, cols. 1-2.

32. Meyer, "A Plea For World Government," *American Academy of Political and Social Science Annals*, CCLXIV (July, 1949), 12.

33. *Peace or Anarchy* was published in Boston by Little, Brown & Co. See also his debate with Thomas J. Hamilton published in the *New York Times*, February 16, 1950, Sec. VI, 11, 16, 18.

34. "A Bargain Counter for Ideals," *Saturday Review of Literature*, XXVI (October 16, 1943), 26.

35. F. L. Schuman, "Toward the World State," *Scientific Monthly*, LXII (July, 1946), 10.

36. Henry Stimson, "The Decision to Use the Atomic Bomb," in *The 1940's: Profile of a Nation in Crisis*, ed. Chester E. Eisinger (Garden City, New York, 1969), 73.

37. Vernon Nash, "Utopia or Cataclysm," *Christian Century*, LXIV (November 26, 1947), 1454. See also Norman Cousins, "Strange Doings," *Saturday Review of Literature*, XXVIII (June 23, 1945), 20. For the same position argued by a man who was later to become President of the UWF and still later the Secretary of the Air Force, see Thomas K. Finletter, "Timetable For World Government," *Atlantic*, CLXXVII (March, 1946), 53-60. The idea of an absence of options has continued to the present. See Freda Kirchway, "One World or None," *Nation*, CLXI (August 18, 1945), 149-150; G. A. Borgese, *Foundations of the World Republic* (Chicago, 1953); Bertrand Russell, "Only World Government Can Prevent the War Nobody Can Win," *Bulletin of the Atomic Scientists*, XIV (September, 1958), especially p. 261; Paul S. Andrews, "Blueprint for a Peaceful World," *Current History*, XXIX (August, 1960), 75-81; Ake Sandler, "A World Constitution," *Bulletin of the Atomic Scientists*, XXIV (April, 1968), 38. Today, of course, the fact that so few believe in the possibility of nuclear war makes such a disaster more probable in the view of theorists such as these.

38. Meyer, *Peace or Anarchy*, 66-67.

39. *Ibid.*, 73.

40. *Ibid.*, especially pp. 106-107. See also his article, "We Must Have World Government NOW," *Scholastic*, LIII (October 20, 1948), 10-11.

41. See *Saturday Review of Literature:* August 23, 1958, 22; January 15, 1966, 28; December 23, 1950, 22-23.

42. Cousins, "Strange Doings," 20.

43. *The Vital Center* (Boston, 1949), 240.

44. "The American Adventure in Federalism," *Current History*, XXXIX (August, 1960), 92-95, 100.

45. *World Politics in an Age of Revolution* (New York, 1965), 133. Much has been written about whether a government can create a sense of shared values and interests. Numerically, at least, those who argue (against the UWF) that a viable community has to exist before federalism can be effective have the advantage. Wagar, for example, pays little attention to the UWF movement in *The City of Man*, considering it unrealistically legalistic in its effort to impose government upon a situation just because it seems necessary (see 228, 293). Another theoretician who denies the equation of need with possibility is Reinhold Niebuhr. See "The Myth of World Government," *Nation*, CLXII (March 16, 1946), 312-314; "The Illusion of World Government," *Foreign Affairs*, XXVII (April, 1949), 379-388; and "The Reach for One World," *New Republic*, CXXIX (November 23, 1953), 16-17.

Other writers believing that a sense of world community must precede world law include: Ralph Barton Perry, *One World in the Making* (New York, 1945); Quincy Wright, ed., *The World Community* (Chicago, 1948); Hans J. Morgenthau, *Politics Among Nations* (New York, 1949), especially pp. 216, 404-406; Werner Levi, *Fundamentals of World Organization* (Minneapolis, 1950); Gerard J. Mangone, *The Idea and Practice of World Government* (New York, 1951), and "The Fallacy of World Federalism," *Current History*, XXIX (September, 1960), 163-168; Inis L. Claude, *Swords into Plowshares* (New York, 1956), especially p. 378.

46. Hornaday, "Nations Move To Free Union," 2. Streit's book was published in New York by Harper & Bros. in 1939.

47. By 1958, when Elton Atwater *et al.* published *World Affairs* (New York), *Union Now* had sold over 300,000 copies in 17 editions (see 564).

48. Piotr S. Wandyez, "Regionalism and World Federalism," *Current History*, XXIX (August, 1960), 87. Other supporters of regional federation include: Pitman B. Potter, "Universalism Versus Regionalism in International Organization," *American Political Science Review*, XXXVII (October, 1943), 850-862; Edward R. Lewis, "Are We Ready For A World State?," *Yale Review*, XXV (March, 1946), 491-501; F. S. C. Northrop, *The Taming of the Nations* (New York, 1952); and Nelson Rockefeller, *The Future of Federalism* (New York, 1968).

49. Schuman, "Toward The World State," 11. Bowles, "World Government—'Yes, But,'" *Harper's*, CXCVIII (March, 1949), 26.

50. "What About World Government," *New Republic*, CXII (May 22, 1950), 16. See also James T. Shotwell, *The Great Decision* (New York, 1945), especially p. 216. K. C. Wheare, *Federal Government* (New York, 1964), 38-39, argues that the desire to unite for economic, military or political reasons seems to be much more crucial to the creation of a lasting federal government than community of race, religion, nationality or social institutions.

51. "Einstein on the Atomic Bomb," in *The 1940's*, ed. Eisinger, 100.

52. "Toward The World State," 12.

53. Quoted by G. A. Bernstein, "World Government—Progress Report," 629.

54. *New York Times*, February 23, 1947, p. 25, col. 4.

55. "World Government—'Yes, But,'" 22.

56. For Meyer's endorsement, see *Peace or Anarchy*, 235.

57. Divine, *Second Chance*, 229.

58. *New York Times*, June 16, 1956, p. 39, col. 3. As recorded in the Summer, 1952, issue of *The Federalist* (p. 6), that year's General Assembly of the UWF unanimously approved an offer made by Atlantic Union to work together toward shared objectives. But this newly accepting attitude was based on present weakness rather than resulting from a theoretical basis self-confident enough to welcome support from any direction.

59. *World Federalist*, July/August, 1969, 2.

60. *New York Times*, February 21, 1950, p. 11, col. 1.

61. A list of a few of his other books, all published in New York by Hallmark, gives an idea of the tenor of this book: *Strikes . . . And the Communists Behind Them; Communist Carpetbaggers in Operation Dixie; Fifth Column vs. The Dies Committee; Vote CIO . . . and Get A Soviet America; Behind The Lace Curtains of the YWCA.*

62. *The Federalist*, February, 1952, 8.

63. *New York Times*, June 25, 1952, p. 18, col. 3.

64. See *The Federalist*, November, 1951, 8.

65. *New York Times*, February 25, 1950, p. 7, col. 6.

66. *The Federalist*, Summer, 1951, 7.

67. *Ibid.*, 19, and February, 1952, 7.

68. *New York Times*, June 7, 1950, p. 23, col. 5.

114

69. "The Climate of Freedom," *Saturday Review of Literature*, XXXV (July, 1952), 22.
70. *Ibid.*
71. *The Federalist*, April, 1953, 10.
72. *Ibid.*, October, 1953, 7.
73. *Ibid.*, June, 1953, 9.
74. *Ibid.*, July, 1956, 6.
75. *Ibid.*, February, 1955, 5.
76. *The Federalist Newsletter*, June 24, 1961, n.p.
77. *The Federalist*, September, 1962, 8.
78. *Ibid.*, December, 1962.
79. *Ibid.*, October, 1963, 7-8 [reprint of September, 1963, *War/Peace Report* editorial urging merger]; *ibid.*, June, 1965, 2. SANE, although generally considered less conservative, shared members, leaders and problems with the UWF. Mutual spokesmen included Donald Harrington, Oscar Hammerstein II, Walter Reuther and Donald Keys. Cousins joined Clarence Pickett (American Friends Service Committee) as co-chairman when SANE was organized in 1951 and wrote the early advertisements. And Cousins was a primary figure in the 1960 purge of alleged Communists which seemed so McCarthyite to younger or more radical members of SANE. For accounts of the participants in the organization, growth and decline of SANE see: *SANE World*, April 15, 1964, 1-2; *Time*, April 27, 1962, 22-23; Nathan Glazer, "The Peace Movement in America," *Commentary*, XXXI (April, 1961), especially pp. 290-293; and Lawrence S. Wittner, *Rebels Against War*, 245, 258-261.
80. *The Federalist*, November, 1963, 8.
81. *Ibid.*, July/August, 1964, 9; and July, 1966, 2.
82. See a typical letter in *The Federalist*, September, 1966, 5.
83. *The Federalist*, April, 1966, 6.
84. *Ibid.*, July/August, 1967, 1, 4, 12.
85. *World Federalist*, March/April, 1969, A-4.
86. Annual conventions are still held; Norman Cousins is still the president of the World Association of World Federalists.
87. Andrews, "Blueprint For a Peaceful World," 77.
88. *New York Times*, November 22, 1964, p. 123, col. 4.
89. For President C. Maxwell Stanley's assertion that the influence of the UWF has never been greater, see *The Federalist*, September, 1964, 4.
90. *The Federalist*, December, 1967, 4.
91. "The Soviet Union and World Government," *Christian Century*, LXV (January, 1946), 40. It is interesting to note that Robert Divine identifies the *Christian Century* as "idealistic," comparing it with the "realistic" *New Republic* and *Nation*. He makes this distinction clear in his discussion of men such as Charles Beard (who "viewed Wilsonian internationalism sardonically"), Carl Becker (who "warned against trying to escape the harsh realities of the world through wishful thinking") and Reinhold Niebuhr (who reinforced their "realistic view of the future"). Thus the liberal's self-perceived choice between idealism and realism remains, dominating over the sort of belief that makes ideologies vigorous—the conviction that the two are the same. See Divine's *Second Chance*, 320, 174-175.
93. October 14, 1946, 45.
94. *Newsweek*, September 20, 1948, 33.
95. Alan Cranston, "What About World Government," *New Republic*, CXXII (May 22, 1950), 16.
96. Francis H. Russell, "Toward a Stronger World Organization," *U.S. Department of State Bulletin*, XXIII (August 7, 1950), 220, 222. This is the printed version of a speech Russell gave as Director of the Office of Public Affairs to a UWF meeting in Washington, D.C.

Student Organizations and the Antiwar Movement in America, 1900-196[

Patti McGill Peterson

"No more war" has been an important rallying cry for the youth movement in the United States. This has been recently apparent in the student movement of the past decade in which opposition to the war in Vietnam played a crucial role. Even earlier the antiwar issue played a significant role in the historical development of student political activism. As early as the Civil War students participated in anticonscription campaigns. ROTC and militarism on the campus were denounced by antiwar students in the 1920's and the antiwar issue provided the cement for the coalitions within the student movement of the Thirties. As in the 1960's, antiwar spirit kept the student movement of the 1930's alive. By the same token, the peace movement in this country owes a good measure of its vigor to student support.

The history of student antimilitarism and antiwar activism is rich in its diversity. From 1900 to 1960 a variety of student organizations engaged in the antiwar movement in changing historical climates, and they drew

The peace movement in the United States has derived a great deal of its vitality from student antiwar activism. In turn, a historical examination of the student movement indicates how important the peace issue was as a focus for student activism. The antiwar issue has had the power to draw together many different types of student groups into antiwar coalitions. During the period 1900 to 1960 a wide variety of student organizations, representing a spectrum of ideological perspectives, engaged in the antiwar movement.

A significant part of students' antiwar ideology was shaped by their affiliation with "parent parties." The youth affiliates of the Communist and Socialist parties provided leadership in student antiwar coalitions. During the periods of most intense student antiwar activism it was the radical political activists, not the pacifists, who supplied the leadership for the student antiwar movement. During the decades when radicalism was in a state of decline the pacifists attempted to provide leadership for the student peace movement, but were never able to restore the momentum that more radical leadership had been able to maintain.

The antiwar movement has attracted only a minority of students. This minority has been further reduced in effectiveness by its fragile leadership and the tension of competing ideological allegiances. Its existence has been significant, nonetheless. It has been a vehicle for the increasing self-consciousness of young people and it has provided them with alternative policies and perspectives when civilization has been tested by war.

their antiwar feelings from many ideological perspectives. As in the general peace movement, the ideological basis for student antiwar activity had a multi-dimensional character.

The Beginnings of Student Antiwar Activism: 1900-1920

Less than four percent of college-age youth attended an institution of higher education in 1900. The class composition of the student population was relatively homogeneous. Upper–middle-class Anglo-Saxon Protestants constituted most of the college and university enrollments. Student life of the early 1900's has been characterized as politically apathetic and generally escapist. Conventional national patriotism was all but universal.[1] Somewhat ironically, it was in this climate that more politically conscious student groups first emerged and took up the antiwar issue.

Between 1900 and 1915 both the Intercollegiate Socialist Society (ISS) and the Young Peoples Socialist League (YPSL) were founded. The ISS, the first president of which was Jack London, the naturalist author, was founded in 1905 by a group of non-students to promote the discussion of socialism among college students. By 1917 it had attracted approximately 2,000 members, mostly middle-class collegians.[2] It was not affiliated with the Socialist Party and ideological views varied greatly within ISS campus groups. In 1913 the YPSL became the official youth group of the Socialist Party. The majority of its membership were of working-class background and most were of Jewish immigrant parentage. Most of YPSL's collegiate members also attended city colleges in New York and New Jersey. Its ideological position was clearly that of the Socialist Party. By 1917 the YPSL claimed a membership of nearly 10,000.

When the entry of the United States into World War I seemed imminent, both the ISS and the YPSL were forced to take stands on the war issue. The ambivalence of the ISS reflected the group's composition and its lack of commitment to any particular political position.[3] The study of militarism, its cause and effect, had not yet been made a special course of study and discussion among the ISS chapters.[4] There was considerable disagreement among members on the war issue at the organization's 1916 convention and summer conference.[5] The ultimate result of this was that in order to accommodate the variety of views of its members and to prevent the organization from splitting apart, the ISS took no official position on the war. It did go on record opposing the introduction of military training on college campuses and continued to discuss the pros and cons of pacifism.

It is clear that an antiwar position had not become a central part of the Society's concept of socialism. The ISS declared that its purpose was the study and discussion of socialism; it emphasized even more strongly that it was not "an anti or pro-militarist, anti or pro-war, anti or pro-conscription organization."[6] In fact, an examination of the *Intercolle-*

giate Socialist, the official publication of the ISS, during the war years indicates evidence of some super-patriotism and some real unfriendliness toward the Socialist Party's position on the war. J. G. Phelps Stokes, the President of the ISS until 1918, struck up the call for patriotism:

> In the midst of war the non-resistant attitude may be the most selfish and immoral imaginable. . . . From the earliest days of this republic the obligation of universal service, in emergencies, has rightly been incumbent upon all who are physically capable of serving. . . . Individual rights must be subordinated to public needs. . . . Every American should put his services at the disposal of the President, the ablest and wisest leader of the whole people available at the present time.[7]

By contrast, the Young Peoples Socialist League came out vigorously opposing war, adopting the revolutionary socialist position of Karl Lieb-knecht and Rosa Luxemburg that wars only serve to kill off the working class. Beginning in 1914, the *Young Socialist Magazine,* the YPSL's official organ, devoted a great deal of space to warnings about the horrors of war. After United States entry into war, convention resolutions put "yipsels" on record opposing all wars, denouncing the war as a crime against humanity and opposing conscription. Some YPSL members even resolved to consider participation in the Red Cross movement as supporting the government and advocated that any member volunteering for such work should be expelled from the organization.[8]

Beyond some strong antiwar statements the members of the YPSL do not appear to have been engaged in much antiwar agitation outside their own circles. After 1914 the local and state organizations continued to report educational lectures, social gatherings and essay contests instead of energetic antiwar activity. In large part this reflected the Socialist Party's attempts to keep the YPSL away from direct political action. However, some antimilitaristic action was directed by the YPSL at urban high schools in New York and New Jersey. YPSL's Inter-High School Anti-Militarist League was created to offset "the military hysteria of the Boy Scouts." The League promoted a few strikes against compulsory military drill in high schools. Some direct contact with the police was experienced in the summer of 1917 when YPSL antiwar meetings were broken up and declared illegal. Even minimal agitational activity by youth was considered threatening by authorities.

From 1900 to 1917 many peace groups were active among less politically oriented students. The American School Peace League was founded primarily to promote the cause of peace among younger students at the primary and secondary education levels. An official National Education Association endorsement indicates that the League's peace activities were not considered threatening although the American Legion objected to this endorsement. At the college level the Intercollegiate Peace Association, the Collegiate Anti-Militarist League, the Christian Students Federation and the Cosmopolitan Clubs were all engaged in promoting internationalism and peace. Much of their work took the form of lectures and discussion meetings. None of these groups viewed war in the political and social terms that the young Socialists did. Nor was pacifism a requirement for membership. When in 1916 many elder pacifists and churchmen rejected the proposals for a general arms embargo and in the next year were won over to Wilson's "war to end all wars," their student counterparts followed in large number without much apparent disillusionment.[9]

The largest Christian student group in existence prior to the outbreak of World War I was the Student Christian Volunteer Movement (SCVM). The participation of some Christian students in settlement-house work helped to bring concern for social problems in the United States to the organization. Even so, most of its activity in the first two decades of the twentieth century was directed toward overseas religious mission work. In 1917 the SCVM through its official organ, the *North American Student,* took a pro-war position and carried many articles on valuable war services performed by students.

The climate on American campuses during World War I was filled with the patriotic spirit of wartime mobilization. Institutions of higher education responded readily to the call for war. College curricula were mobilized willingly in response to requests by the United States Bureau of Education which conjured up frightening images of "Bad Kaiser Bill," and the Bureau's bulletins served as constant reminders of the dangers of unpreparedness. Scientific research was oriented to war needs in most institutions. At Yale a new three-year "military course" was cited as an alternative to the regular course of studies and at little Reed College in Oregon the college catalog contained a twelve-page supplement for "war studies."[10] It was hardly a milieu for antiwar thoughts or actions.

The Red Scare and the Palmer Raids of 1919-1920 quickly singled out many of those who had been prominent antiwar activists and especially inhibited the Socialist movement. Those who did continue outspoken opposition to government policies did so at the risk of having their remarks labeled seditious. Added to this atmosphere of political repression was the beginning of the "Roaring Twenties" which seemed to mute concerns about war at the turn of the decade.

The various student groups concerned about peace before the war might have had a greater impact on the campus had the various groups been able to appeal to larger numbers of students and, perhaps even more important, been better able to cooperate more among themselves. However, the antiwar issue was not able to draw students from their various ideological perspectives into a common cause. Of course, many of these groups were neophytes to debate about war or were still building membership when war broke out in Europe; but in any case, no attempt was made to formulate a united call to resist. Like the traditional peace movement most student groups were able to rationalize the existence of war. Little radical pacifism was evident among the religious student groups. This was of significance since more students were affiliated with religious organizations than other types of organizations. Strong opposition to the war from their ranks might have had political impact. Ironically, the youth group that remained firm in its antiwar stand was the YPSL which had the smallest collegiate following. The young Socialists, however, made few attempts to convince others of the correctness of their position. Except for a small group of steadfast pacifists, they remained alone in their adamant opposition to the war. In short, a viable peace movement did not exist as yet among students.

Peace Concern Among Students: the 1920's

If the war had dealt a devastating blow to the cause of peace, its aftermath, the Roaring Twenties, seemed to hold up the speakeasy and the college campus as great places to escape from the serious cares of the world. Yet college students of the Twenties have perhaps been too hastily stereotyped by the gay abandonment of the flapper. In 1935 James Wechsler noted two major trends of revolt among students during the 1920's: a revolt in morals and manners, escapist in character, and a serious desire to remake America out of the ruins of World War I.[11] H. L. Mencken, denouncing the masses as well as the "booboisie," provided an ism for those involved in the former. Devere Allen personified the latter. Later a prominent figure in the peace movement, Allen's pacifism was nutured while a student at Oberlin. His ideas were developed during wartime while the editor of Oberlin's *Radical Patriot*. In 1919 Allen was instrumental in organizing Young Democracy and became editor of its magazine. He attempted to take pacifism out of the realm of the merely personal religious commitment of students, more typical of the pre-World War I era, and to put it in new terms of a social and political critique of American society. Along with other student groups, Young Democracy viewed the League of Nations idea as a bright ray of hope for the future of peace.

New organizations grew out of this decade, but it is also important to note that the war and the Palmer Raids did not totally destroy the groups that had been active before the Twenties. The YPSL was most devastated by the raids and it was not until about 1925 that it began to recoup its strength. By the late Twenties the YPSL was calling for the release of political prisoners who had resisted the war, condemning once again the military hysteria of the Boy Scouts, and demanding an end to ROTC on the campus.[12] However, except for strong antiwar resolutions and an antiwar rally sponsored by the YPSL in New York in 1927, most of its energies were devoted to the more mundane problems of bringing the organization back to life. The Intercollegiate Socialist Society also survived and became the Student League for Industrial Democracy (SLID) in 1928. ISS chapters were active but found it difficult to sponsor liberal pacifist and radical speakers on campuses because of the reluctance of college administrations to have them.[13]

While the more radical and politically oriented groups struggled to recover from the repression brought about by the Red Scares, the Christian student groups seemed more vital than ever and perhaps paradoxically leaning more to the left. Student pastors and YMCA leaders became important figures in the struggle against campus militarism. The YMCA and YWCA in particular were quite active in campaigning against militarism. At the annual National Conference of Christian Students in 1927, jointly sponsored by the YMCA and YWCA, increasing radicalism and antimilitarism were in evidence. A majority of the delegates voted that the economic system of the United States based on production for profit was wrong. On the question of war 327 students indicated that they would not support any war, 740 voted to support only some wars, 356 were uncommitted, and only 95 students voted to support any war declared by their country.[14] Earlier in the decade, at a Student Christian Volunteer Convention, approximately 700 students took a strong pacifist stand under the leadership of the Fellowship of Youth for Peace, a group which later affiliated with the Fellowship of Reconciliation.[15]

Among the new groups appearing on the scene were the National Student Federation of America, the Young Communist League and the New Student Forum. Of these, the New Student Forum (NSF) concerned itself most with the antiwar issue. The NSF was the product of a merger in 1922 of the National Student Committee for the Limitation of Armaments and the Intercollegiate Liberal League. Under its auspices the *New Student* was published. Although certainly not radical, it was nonetheless an important weathervane for concerns of more politically and socially concerned students during the Twenties. It devoted a great deal of coverage to peace issues and pacifist views, seeing war as part of America's scientific spirit with no moral purpose. The *New Student* became the voice of student opposition to campus militarism and to the ROTC and encouraged students in their activities against it.

Amidst the more publicized fad of goldfish swallowing, these groups helped to keep antimilitarism alive on the campus. Major campaigns against compulsory military training in the colleges occurred in the Twenties. At large midwestern universities thousands of students voted to abolish compulsory ROTC and in the East similar protests took place.[16] Students who refused to participate in ROTC training were expelled. ROTC commandants recommended the dismissal of faculty and staff encouraging unpatriotic behavior on the part of students. The American Legion acted as patriotic watchdog. In one case American Legion officials boasted that they had brought about the dismissal of two professors because they had supported the right of the student Liberal Club to criticize "American military imperialism in Mexico and Nicaragua."[17]

Important to the future of the antiwar movement among students were the numerous conferences that placed many different kinds of student groups in contact with one another. At these interdenominational and intercollegiate conferences students from a wide variety of ideological perspectives had an opportunity to discuss militarism on the campus.[18] One such meeting was the conference of the American Federation of Youth held in 1927. It provided a forum for approximately fifty youth organizations. Mordecai Johnson, President of Howard University, called upon the delegates to resist being "drafted as cannon-fodder for future imperialistic wars." The groups attending went on record favoring a nationwide program to combat compulsory military training, militarism and imperialism.

In the prosperity of the late Twenties it might have been predicted that concerns about militarism on the campus would atrophy. The *New Student* had lost much of its reforming fervor by 1928. Although there were some active student groups, there is no evidence that a student movement with a large base of support existed. Yet this decade would be separated from the next not by a war and the Palmer Raids and their effect of promoting patriotism, but by an economic depression. The combination of that depression and the rumblings of another war in the Thirties helped to build and sustain a student movement of scope and intensity previously unknown in American society. It would not have been easy to predict the political radicalization of students during the 1930's from the vantage point of 1928, and yet seeds of discontent were planted prior to 1930 in the form of increased criticism of "the system" among student groups. These organizations reflected to lesser and greater degrees a growing awareness of the political role of youth in the United States.

Students and the Antiwar Movement of the Thirties

The depression was the spawning ground of the student movement of the 1930's. The economic crisis became a social and political crisis which affected all segments of the youth population in the United States. In 1930 approximately one-fourth of the unemployed were between the ages fifteen to twenty-four. This helped to foment an unprecedented amount of discontent among students. The depression had the effect of economically disinheriting college graduates and made the future dim for those studying toward degrees. The membership of the Communist and Socialist youth groups increased substantially and pacifist student groups moved further to the left. Because students were so active in the 1930's, that decade has received far more attention by scholars and observers than those preceding or following it.[19]

A radical critique of war was central to the student movement of the Thirties. In their search for answers to the problems facing American society many students were attracted to solutions offered by radical political groups. The young Communists and the young Socialists stressed the idea that war was an outgrowth of the profit system. This critique pervaded many of the religious pacifist student groups. The climate on college campuses was distinctly antiwar. An analysis of the results of various peace polls conducted on college campuses revealed that of an approximately 22,000 students covered, eight thousand considered themselves pacifists and seven thousand would refuse to become part of an American Expeditionary Force.[20] A poll conducted by the Intercollegiate Disarmament Council in the early Thirties indicated that 92 percent of the respondents (24,345 students) wanted a worldwide reduction of armaments, and 63 percent voted for independent disarmament by the United States regardless of what other countries did. Devere Allen reported that the antiwar attitudes revealed by these surveys were so drastic that several institutions forbade their students to participate in similar polls of opinion.[21] Clearly those organizations that could capture the growing antiwar spirit and radicalism of American students would play a leading role in the movement of the Thirties.

The groups that had been active in the Twenties grew and increased their activity in the Thirties. Among the most active in 1935 were the SLID and the YPSL, many of whose members held joint membership in both organizations.[22] Religiously affiliated student groups such as the FOR and the YMCA and YWCA continued their activity. The Young Communist League (YCL) and the National Student League (the Communist Party-affiliated national student group) were relative newcomers to student antiwar activity. They would play, however, a key role in the student movement of the 1930's. Aggressive fascism in Europe and the liberal politics of the New Deal paved the way for increasing cooperation among Socialist, Communist and liberal groups. In 1935 this cooperation was formalized in the Communist-promoted "United Front," of which youth groups played an important part. It provided the impetus for the largest student antiwar coalition known in the United States before the Sixties.

Neither the Socialist Party nor the Communist Party had been much concerned with college students prior to 1930. Most of their youth work had been directed at young workers and high school youth. The Thirties, however, opened a new field of possibilities for organizing students. The Communists attempted to keep a fairly strict division between young workers and students. For this reason and to give the appearance of being a broadly based organization, the National Student League was created. The Socialists, on the other hand, had a more complicated situation in the student field. The SLID had become more radical and now contained students committed to the Socialist Party's platform. Although student members of the YPSL joined SLID chapters, the official youth position of the Socialist Party was still that of the Young Peoples Socialist League, not that of the Student League for Industrial Democracy. Even though many YPSL members had joined the SLID, the latter was not bound to follow the Socialist Party's directives. This situation tended to give the Communists an important edge.

During the Christmas holidays of 1935 at a convention in Columbus, Ohio, the NSL and the SLID created the American Student Union (ASU).[23] The ASU more than its New Deal counterpart, the American Youth Congress, provides a forum in which political positions and the antiwar concerns of student groups in the 1930's can be viewed. The NSL was following Communist Party directives to create United Front organizations. Many members of the SLID tended to be somewhat skeptical of the Union. However, young Socialists, such as Joseph Lash, the Executive Secretary of the SLID, became convinced of the need for unity and swung the SLID to the United Front position. The disunity in the 1935 gathering could be seen in the existence of strong factions on the war question. The young Communists held separate meetings each night during the convention and developed strategy to get the ASU to endorse a collective security position. But many YPSL and SLID members remained hesitant about the Union for this reason. About 500 delegates attended the first convention and nearly half of them were neither Socialists nor Communists. The National Student Federation of America (a conglomeration of college and university student governments) and some pacifist groups had representatives at the Convention. The concept of collective security troubled the pacifists and the Socialists, and the antiwar position of pacifists and Socialists disturbed the Communists. The Union rested on a tenuous blend of the anti-fascist concerns of the young Communists and the antiwar spirit of the Socialists and pacifists.

The NSL and the SLID clearly provided the leadership for the Union at its inception, but both tried to keep questions of ideology at a minimum in deference to their desire for a broad coalition. The young Communists in particular were willing to make many accommodations in the interest of an anti-German alliance, and they cooperated in making the ASU an antiwar organization in order to please the other factions. Nevertheless, suspicions among the political elements of the ASU remained. The young Communists viewed the young Socialists as propagators of "treacherous pacifist dope." In turn a strong faction of the YPSL felt that the Socialists must form a left opposition committed to revolutionary antiwar principles to which they felt the young Communists were not committed.[24]

Two tactics seem to stand out in the student antiwar struggle of the Thirties: the Oxford Movement and the antiwar strike. In 1933 the Oxford Student Union, reflecting the strong pacifist currents in England, passed a resolution stating that under no circumstances should one fight for King and Country. The ASU picked up the resolution, adapting it to America's needs as a means of involving large numbers of college youth in the antiwar movement. Between 1936 and 1938 the Oxford Pledge was administered to thousands of students across the United States. In taking the pledge American students refused to support the United States government in any war it might conduct.

The antiwar strike became an increasingly popular tactic. In 1934 about 25,000 students participated in the first nationwide antiwar student strike. Three years later 500,000 students participated in the national antiwar strike coordinated by the United Student Peace Committee.[25] The strikes were of very limited duration, usually consisting of leaving classes for one hour. No all-day student strikes were endorsed by the ASU. Even so, some university administrations acted quickly and forcibly against the strikers: at Berkeley, for example, twenty students were arrested in 1935 for handing out announcements calling for a student strike. "Peace Assemblies," more acceptable to college administrations, also took place on many campuses as ASU-sponsored events.

By 1936 the marriage of incompatible elements began to disintegrate. The central issue of the ASU convention in that year was peace. The young Communists in their desire to support "the anti-fascist struggle" in Europe continued to be annoyed by the "stubborn pacifism" of the Socialists, Christians and liberals. Those groups in turn accused the Communists of attempting to undermine the ASU's antiwar program. In 1936 the YPSL sponsored an anti-collective-security resolution that was almost adopted. The convention, to avoid an irreparable split, finally voted to leave out any specific reference to collective security. However, by 1937 the Communists had gained control of the ASU through the defection of Socialists (SLID members) on the Executive Committee to the Communist collective-security position. At the 1938 ASU convention the Oxford Pledge was dropped as a program plank. The young Communist strategy now was that of outright cooperation with New Deal policies at home and abroad. The discontent of the pacifists and antiwar Socialists with this new direction was summed up by the "yipsels":

> The American Student Union, founded as the agency of American students to combat war, war preparations and militarism, was converted, at its third congress, into an agency to support war when it comes, to justify war preparations and to condone militarism. This change, brought about largely by the Communists within the Student Union, foreshadows a campaign by the united jingoists to sweep the campus into the war camp, as was done in the pre-war months of 1916-17.[26]

The antimilitarism and pro-peace orientation of the ASU was its unifying force. In 1938 the ASU claimed a membership of 20,000. By late 1938 many of the YPSL and SLID members had left the organization. However, the fatal blow for it was the Hitler-Stalin non-aggression pact.

The young Communists, firmly in control of the ASU, discarded collective security and defended the Soviet attack on Finland. By 1940 the ASU membership had dropped to less than 2,000 youth. Socialist and pacifist students had been important components of the Union. They had supplied it with a strong antiwar basis which had attracted thousands of students.

It was the youth group of the Fellowship of Reconciliation (FOR) which attempted to fill the vacuum created by the demise of the ASU. The YPSL and the SLID were plagued with factions in the late Thirties. The FOR urged students to participate in the antiwar strike of 1939 which had been abandoned by the ASU. Christian pacifist students had not had the commanding hand in the coalitions of the student movement but they were a very important element. The Methodist youth group was the most radical denominational group, and some of its national executives belonged to the YPSL. The YMCA and YWCA also were important to coalitions. In attempting to provide leadership among antiwar students, the FOR youth secretary thought that those students disillusioned with the ASU would be new recruits for pacifism and would turn to the FOR. Its youth section was tireless in its door-to-door campaigns and literature distributions. However both the young Communists and the young Socialists viewed the FOR and other religious pacifist groups somewhat contemptuously as religion and reconciliation oriented without a solid radical critique of society. Although its leadership among Christian pacifist groups was important, the FOR had only a small sympathetic audience and was unable to pull the liberals and the Socialists who had left the ASU into a renewed antiwar campaign.

The Student Movement in the 1940's and the Cold War Era

The entry of the United States into World War II dealt the final blow to the student movement of the 1930's. It placed the peace movement in a general state of confusion. By 1942 pro-war sentiment had captured the American campus. The draft and volunteer enlistment cut into the male population of the college campus and colleges mobilized for war preparations in the early Forties. "Higher Learning" was again sacrificed to wartime efficiency. About 440,000 students were enrolled in Engineering, Science and Management War Training courses set up by the Army and Navy. Even before Pearl Harbor two hundred youth leaders signed an appeal for a declaration of war.[27] The Student Defenders of Democracy was formed in New York in January of 1941 and claimed about 5,000 members after one year of existence. It resolved to aid the allies, to oppose isolationism, to encourage foreign people to support exile governments of their overrun nations, but to work for a just and lasting peace after the defeat of the aggressors. During the war, colleges and universities had Student War Councils to organize student activities in war services. All of this served to reduce the antiwar movement to a murmur.

The two decades between 1940 and 1960 had very negative effects on left-wing student politics in the United States. The young Communists and the young Socialists lost their hold on the campus.[28] For example, a postwar convention of the SLID held in 1946 was attended by only forty delegates from twelve schools.[29] During the early Forties the FOR was instrumental in organizing the Youth Committee Against War. The second annual meeting of the Committee held in December of 1940 was attended by 400 youth, many of whom were FOR members. It passed an eight-point program to keep the United States out of war and upheld the right to conscientious objection. The Committee also made the Oxford Pledge part of its program.

The FOR youth section claimed an increase in membership of 1,400 members in 1941 and carried on an array of activities. It remained active during the war years. Under the leadership of A. J. Muste the FOR stanchly supported an anticonscription campaign.[30] Non-violent civil disobedience was a topic studied in many of its campus groups. Sporadically FOR groups on campuses sponsored antiwar activities and pacifist retreats.[31] Nevertheless, it was unable to revive the broad student antiwar movement of the 1930's.

A small number of peace-oriented student groups sprang up after 1945. One such group was the Youth Council on the Atomic Crisis whose negative reactions to the Japan bombings caused it to dedicate itself to the peacetime use of atomic power. As the League of Nations concept excited the imaginations of some students in the 1920's, so did the idea of a world government appeal to some peace-oriented students in the late 1940's. The United World Federalists (UWF) caught up this spirit. By the end of 1948 the UWF claimed about 40,000 members. However, the junior wing broke with the UWF because of some generational frictions. Some students felt that the UWF's goals were too esoteric while others felt the adult members were businessmen who viewed world government as a business operation.

The American Youth for Democracy (Communist) and the Wallace campaign diverted some student activity but generally the tone of student politics in the late Forties and early Fifties was set by liberal, anti-Communist groups such as Students for Democratic Action and the CIA-financed National Student Association. The largest of these, the NSA, reflected the postwar desire for international cooperation. The NSA, however, was very much a product of the Cold War and it grew from a solidly anti-Communist base.

By the 1950's the college campuses reflected the impact of the veteran, growing conservatism and the beginning of serious red-baiting. Applicants for Navy ROTC were asked to identify any persons they might know who had been associated with "subversive organizations." As a counterpart to McCarthyism, right-wing student groups such as Students for America began to appear, and the climate was right for the emergence of the Young Americans for Freedom in the early Sixties. The increased military prowess of America was important to all these groups.

Although right-wing and liberal anti-Communist groups were prominent in the Fifties, the student populace could not be labeled pro-war. A poll taken in 1953 suggested some antiwar spirit among students. Of those who responded 26 percent indicated they were strongly opposed to the Korean War and 36 percent indicated that they had reservations.[32] Even with evidence of these feelings, the student peace movement continued to suffer a decline in the 1950's. The War Resisters League was reduced to a small core of supporters and the membership of the FOR dropped by about 3,000 members. The college section of the FOR under the direction of Bayard Rustin conducted peace caravans through the United States, but attempts to bring youth together in large antiwar conferences similar to those of the 1930's were not very successful. The conferences that did occur were confined primarily to religiously oriented students and did not attract large numbers of participants.[33]

Nevertheless, the FOR did survive the apathy of the Fifties as did other leftist student groups. The Socialist groups, the YPSL and the SLID, continued to function with small memberships of two hundred each. The Communists changed the name of their student group from American Youth for Democracy to Labor Youth League (LYL), reflecting shifts in Party policy. The LYL maintained a small number of chapters during the Fifties, mainly on metropolitan campuses. But it was the religious pacifist groups like the FOR who were responsible for keeping the peace issue alive.

Along with already established pacifist organizations, the newly emergent National Committee for a Sane Nuclear Policy (SANE) and the Student Peace Union (SPU) created a more vitalized peace movement in the late 1950's. The student affiliate of SANE was founded in 1958, and although it included many left-wing students, it generally followed SANE's liberal politics. Its major focus was on ending nuclear testing. The Student Peace Union was founded in 1959 by a combination of pacifists and Socialists in the midwest. For a period it was the largest radical student group in the United States with a national membership of about 5,000. The SPU, more radical than SANE, took a "third camp" position, favoring the militarism of neither the Soviet Union nor the United States.[34] It proclaimed itself as "a bold new effort to tear away at the apathy which enshrouds our campuses today," but reached its height in about 1961 and declined after that. An SPU-inspired campus event which attracted students was the antimilitary ball. Creative antiwar skits and folk songs were an integral part of these social functions. Atmospheric weapon testing was an important demonstration focus for both SANE and the SPU. When the Soviet Union and the United States signed the atmospheric test-ban treaty in 1962 the peace movement found itself devoid of an important central issue.

As the Twenties helped to lay some of the foundations for the antiwar movement of the Thirties, so the Fifties offered a legacy to the Sixties. Non-violent civil disobedience as a protest tactic was developed by FOR youth-section leaders whose ideas would be important to the Sixties.[35] The horrors of McCarthyism often tend to overshadow the fact that a peace movement did begin to emerge on the college campus in the late Fifties and that it too contained the non-violent sit-in as a protest tactic. Similarly, the attempts of the Student Peace Union to develop an ideological framework not dictated by any parent party would have fundamental relevance to the politics of the New Left.

For all its indebtedness to the past, the student antiwar movement that formed around the Vietnam War in the next decade displayed some important departures from the previous fifty years of antiwar student activism. Tidy comparisons often lead to gross oversimplification. However the new trends in the Sixties offer discernible contrasts. For instance, the movement that emerged then was not as dependent on "parent groups" for direction as were earlier movements. In almost all instances during the period 1900 to 1960 the antiwar activities of students were a direct outgrowth of close affiliation with such groups as the Communist and Socialist Parties or the Fellowship of Reconciliation. The "antiwar heroes" of the earlier period were older men like Eugene Debs and A. J. Muste. Except for the incipient revolt against the older generation in the 1920's and the SPU's attempt to define its own position, the period 1900 to 1960 can be characterized as a movement seeking direction from older antiwar advocates. A new group of young "anti-war, anti-heroes" such as Tom Hayden and Abbie Hoffman emerged during the Sixties.

The nature of the antiwar tactics employed also distinguishes the Sixties. The tactics employed from 1900 to about 1960 were non-violent and legal direct action. Prior to the 1930's the YPSL was the only student group which had employed the strike as an antiwar tactic. The anti-ROTC campaigns of the Twenties were carried out principally through petitions and campus votes. Even during the Thirties the antiwar student strikes and demonstrations were of short duration and non-violent. The Sixties marked the era of the "obstructive demonstration" and a new tactical approach of "violence for violence" to counter war-making efforts.

Finally the war in Vietnam did not induce the patriotic reactions that earlier wars in the century had induced. Sending troops into combat therefore did not weaken student protest, but rather invigorated it. Most important, the antiwar movement among students in the 1960's had more significant political impact than any of the earlier movements.

In retrospect it seems somewhat ironic that pacifist students have not had the principal leadership position in the student antiwar movement in the United States. Student pacifists waged no real opposition to World War I. A few liberal pacifists were sympathetic to the antiwar position of the YPSL in 1917, but like the elder pacifists few challenged Wilson's war to end all wars. During the two most intense periods of student anti-war activity, the 1930's and the 1960's, leftist political groups commanded the direction of student antiwar activism. The role of pacifist groups during the Thirties strongly suggests that pacifist groups were conveniently manipulated by more politically oriented student groups. Pacifist groups certainly have made major contributions to the cause of peace among students, but their role has been more subtle than that of leftist antiwar groups. It was only when the more radical elements were unable to function in the Twenties and Forties that the pacifists stepped into the leadership and valiantly attempted to sustain the peace movement of the campus.

It is clear that antiwar student protest has been most intense and far-reaching when led by radical political groups. During these periods the antiwar issue has been connected to other social problems. When war has been tied to other social evils it has tended to radicalize more students. Certainly this has been true in both the Thirties and the Sixties. In the former the dynamic combination was the depression and an impending war and in the latter it was the ferment of the Civil Rights movement and the war in Vietnam. In these decades when radical groups provided antiwar leadership a pervasive critique of American society was set forth and broad coalitions could be formed. This brought less radical students into contact with leftist politics; but it also meant some compromise, both ideologically and tactically, on the part of more radical elements.

The major problem which has plagued radical student groups that have participated in the antiwar movement is their suspicion of one another. This was quite evident during the Thirties. Because of their commitment to the ideological position of their parent parties the young Socialists and the young Communists remained mutually hostile to one another in the midst of apparent cooperation. The hostilities among leftist political groups resulted in shaky antiwar coalitions. Also, because ideological agreement within each of these groups was of great importance, factions were far more debilitating, so that the leadership of the student antiwar movement was very fragile leadership.

War and the antiwar issue have also been important in intensifying generational differences. Karl Mannheim in his *Essays on the Sociology of Knowledge* cites war as a critical factor in the shaping of generations. Simply stated, war precipitates the political and social crises that have the capacity of molding the world view of a generation, distinguishing it from the next generation. This has yet to be empirically tested, but if the milieu in which one comes of age has anything to do with one's outlook, then antiwar protest must have a significant impact on youth still in the process of developing their perspective on the world. Just as wars have produced unifying bonds of patriotism, so too antiwar spirit has united those of divergent backgrounds and interest under a common cause. The antiwar movement of the 1930's for example had the effect of bringing together anti-imperialists, a variety of antimilitarists, pacifists and radicals on domestic issues, and challenging their values and conceptions of society. It has been discovered that the parents of activists of the past decade are decidedly more liberal in political outlook than others of their social status.[36] These parents received their college education in the Thirties, a time of political ferment on the campuses. They graduated to the call to arms in World War II. Although it is not possible to calculate precisely the effect of the war and antiwar sentiment on them, or of the carryover to their children, it is worthy of serious consideration.

Militant patriotism has mobilized vast numbers of citizens, young and old. The antiwar movement has attracted a small minority. The minority of antiwar students has been further reduced in effectiveness by its fragile leadership and the tension of its competing ideological allegiances. Its existence has been significant, nonetheless. It has been a vehicle for the increasing self-consciousness of young people, and it has provided them with alternative policies and perspectives when civilization has been tested by war.

State University of New York
Oswego

notes

The research for this paper was conducted under a National Endowment for the Humanities project grant under the direction of Philip G. Altbach at the University of Wisconsin.

1. Laurence R. Veysey, *The Emergence of the American University* (Chicago, 1965), 278.

2. The group of "young rebels" who founded the ISS contained Jack London, Upton Sinclair, Charlotte Perkins Gilman, Clarence Darrow and Morris Hillquit among others. The origins of the ISS are discussed in Harold Lewack, *Campus Rebels: A Brief History of the Student League for Industrial Democracy* (New York: Student League for Industrial Democracy, mimeo, 1953). The early issues of the *Intercollegiate Socialist* are an important primary reference for the early development of the ISS.

3. A questionnaire sent to the ISS membership in 1913 showed that some members considered themselves non-socialists and even anti-socialists. Those who did view themselves as socialists represented a gamut of positions.

4. A. T. Trachtenberg, "The ISS and the War," *Intercollegiate Socialist*, II (October-November, 1914), 19.

5. For a more detailed account of the Convention and Conference proceedings of 1916 see Harry W. Laidler, "Intercollegiate Socialist Society Convention," *Intercollegiate Socialist*, IV (February-March, 1916), 12-21 and "ISS Summer Conference," *Intercollegiate Socialist*, IV (October-November, 1916), 4.

6. "The Coming Year," *Intercollegiate Socialist*, VI (October-November, 1917), 4.

7. J. G. Phelps Stokes, "Universal Service in Peace and War," *Intercollegiate Socialist*, VI (December-January, 1917-18), 12-15.

8. The convention resolutions on the war of various statewide and citywide YPSL units are reported in *The Young Socialist Magazine* (June, 1917).

9. Good general accounts of pacifists during this period can be found in Merle Curti, *Peace or War: The American Struggle 1636 to 1936* (New York, 1936), chapters 6 and 7; Charles Chatfield, "World War One and the Liberal Pacifist in the U.S.," *The American Historical Review*, LXXV (December, 1970), 1920-1938. It should be noted that pacifism before World War I for the most part meant a desire for international cooperation. Under the pressure of the war the definition narrowed to indicate complete opposition to war. See Chatfield, 1920. Pacifism will be used in the latter sense for the remainder of this paper.

10. For a fuller discussion of the role of militarism on the college campus, see Arthur A. Ekirch, *The Civilian and the Military* (New York, 1956).

11. James Wechsler, *The Revolt on Campus* (New York, 1935), and Mollie C. Davis, "Quest for a New Order: Ferment in Collegiate Culture, 1921-1929" (unpublished manuscript used with permission of the author), offer good accounts of student outlook during the Twenties.

12. "Resolutions Passed by the Inter-State Conference of the Young Peoples Socialist League," (Pamphlet of February, 1929). A copy of this is in the Duke University Socialist Party of America Collection, YPSL files.

13. For example, at the University of Wisconsin the administration attempted to prevent the visit of Red Kate O'Hare. John Nevin Sayre and Kirby Page were also regarded as "dangerous speakers."

14. For detailed reports of the convention see "YM and YW Conferences," *New Student*, VI(January 12, 1927), 1, and Kirby Page, "National Conference of Christian Students," *The World Tomorrow* (February, 1927).

15. "Student Volunteer Convention," *New Student*, III (March 15, 1924), 2.

16. "Anti-ROTC Campaigns," *New Student*, IV (May 23, 1925), 1.

17. Wechsler, *Revolt on Campus*, 130-131.

18. In 1926 the LID Intercollegiate Conference and the Interdenominational Student Conference both went on record opposing militarism on the campus.

19. For example, see Wechsler, *Revolt on Campus;* Hal Draper, "The Student Movement of the Thirties: A Political History," in Rita Simon, ed., *As We Saw the Thirties* (Urbana, 1967); or George P. Rawick, "The New Deal and Youth" (unpublished Ph.D. dissertation, University of Wisconsin, 1957).

20. Frank Olmstead, "The Significance of the College Peace Poll" (mimeo, War Resisters League, 1933). This is the text of an address on a nationwide hook-up under the auspices of the National Student Federation, May 15, 1933. A copy of this is in the Duke Socialist Party Collection, YPSL files.

21. Devere Allen, "The Peace Movement Moves Left," *Annals of the American Academy of Political and Social Science*, CLXXV (September, 1934), 154.

22. A motion was passed by the YPSL in 1935 directing its college members to join SLID chapters. By 1935 the SLID had moved considerably closer to the Socialist Party's political position.

23. There are numerous accounts of the founding of the American Student Union. The publications of all the student organizations involved in the ASU carried reports; see also Wechsler, Draper, Rawick, *op. cit.*

24. A discussion of YPSL attitudes toward cooperating with the Communist students can be found in "Trends in the Student Movement" (Report of the National Student Secretary, YPSL, April 10, 1935), Duke Socialist Party Collection, YPSL files.

25. The United Student Peace Committee consisted of the American League Against War and Fascism, ASU, AYC, Committee on Militarism in Education, FOR, Foreign Policy Association, United Christian Youth Movement, Methodist Youth, WRL, NSFA, YWCA and YMCA. It was the ASU's attempt at a larger "united front" for strike planning.

26. Al Hamilton and Alvaine Hollester, "Left Jingoism on the Campus," *Socialist Review*, VI(January-February, 1938), 9.

27. "The Tempo Quickens," *New Masses* (November 4, 1941), 5.

28. The Communists formed the American Youth for Democracy in 1943, but it had no significant impact on student politics.

29. Lewack, *Campus Rebels*, 17.

30. See the pamphlet "Why We Refused to Register" (New York: Fellowship of Reconciliation, 1941).

31. *Fellowship*, the FOR journal, indicates that FOR groups were active at such large campuses as the University of California and the University of Michigan where rallies were held and where antiwar petition campaigns were waged. Some small religious-affiliated institutions actually witnessed antiwar strikes in 1941, but these were rare.

32. Edward Suchman, Rose K. Goldser and Robin Williams, Jr., "Attitudes Toward the Korean War," *Public Opinion Quarterly*, XvII (1953), 173, 182.

33. "Christian Youth Conference on War," *Fellowship*, XVIII (June, 1952), 20.

34. For a general discussion of the politics of the SPU see Ken Calkins, "The Student Peace Union," *Fellowship*, XXVI (March 1, 1960), 5-7.

35. In the late Fifties the FOR listed among its youth section leaders James Farmer, David Dellinger and Bayard Rustin.

36. See Richard Flacks, "The Liberated Generation: An Exploration of the Roots of Student Protest," *Journal of Social Issues*, III (1967).

Kenneth Boulding and the Peace Research Movement

Cynthia Kerman

I

The peace research movement is a kind of interface between the peace movement and general social-science research. Its positive motivation, like that of the peace movement, comes from a social concern to see the devastation of war eliminated from man's experience. Its practitioners, however, and its tools and methods come directly from the social sciences. It works with sample surveys, content analysis, simulation, statistical treatments of past wars, intercultural comparisons of belief systems, images and behaviors. It uses theoretical models drawn from economics, social psychology, sociology, psychology, political science, game theory and operational research.

> The origin of this book in my own mind can be traced back to a passionate conviction of my youth that war was the major moral and intellectual problem of our age. If the years have made this conviction less passionate, they have made it no less intense. . . . In particular, this work is the result of a conviction that the intellectual chassis of the broad movement for the abolition of war has not been adequate to support the powerful moral engine which drives it and that the frequent breakdowns which interrupt the progress of the movement are due essentially to a deficiency in its social theory.
>
> Kenneth Boulding, Preface to *Conflict and Defense: A General Theory* (New York, 1962), vii

The leading professional journal in the field of peace research is *The Journal of Conflict Resolution*, published at the University of Michigan; and its birth, together with that of the Center for Research on Conflict Resolution, may fairly be said to mark the establishment of the peace research movement. It came, like any movement, at its particular intersection of the appropriate personalities and the opportune moment in history.

133

In the winter of 1954-1955, shivering American liberals, pacifists and internationalists found few coals of comfort in current events. The reality of nuclear devastation had been facing the world for nine years. The Korean War, hard on the heels of World War II, had been brought to an unsatisfactory close just the preceding year; and the Cold War threatened to burst at any moment into World War III. The shadow of Joseph McCarthy lay over the land; purges and loyalty oaths and the ugly winds of suspicion were the order of the day, although the Senate censure of McCarthy in December of 1954 gave some promise of a new direction.

In that year at Palo Alto, California, were gathered the inaugural group of scholars at the Center for Advanced Study in the Behavioral Sciences (CASBS). Selected psychologists, economists, biologists, mathematicians, anthropologists and political scientists had come for a year of thought, study and interaction on the sun-washed hills above San Francisco Bay. Out of this confluence of minds, enthusiasm and resources, in reaction against the dreary prospect of events in the world, was catalyzed the peace research movement. It was an effort to use the quantitative, technical tools that had produced a system that seemed bent on destruction in order to transform that system into one that worked for man.

Some of the ingredients for peace research already had been brought together. Since 1950 (the year McCarthy began his anti-Communist campaign) a few young psychologists led by Herbert Kelman and Arthur Gladstone had been putting out a no-budget newsletter called "Bulletin of Research Exchange on Prevention of War." Its editing had been transferred in 1953 to two graduate students, Robert Hefner and William Barth at the University of Michigan, who were scrounging supplies and putting it out in a photo-offset format from the psychology office. They had interested a group of faculty members, including psychologist Daniel Katz and sociologist Robert Angell, in working with them. The economist Kenneth Boulding, though he was there and had been a lifetime pacifist and peace movement supporter, was not especially involved at the beginning.

In the early months of that academic year at CASBS, Stephen Richardson, a junior scholar there, had been sharing microfilm copies of his father's pioneering studies on the quantification of historical data on arms races and wars. These had been written by Lewis Richardson in the 1920's, but had received no recognition and were available only on microfilm in 1954.[1] Kenneth Boulding, Anatol Rapoport the mathematical biologist, and others at CASBS became immensely excited by reading these studies and seeing what could be done with such a technique. (Boulding now refers to those who read Lewis Richardson on microfilm as the "Early Church" of the peace research movement.) When Kelman, also at CASBS for that year, called together a group of socially concerned scholars to consider his "Bulletin" and how it could be improved, it was like a puff of wind on a smoldering fire. The potential they had seen in studies such as Lewis Richardson's blazed into flame with the idea of transforming the Bulletin into a more ambitious interdisciplinary journal, to establish peace research as a professional activity.

In one of Boulding's figurative images, the hand of fate is daily reaching into a bowl containing many white balls and one black one. The white balls represent continuing life as we know it; the black, nuclear destruction. "There is a race between knowledge and disaster," as he puts it, "but in this race the longer disaster is staved off, the better chance we have of acquiring the knowledge to prevent it altogether." Here was a way to encourage investment in this crucial kind of knowledge.

Dry kindling was all about them; they were well placed in the midst of prestigious experts. The initial list of sponsors included political scientist Harold Lasswell, anthropologist Clyde Kluckhohn and biologist Ralph Gerard from CASBS personnel, as well as Boulding, Kelman and Rapoport; with this kind of backing they found they could get others. It seemed natural to center the operation at Michigan, with Boulding already there and Rapoport going there, and to ask Hefner and Barth to begin the legwork for the larger journal. Kelman continued in a consultative role, and several years later came into a closer working arrangement when he also joined the faculty at Michigan.

At a meeting in Ann Arbor in the fall or winter of 1955, the title for the new journal was chosen, *Journal of Conflict Resolution*. By now Boulding was a leading figure in the new movement. He concentrated on the topic of conflict in a faculty seminar in the spring of 1956; he solicited articles for the early issues almost singlehandedly; and he and Barth were the primary fund-raisers. Barth and Hefner moved their operations to a small anteroom outside Boulding's office. Although they had succeeded in getting a small grant from the Graduate School to get it started, there remained the problem of finding a department at Michigan willing to adopt the infant. The winds of the McCarthy era were still blowing and the effort was viewed with a certain suspicion. The political scientists did not feel any particular calling to open their field to intrusion by outsiders from other specialties, and some officials of the University did not think the venture appropriate. Finally Wesley Maurer of the Journalism Department agreed to give it his department's sponsorship and the *Journal* was born, the first issue coming out in March, 1957.

Even then there was grave danger of infant mortality. When they began they had funds enough for two issues and took subscriptions for the first year. At the end of that year they had three issues out and paid for, and no way in sight to pay for the fourth. The editors and managers had just decided to go out of business and were filing down the stairs from Boulding's office when there came a phone call from a woman Barth had talked to, who had a small foundation and had decided to give her last thousand dollars of foundation money to the *Journal*. Boulding ran to the top of the stairs and called the committee back, and they were in business again.

And so the *Journal* did not die. It has not yet reached its final goal, stated in Boulding's editorial in the first issue, to "devise an intellectual engine of sufficient power to move the greatest problem of our time—the prevention of war." But it has achieved its immediate purpose of becoming a professional organ where the theories and research of psychologists, sociologists, political scientists, economists and others could be shared, focusing around the issue of conflict in many forms, and serving as a general exchange of theories and data in the area of international systems. Boulding has continued on the editorial board, and was the *Journal's* intellectual leader in the early years, gathering articles and stimulating research.

The Journal of Conflict Resolution has succeeded in carving out a place for peace research as a new field of scholarship, in which several companions have since joined it. A Peace Research Institute was founded in Oslo in 1959 under the leadership of Johan Galtung, and it started publishing the *Journal of Peace Research* in 1964. Walter Isard in Philadelphia set in motion an annual conference on peace research in 1963, and the proceedings of this group, the Peace Research Society (International), have been published regularly since 1964. And since 1967, *Peace Research Reviews,* edited in Ontario by Alan and Hanna Newcombe, has published a series of topical issues, each gathering together relevant research findings on a selected question.

Just after the *Journal* was rescued as it teetered on the edge of oblivion, there was a further gift to the struggling peace research group at Michigan. Another potential donor to whom Barth had talked inherited a million dollars and decided to give $100,000 of it for peace research, $65,000 of that going to Michigan. This gift did not go just for the *Journal.* By that time the nucleus of interested faculty who had been working on the *Journal,* with Boulding as a pivotal figure, had developed another idea: a Center which would stimulate and encourage research and learning in this new area—conflict and ways of managing it. They had drawn up a proposal for establishing such a center at the University of Michigan, and with this sizeable gift they were able to reach an agreement with the University. This amount was to start the Center and provide research support for three years, and after that the University would continue to support it with a full-time salary for the assistant director and half-time for the director. Boulding and Robert Angell shared the directorship through most of the Center's life, with William Barth serving as assistant or associate director. Funding for secretaries, supplies and any special research always had to be found elsewhere. The Ford Foundation and the Carnegie Corporation have been the two largest supporters of the work of the Center, with the National Science Foundation also funding considerable research. The Regents gave formal approval to the agreement on June 26, 1959, and the Center for Research on Conflict Resolution began operating in July, embarking on a program of conferences and seminars, research and training. Twelve years later, in July, 1971, in a general economy move, the University of Michigan unfortunately saw fit to terminate its support of the Center, so its life in that form has ended. The *Journal of Conflict Resolution,* however, continues to be published.

The Center for Research on Conflict Resolution has served as an institutional base for pioneering studies, resulting in publications such as *Disarmament and the Economy,*[2] the landmark documentation of the potential for depression-less conversion from a defense economy to a peacetime economy, and Boulding's theoretical analysis of many models of conflict, *Conflict and Defense.*[3] In the vanguard of current problem-oriented interdisciplinary approaches, it has drawn students and faculty from many related disciplines to conduct research under its wing.

II

What, then, has been the focus of peace research through its relatively short history? As a clue, we may turn to the pages of the *Journal of Conflict Resolution.* The purpose of the *Journal* is best transmitted through its editorial statement, practically unchanged over the years:

> . . . to stimulate and communicate systematic research and thinking on international processes, including the total international system, the interactions among governments and among nationals of different states, and the processes by which nations make and execute their foreign policies. It is our hope that theoretical and empirical efforts in this area will help in minimizing the use of violence in resolving international conflicts.
>
> The editors believe that concepts, data, and methods from all of the social and behavioral sciences are needed for the understanding of problems in this field and for the development of a systematic body of knowledge. Moreover, we believe that relevant insights can be derived from analyses of interaction and conflict, not only directly at the international level, but also at other levels of social organization . . . . The *Journal* publishes . . . reports of empirical research (basic or applied), theoretical analyses, critical reviews, as well as speculative or programmatic papers with a systematic focus.

We see here an attempt to funnel insights and findings from the many branches of social science into the problem of conquering or controlling war. "Conflict resolution is social technology," as the long-term managing editor, Elizabeth Converse, put it, "and should be based on social science."

The content of the *Journal* over its first twelve years included, as one area of emphasis, studies of national decision-making. How are national decisions made; is it a rational or an irrational process; what are the variables and factors involved; how effective is the communication leading to decision? Studies in this field have included analyses of the attitudes of various leadership groups, of public "war-mindedness," of the relations between leaders and led, and of personality types and persons in stress conditions in their relationship to policy decisions. One experimental game reported, for instance, showed personal "hawkishness" to be related not to aggressiveness or deceitfulness but more to cautiousness and conservatism.[4]

A related area receiving much attention is that of bargaining. Bargaining represents a non-war or constructive way of handling conflict. The concentration naturally has been on international bargaining, but many articles have moved toward a general theory of bargaining. Continuing empirical findings in game theory have been evaluated for their real-life significance for international bargaining. The "Prisoner's Dilemma" game has received the most repeated study since it puts players in a situation where they can choose to compete or cooperate, and each has to guess the other's attitude in order to optimize his own gains. The choice of cooperation is risky: one can lose more by this, but also gain more. The parallel with the international "game" is obvious. Conflict within a group and between groups and how these patterns differ have also been examined, as well as the role of a third party in a conflict situation and its possible applications to the international field (that is, an international peace-keeping organization or some kind of arbitrator).

Wars in general—the actual occurrences of wars and the events leading up to them—have been minutely and quantitatively examined, but here the traditional approaches (the general historical studies of past wars and their effects, or of international trade-linked economic causations) have been significantly absent. How nations choose or stumble into war seems to have been the peace-research concentration; what happens after that, peace researchers leave to the historians. Many articles have dealt with detailed problems, technological and psychological, related to arms control. Whether man *has* choice or control in matters of war and peace was found in several studies to be a culturally differing question, which has interesting implications for international planning.[5]

The peculiarities of international systems have been examined in the *Journal's* pages; the perception of "systemicity" in the world of nations is a distinguishing mark of its peace-research orientation. This involves considering nations as "actors" with varying "attributes" and examining the exchanges of goods and behaviors among them. Perhaps we could spell this out in more detail, drawing on Kenneth Boulding's description of what he calls the "international-systems" approach to learning about what happens between nations. In large part, this sums up his view of the theory aimed at by peace research and of the ways this theory might get intellectual purchase to unscrew from man's history the ancient rusty bolt of international violence.

In the first place, such a system is Copernican. That is, it is viewed as a totality, as if from the outside, not from the point of view of any one nation. Second, it is parametric. This implies the mutual interaction of a large number of variables rather than a simple cause-effect relationship. Third, it does not limit itself to equilibrium models but recognizes the dynamic and cumulative processes in operation. Fourth, it is institutional: the sociological and anthropological effects of organizations, symbolic elements and cultural habits are taken into account, and a wide variety of behavioral principles allowed for. Fifth, it looks not only at the characteristics of the actors in the drama but also at the forms of relations and transactions between them. Sometimes it may even abstract so far as to look at the transactions as if the actors were not there. And sixth, it is aggregative; that is, it looks for ways to condense large masses of heterogeneous information into useful quantitative indices, as the economists have done with the cost-of-living index.[6]

Many difficult conflict-related concepts such as violence, power, utility, rationality, consensus and guilt have been presented in casual use or rigorous analysis in the pages of the *Journal*. The total corpus of this work, built as it is on varying assumptions and disciplines and points of view, does not make up any unified theory of conflict or its resolution, but certainly goes far toward forming the beginning of such a theory. Just gathering various models into one place facilitates their comparison and usefulness.[7] Before the dynamics of conflict can be spelled out, the significant variables have to be abstracted: the types of parties, the types of interactions, the types of objectives. Even what is to be included in the term "conflict"—how broad or narrow a segment of human behavior—is not agreed on. But to those dedicated to the process, as with any social science, there must be a broad area of messiness, of trial and error, of all sorts of theoretical approaches, of wide-ranging sampling of the multiplicity of human behavior, before there can be much narrowing to pattern or certainty. Empirically observing behavior; examining what people do in a given situation; processing data through the intellectual, theoretical, rational mold; and insisting on learning prior to doing are the distinguishing marks of the peace research movement as against the peace movement.

The "social-scientific revolution in the international system," as Boulding terms it, which can be identified with the peace research movement, depends on a group of scholars who combine a moral commitment to stable peace with a devotion to the intellectual method. Among them will surely be those (to use here a limited, purely quantitative measure) who have contributed the largest number of articles to the *Journal of Conflict Resolution* in its first twelve years: Anatol Rapoport, David

Singer, Kenneth Boulding, Inis Claude, Elton McNeil, Bruce Russett and Quincy Wright. Boulding, in referring to the development of theoretical insights in the international systems field, mentions Lewis Richardson, Quincy Wright, Thomas Schelling, Karl Deutsch, David Singer, Charles McClelland, Robert North, Morton Kaplan "and others among whom I might include myself." There is an overlap in theory development, however, between the peace researchers and the strategic theorists such as Schelling and Herman Kahn. The methods of looking at the material are similar, but the main difference is in the choice of problems and in the constraints programmed into the stipulations.

> At many points peace research and national security research overlap. In these days, certainly nobody regards war as anything but a cost to be minimized in the interest of certain other values. Nevertheless, there is a difference between those who regard it as a tolerable cost and those who regard it as an intolerable one.[8]

It would be well, perhaps, to look at some of the personal factors that bring a man in one direction or another. It is a reasonable assumption that this combination of a moral, emotional response with an intellectual way of dealing with a problem belongs to a particular personality package containing a strong double thrust of moral outrage and intellectual commitment. The background and events that brought Kenneth Boulding to his position in the peace research movement provide an appropriate case history of one of its major figures.

III

A careful examination of the people and organizations surrounding Kenneth Boulding in his youth must lead one to conclude that it was not the pull of "significant others" nor "reference groups" that led him to his deep and lasting commitment to pacifism or non-violence. Neither of his parents was a pacifist; his church, the English Methodist chapel, did not preach it; none of his good friends endorsed it as thoroughly as he; none of his teachers taught it. Pacifism was a wispy, almost invisible thread in the culture he grew up in, which was the port city of Liverpool in the second decade of this century. Yet as a young boy he found it and made it his own. A private inner response to large outward events, without the mediation of familiar people, must have characterized the process.

Boulding was four years old when World War I began. The war had an immense impact on him, both direct and indirect. His father, a plumbing and heating contractor, had a business office in the inner city of Liverpool. But the family in a time of relative prosperity had taken a house across the River Mersey, in the Liverpool equivalent of the suburbs, where they had a tree and a garden, green things around them, salt air and beaches nearby for sand castles. But with the coming of the war, the decline of his father's business forced the little family back to the rooms above the business in the inner city, a row house whose only yard was a covered pavement in the back, full of heating equipment. It was a move from openness, freedom and light to constriction, crowded living and dirty pavements; and both young Kenneth and his mother (a country girl who had always felt pent up in Liverpool) were completely miserable at the move. It is likely that when he asked "why?" as a child of four must do, he was told, "Because of the war." "The war" could well have assumed the proportions of a personal enemy from that moment.

There were other less direct war-borne experiences. His father was not accepted for the army, but his uncle was conscripted and later returned with permanent damage from shell shock. Cousins, friends and neighbors of the family were killed or maimed, and Mrs. Boulding was often called on to do the comforting. Once she took small Kenneth with her (he was eight or nine) to visit her aunt, who had lost her reason shortly after a son was killed. It was a frightening experience for him, and would have increased the negative emotional freight carried by the image of "war." The military system impressed him as fantastically intrusive, taking away the autonomy of private lives, the terribly important right of making choices.

In addition, there was an individual reason for Boulding's seeking other than violent methods of settling conflict: he was not well coordinated physically, was frequently sick, and found his mental equipment far superior to his physical capacity to resist aggression. And, with his thorough grounding in the Bible in a church-centered family, a logical little boy could find strong support for his non-violent inclinations in the Sermon on the Mount.

Very early, then, and almost independently, Kenneth Boulding came to his personal commitment to pacifism. By the time he was about fifteen, he was publicly espousing the cause of the League of Nations against that of the military, both vocally and in his school paper. At about the same time he made a lifetime pledge to Christianity. This took the shape of formally joining the Methodist Church; but in his search for a deeper expression of the experience of worship, and at the same time for the roots of the Christian pacifist position, he sought out and began attending the local Quaker Meeting. He became a Quaker during his college years. This was an institutional connection which could bolster the antiwar position he had adopted, and it was also a place where he found an extension of his religious experience which did not conflict with his deepening intellectual grasp on the world.

From the beginning, the intellectual mode was the one in which Boulding could best respond to his environment. Not very good at locomotion or reaching out physically, he reached out mentally. He was good at arguing, asking questions and thinking things out. He was an only child and an only grandchild, so that surrounded by an adult world he had to learn early to interpret and use adult communication. Hampered by an incapacitating stutter and a rejecting slum-school first experience of education, he was fortunate in having parents who, though of working-class background and very little income, valued his potential and the process of education enough to find a better school that would accept him. From the time he was nine, his teachers worked with him to prepare him for the series of examinations that won him scholarships, first to secondary school and then to Oxford. His continuing intellectual excellence brought him repeated scholarships for graduate work at Oxford and then at the University of Chicago.

There was a considerable inner battle in the adolescent Kenneth Boulding between the attraction of the exact sciences and that of literature and philosophy. He had high ability in both and went to Oxford on a scholarship in chemistry. At the end of his first year, finding the laboratory deadening and the pull of the literary very strong, he changed fields to Politics, Philosophy and Economics, with his main work concentrated in economics. In later years his concentration has broadened to touch on all these fields. The social sciences, to which he has given his professional life, are in a way a combining of his bent for science with the humanism and respect for life which he endorsed so early.

IV

The ideas which he developed in the area of international systems and peace research have been sophisticated and refined over time, but it is surprising to find how many of them echo thoughts he expressed very early. They are founded on enduring attitudes about man and his place in the world. As they have continued through his life, they have carried three major themes: man is good; the war system is evil; more powerful knowledge is the way of transforming the system. On each of these themes he found in the surrounding culture some supporters and some detractors. The Quaker tenet of the potential goodness in all men has been shared through the years by liberal Social Gospelers and Christian pacifists, but it stands in contrast to the conviction of original sin on which the Constitution of the U.S. was built and to the garden-variety of this belief reflected in the saying, "We'll always have wars because you can't change human nature." Its corollary, that it is the system which gives man trouble, particularly the national state in all its ramifications, has its swelling ranks of supporters today within the counter-culture. With the third theme, however, that of the route to salvation through knowledge, much of the counter-culture would part company. Here Boulding makes a strange alliance for a humanist, for he is not speaking of traditional wisdom but of technical, quantitative, hard-data knowledge, the kind that inventors and engineers and space-station builders use, the kind that has produced our burgeoning technocracy—but he wants this knowledge applied to social forces.

Beyond the high school and college essays, Boulding's first published international-systems writing was a pamphlet called *Paths of Glory*. An explanation of the non-violent method of defense, it was published in 1937 by the Northern Friends Peace Board, a Quaker committee which concentrated on peace education. Boulding served on this committee while working at his first teaching job at the University of Edinburgh. In 1937, in the United States for a Quaker conference, he was offered a job at Colgate University and made the momentous decision to leave Britain, at least for a trial year. Part of his reason for being attracted to America was his sense of its openness to new and better kinds of social organization, its looseness, plurality and humanness in contrast to his experience of class constrictions in England and the kind of traditional rigidities that left only one way of doing anything. He hoped, too, for a minimizing of the sacredness of the state which a long tradition of divine right of kings had helped to implant. The year became a lifetime.

World War II, subjecting all his school friends and his relatives to bombardment and the continual terror of invasion, put a heavy strain on his pacifism. In the teeth of Hitler's unbelievable affronts to human life and dignity, it became harder and harder for him to cling to his commitment to love his enemies. Only a kind of mystical experience that came to him at a time when hate was almost overwhelming brought him back to a sense of kinship with all men in suffering, sin and hope. He came again to the certainty, as he put it in a sonnet he wrote at about that time, "though love is weak and hate is strong,/Yet hate is short, and love is very long."[9]

Teaching and writing in the field of economics, he carried on at the same time his inner struggle to preserve his love for mankind, poured out in a series of sonnets written over the war years and published as *There is a Spirit: The Nayler Sonnets* (1945). All of his best friends who joined him in pacifism in adolescence rejected the stand when war came, and some rejected him for clinging to it. But stubbornly he stuck to his themes of the goodness of man, the evil in the system, and the logical arguments against war. In a 1942 pamphlet, *New Nations for Old*, he argued for the early end of the war system on two counts, its moral cost and its financial cost: its increasing horror and increasing unprofitability. He did not expect men to become perfect but did not feel this was necessary. The key to his hope was the proposition "that war, as a specific human institution, is the result not of conflicts, nor of human wickedness, but of the political organization of the world into a number of separate, sovereign and irresponsible countries."[10] As he pointed out, there are ways to handle conflicts and wickedness (as is normally done within a country), without war: "the trouble with the world has not been so much a lack of good will, as a lack of knowledge as to how to make good will effective." Consequently, he recommended an international organization not with a military function but as a center of research and information, a clearing house for statistics and a place for administration of practical problems. The major obstacle he saw was the lack of a sense of responsibility for people outside one's own borders. It was the concept of the sacredness of the nation which got in the way of the needed extension of the sense of community.

Here already were two of the elements which run through all his succeeding writing on the subject: the view that the national state is obsolete and the reliance on research, statistics and information as a way out of reliance on military force. The third constant, present in the 1942 pamphlet and strikingly brought out in another pamphlet in 1967, is taking man as he is—believing he wants pretty much the right things—and concentrating the effort in making the system work for him, not against him.[11]

Boulding pointed out the obsolescence of the national state as early as 1931 in a prize essay at New College, Oxford. The echoes of this theme have sounded through articles and books to the present; and in *Conflict and Defense* he refined and extended it. Sovereignty depends on the ability to protect from attack. There used to be an area of safety for each country where the cost of transporting violence was too great for an attacking country. But the increasing range of the projectile has effectively reduced the distance between countries, and the increased efficiency of warheads makes it possible to pack incalculable destruction into one missile, so that no nation any longer has an area it can protect: "we can only continue to have a world of separate nations if none of them wants to upset the existing structure, for none can be defended." Boulding's perception of the shaky condition of the national state as an institution, an intuition based on moral and economic grounds in 1931, was documented in 1962 by a theory of conflict and data about man's technical progress. When the range of the deadly missile is half the diameter of the earth, sovereignty becomes, in fact, a fiction.

The vision of the state as the servant, not the master, of man is clearly Boulding's point of view. When an organization ceases to serve, it should cease to exist and not be propped up with false legitimacy.

> The nation-state can no longer be treated as a sacred institution; there must be a deflation of the emotions and values that attach to it, a decline, if you will, in the passion with which people love their countries and an acceptance of the nation-state and the nation-state system as essentially mundane institutions designed solely for public convenience.[12]

If one views war not as the inevitable result of the conflict of human interests but as the rupture of an existing social system, then it is wise to find ways to identify the stresses and strains that can lead to such a break. One such effort has been Boulding's exploration of the theory that wars tend to happen when one country overtakes another in power, a factor closely related to the per capita GNP. If this could be demonstrated, then the overtakes in GNP—which can be roughly predicted from collectable data—would give a considerable clue to coming stress points. There are no doubt other kinds of data which put together would greatly sharpen the effectiveness of this kind of prediction. And so Boulding gradually refined the second theme from that early pamphlet, an international clearing house for statistics.

Quincy Wright's parallel development of the concept of a "World Intelligence Center" no doubt fed into his thinking.[13] Through interchange and discussion the idea emerged for what Boulding likes to call "social data stations." These would serve as a world network of weather stations, collecting and processing data on populations, rates of economic growth, surpluses and shortages, attitudes, tension levels, shifts in power relationships of classes or groups within a country, voting trends, images which nations have of one another—all sorts of social indicators which could be put together to identify social temperature and pressure and predict cold and warm fronts. Karl Deutsch, Robert Hefner, David Singer, Bruce Russett and other peace researchers have actively worked on the identification of such social indicators.

Boulding urges the development of indices from this mass of information comparable to the economic indices of prices and national income, by which the direction of change can be identified early:

> The problem of the maintenance of peace is one of "conflict control." We are faced in international relations with dynamic processes of action and reaction in fear, armament, and in the images which nations have of one another which go either from bad to worse or from bad to better. If they go from bad to worse too long, the result is a breakdown of the system in war. The great problem of the maintenance of peace is how to identify these movements, to catch them young, and to deal with them before they become unmanageable.[14]

The situation at present, he feels, is so foggy that most international decision-makers do not know when they take a step whether they are going up or down, and the information from social data stations would at least tell them which way was up.

But while Boulding was building and modifying his intellectual engine for the prevention and control of war, he was also involved in actively witnessing in response to his conscience against the system which planned and executed wars. He and his wife, Elise, wrote and sent out in 1942, against the advice of their friends and his employer (at that time the League of Nations Economic and Financial Section, based in New Jersey), a statement asking all peoples to renounce their national allegiances and throw down their weapons. Notified that he would be fired if he sent this out, Boulding resigned his job and made plans for an uncertain future. But the Quaker president of Fisk University invited him to the economics department there, and after a year at Fisk

Boulding went on to Iowa State College. Although ready to go to jail rather than to Civilian Public Service camp or the army, he was taken off the draft hook by being classified 4-F. During the war, while other economists were addressing themselves to the wartime economy, he was writing *The Economics of Peace,* aimed at the problems of reconstruction and development. He fought a legal battle to become naturalized as a U.S. citizen—till then denied to pacifists—which he won in 1948 without taking the oath to bear arms.

This was not the end of the moral hurdles related to war and peace. In April, 1958, in response to continued nuclear testing, Boulding initiated a "vigil" by the flagpole in the center of the University of Michigan campus, as a symbolic act of penitence and non-consent. In 1960 he stood in front of the Pentagon in another protest vigil with a thousand other Quakers. In April, 1961, he turned down an appealing offer of a visiting lectureship in Hawaii because it required a stringent loyalty oath. He gave the Students for a Democratic Society in their early days a good deal of inspiration and encouragement; for a time the SDS shared office space with the Center for Research on Conflict Resolution (in the old ROTC building!). In March, 1965, he helped to plan and conduct the first "teach-in" on the Vietnam war, in which between two and three thousand students spent all night talking, listening and debating; it was a meaningful alternative to the threatened strike against classes during the day. An observer, Rose Kelman, reports her memory of that occasion:

> The night of the first teach-in—do you remember?—it was about 12:30, black night and bitter cold, and the bomb scare and everything, everybody out on the quad—and Kenneth was supposed to speak. And I can't remember anything else about it but these words: "I see a sneer across the face of America . . . and I don't like it." I don't know if I heard anything after that.

Boulding found ways from time to time to reach into officialdom: to testify before a Congressional committee, to bring facts and moral issues about Vietnam to a talk with a governor. In the fall of 1966 the Boulding protest was turned to the political process when Elise Boulding was asked to serve as a write-in peace candidate for Congress, and Kenneth worked with her on her campaign.

And yet the war went on. There seemed to be no way to reach the decision-makers.

The "love affair with America" that drew Boulding to make his home and his citizenship here had certainly gone sour. The violence of his reactions to the war policies of the government was related to the intensity of his idealism about his chosen country in the early years. He had never fooled himself about the two faces of the national state, but he had hoped for better from the one state that had deliberately embarked on a path based on a respect for life, liberty and pursuit of happiness. On a scrap of paper with no date he jotted three bitter incomplete lines:

Don't love your country any more
She's a bitch, she's a bastard, she's a whore
She burns up babies, she roasts them slow . . .[15]

And yet, and yet—disillusioned, betrayed—what does one do? An irresistible, persistent non-violence, though it brings Kenneth Boulding to despair, forbids him destruction and revolution. Whatever the roots of this non-violence, it will not let him go. So he must part company with those who despair of peaceful protest and feel the society must be destroyed: the black militants, the Weathermen, the Communists, the New Left. The costs of violence are always in his mind, the costs of revolution: one, two or three generations to get back to the level of living that people had before. The shattering of lives, the building of the habit of violence: "Revolutions have a way of eating their own children." The counterproductiveness of uncontrolled anger has been a repeated theme of his. An anarchist who must have order, he is a revolutionary who cannot stomach revolution.

The position of non-violence is real and active in his life. It is logical and is based on a sound conception of humanity and of the will of a loving God (if such there is). It is perhaps the only way we can thread our steps across the swinging bridge over the gulf between what is and what ought to be. But the position would be just as logical and tenable for many people who have not chosen to adopt it. Why has he?

As social psychologists Smith, Bruner and White have pointed out, attitudes or opinions serve several functions. The first one we have referred to, object appraisal as a cognitive activity; this is the commonly understood function of perceiving and valuing elements of reality. There is also a social function for an opinion, as a vehicle by which we orient ourselves to membership groups or reference groups in our environment. The third function is psychological: attitudes serve partly as the means by which internal problems are externalized and acted out in the everyday world. A fear or a wish may quietly influence which objects we perceive in our environment; and our positive or negative attitudes toward the objects we perceive are also influenced by fears or wishes often unknown to us.[16] None of these considerations, of course, influence the validity, the rightness or the genuineness of an opinion; these qualities must be judged on other grounds. The more we can understand of the three functions, however, the better we can understand why a person believes and acts as he does.

The objective function of attitudes, as instruments with which to appraise reality, is illustrated by Boulding's systematic and polemic works. What gives his writing such insight is his habit of examining his own attitudes systematically, as working hypotheses. But they have had, as well, a socializing value for him. Boulding's pacifism helped to define his relationship to groups. It partly came out of an intensification and purification of the faith of the Methodists, and then it led him to, and was reinforced by, his association with Quakers. Throughout his life he found like-minded people with whom to ally himself, including his colleagues in the Center for Research on Conflict Resolution and, most notably, his wife,Elise.

His pacifist attitudes may also have a psychological function as a defense against aggressive tendencies, although it is possible only to make suggestions about their inner workings. Perhaps there is an observable clue to their operation in the fact that he seems to delight in shocking people with his rhetoric, although he usually cloaks the barb in humor. Sometimes, however, his indignation almost gets away from him. His hostility toward the irrational actions of militant youth recently has been more and more expressed. At times he seems to be stirred by wrath of cosmic proportions; and occasionally a colleague, and sometimes his own later, cooler judgment, has toned down a too-violent letter he has written when feeling some essential value subverted.

These are traits consonant with his childhood history and adult temperament. His early family climate, though loving, was not without strain; but it was one where the expression of hostility was definitely discouraged and where young Kenneth had in fact often to take the role of harmonizer among parents, aunts and grandparents, composing funny poems or putting on a show to set them laughing. Perhaps, at four and a half, he felt so threatened by rejection or separation when his gay and lively mother became depressed and miserable that even the awareness of hostility was too much for him to let into perception at later times. Perhaps there is something in him that he senses below the level of awareness—as there is in most of us—which would really like to rebel, to destroy, to shatter; but it has remained terribly important to him to keep it within bounds. Indeed, there is a passage in one of his books where he is discussing the high valuation we place on scarce goods, in which he states, "The violent make a religion of love." And one day in a seminar he reported an earlier conversation: "Bob Angell asked me once, 'How is it you're a Quaker and so violent?' and I answered, 'If I wasn't so violent I wouldn't have to be a Quaker.'" Some of the power of the moral outrage probably comes from this pent-up violence, and the intellectual mold into which it is poured comes from the need to hold it in bounds.

In such a case, the rebelliousness of youth, the dichotomy of our times, the looseness or freeness of life-styles in resistance to the dicta of society, the overturning of the university and the world of rational intellect, the letting in of violence as a conscious mode of behavior—all could serve as deeply unsettling movements to one who has held such forces in tenuous balance in himself over a long lifetime.

And so he has moved in the other direction. The turning point was thoughtfully marked by his 1965 article after the teach-in, "Reflections on Protest."[17] Despairing of protest, others have turned toward violence, but he has turned toward knowledge. Peace research, rather than the peace movement, now looks to him like the wedge to crack the war system. The moral commitment is still strong, but irrational acts appear more and more dangerous at a time in society when all bounds are loosening and nothing seems to hold any more. The strong way, the only way, is the way of control and discipline and hard, tough knowledge. If peace research can keep honing in and building that intellectual engine to life the scourge of war off man, Boulding's hand and mind are likely to be in it.

Villa Julie College

notes

1. They have since been published: Lewis Richardson, *Arms and Insecurity* (Pittsburgh, 1960), and *Statistics of Deadly Quarrels* (Chicago, 1960).

2. Kenneth Boulding and Emile Benoit, eds. (New York, 1963).

3. New York: Harper and Row, 1962, and Harper Torchbooks, 1963.

4. Marc Pilisuk, Paul Potter, Anatol Rapoport, and J. Alan Winter, "War Hawks and Peace Doves," *Journal of Conflict Resolution*, IX, 4 (1965), 491-508.

5. Robert C. Angell, Vera S. Dunham and J. David Singer, "Social Values and Foreign Policy Attitudes of Soviet and American Elites," *Journal of Conflict Resolution*, VIII, 4 (1964), 329-491; and Zbigniew Brezinski, "Communist Ideology and International Affairs," *Journal of Conflict Resolution*, IV, 3 (1960), 266-291.

6. Boulding, *The Impact of the Social Sciences* (New Brunswick, N.J., 1966), 70-73.

7. Clinton Fink has done a masterful job of pulling together many segments of conflict theory from the history of the *Journal*, as has Elizabeth Converse in the summation of the problems treated over the years, in the special review issue of December, 1968 (XII, 4). I have depended on their summaries for my very brief capsule history.

8. Boulding, "Social Sciences," *The Great Ideas Today*, eds. R. M. Hutchins and M. J. Adler (Chicago: Encyclopedia Britannica, 1965), 278.

9. "Nor to revenge any wrong," in Boulding's one published book of poetry to date, *There is A Spirit: The Nayler Sonnets* (Nyack, N.Y., 1945), 3.

10. Both quotations in this paragraph are from *New Nations for Old*, Pendle Hill Pamphlet #17 (Wallingford, Pa., 1942).

11. Kenneth Boulding and Milton Mayer, *The Mayer/Boulding Dialogue on Peace Research*, eds. Cynthia Kerman and Carol Murphy (Wallingford, Pa., 1967).

12. Boulding, *Beyond Economics*, 299-300.

13. Quincy Wright, "Project for a World Intelligence Center," *Journal of Conflict Resolution*, I, 1 (March, 1957), 93-97.

14. Boulding, *Perspectives on the Economics of Peace*, Part I of *Economic Factors Bearing Upon the Maintenance of Peace* (New York, 1961), 23.

15. Personal papers; by permission of Kenneth Boulding.

16. M. Brewster Smith, Jerome Bruner and Robert W. White, *Opinions and Personality* (New York, 1956).

17. *Bulletin of the Atomic Scientists*, XXI, 8 (October, 1965), 18-20.

Peace Education at
the Crossroads [1]

A. Michael Washburn

Suddenly, peace education is the thing, after twenty years of resistance and indifference on the part of the education establishment. Peace courses and programs have begun or are being planned in many parts of the country, in colleges of all sizes. As they become more widespread, the inevitable questions are beginning to be asked: How big is this movement? Who is behind it? What are its origins? How are students reacting? What do they actually study in a peace course? Those who study political trends in this country will also want to know: How likely is it that the peace education movement will achieve great stature and wide adherence in the academic world? How significant a political factor could it become?

> In the wake of academic upheaval and the emergence of peace research in the Sixties, many universities are establishing peace education programs. The director of the World Law Fund's University Program warns, though, that if this new movement is to become more than a passing fad it must develop a cohesive sense of purpose.

Unfortunately, at the present time my own answers to these last two questions must be: "Not very likely; not very significant, unless. . . ." Why? For peace people, the barriers to recognition and power are formidable because peace courses are often viewed as a direct challenge to traditional world-affairs courses. In addition, what is taught in these courses can be highly critical of American foreign policy since 1945, indeed of the nation-state system itself. In short, peace education calls into question the prevailing institutionalization of our country's thinking and teaching about international problems. Largely without prospect of significant financial support and with no leaders having the political influence or stature of a Henry Kissinger, a John Kenneth Galbraith or even a Paul Ehrlich, the peace education movement must rely for the moment on sheer, brute intellect. It can only achieve power through the force of its analysis and the strength of its prescriptions for changes in policies and institutions.

Herein lies the source of my pessimistic assessment of the movement. It simply does not yet have the unity, clarity and forcefulness of vision to take on the academic foreign-policy/international-relations establishment issue by issue, research design by research design, recommendation by recommendation and come out ahead.

Although no actual surveys have been conducted to measure the extent of peace education programs on the college level, it is estimated that a minimum of 150 institutions have courses related to peace. Perhaps most indicative of the rising interest in peace education are the rapid growth of the Consortium on Peace Research, Education and Development (COPRED)[2] and the increasing demand for the services of the University Program of the World Law Fund, a privately supported foundation engaged since 1961 in a program of peace research, materials production, educational consultancy and teacher training. The Fund seeks the introduction of the subjects of world order and peace into the courses of all major educational systems of the world—on the graduate, undergraduate and secondary school levels.[3]

The purposes of COPRED are to stimulate and support peace research and education activities and to perform a variety of clearinghouse, synthesis and contact functions for all people in the field. Its first meeting was convened in May, 1970, by Kenneth and Elise Boulding. Just one year later the number of member organizations had reached 54, including 43 university research and teaching institutes or programs, and six professional associations such as the International Studies Association and the Conference on Peace Research in History.[4]

Other organizations service peace education, too. The American Friends Service Committee has long made this a major thrust of its work, and the World Without War Council is developing curricular materials, largely in the context of adult and religious education programs. Especially useful are its compilation of relevant films and its book-length annotated bibliography *To End War*.[5] The Center for Teaching About Peace and War, at Wayne State University, directs its attention primarily, but not exclusively, to secondary education.

Workshops Popular

In the last year staff members of the World Law Fund's University Program visited close to 50 campuses, sometimes at the invitation of the schools and at other times on its own initiative to stimulate interest in peace education. The Fund also cosponsored workshops last summer for faculty members and students at Colgate University and Pacific University. These meetings elicited three times as many applications as there were spaces available. In addition, 300 peace related courses are using

World Law Fund materials, and almost 2,000 faculty members are receiving the Fund's *Progress Report*. Especially interesting is the small but rising number of university administrators and officials who are requesting Fund materials and counsel.

The peace education movement is part of the larger trend toward the acceptance of courses in social problems as necessary and legitimate components of the college curriculum. Its strong emergence is one culmination of the turmoil of the Sixties: Vietnam and students' disgust at the close ties between the academic community and the military foreign-policy establishment; the depersonalization, overspecialization and insensitivity to value questions of much of American education; the emergence of the counterculture with its emphasis on community-building and rebellion against individual competition and achievement; and finally, the struggle to find workable strategies for effecting fundamental change in important American institutions.

No institution has been more shaken by these upheavals than the university. The resulting fluidity in course requirements and offerings has finally made it possible to start peace programs on many campuses.

Still, there is an enormous distance to go before even a significant minority of American undergraduates will have an opportunity to confront in the classroom the problems of global survival and to work out solutions to what they can and will do about them. Resistance from the existing academic disciplines is still quite strong on most campuses. The peace education courses that exist are not always well publicized and are often understaffed. Every institution is critically short of money and torn by budgeting arguments. Information about peace education is scarce and fragmentary; the major publishers are only beginning to take this potential market seriously enough to publish and promote new teaching materials. Training opportunities for interested faculty members are practically non-existent.

None of these difficulties is insurmountable, however. Ironically, the major obstacle to the establishment of peace education as a significant force in American education and politics is the peace educator himself. A fair evaluation of peace education as it exists today would have to concede that a widely accepted definition of the scope, content and purposes of the field does not yet exist. Peace educators do not yet share a minimum understanding of what constitutes an exciting and responsible program. In fact, this question is rarely raised in the fraternity. A *laissez-faire* attitude prevails, on the assumption that all peace efforts are positive.

These are some of the various goals that have been articulated for peace education:

> To prepare students for peace research careers.
> To prepare people and ideas for the governmental policy-making process.

To give some sense of world problems to all American undergraduates.

To feed and serve a "revolutionary" movement in America.

To stimulate mass involvement in the invention and implementation of a new world political system.

My own view is that very few programs already in existence encompass more than a very narrow combination of these purposes. Many programs, for example, are either too research-oriented and traditionally academic or are very unstructured and ideologically parochial. Too many have no clear purpose at all.

In this age of high-flying fads, I would estimate that peace education has less than five years to get itself together. That requires the development of an approach to world problems that is cohesive and comprehensive, that has intellectual and moral power. Peace education must transform itself from a momentarily attractive answer to the problem of academic irrelevance into a pervasive factor in American life and thought.

The future of peace education depends on whether there is inherent in the current diversity of approaches the seeds of a major advance in our understanding of the problem of creating a minimally just and peaceful world system. I believe the potential is there, and recent developments in several branches of the field seem to be pointing toward an exciting synthesis. Before drawing these strands together, let me review some of the major approaches to peace education and research.

Basically, the differences among approaches derive from different ideas of the nature of peace, from different conceptions of the kind of changes in people and in institutions that will be necessary to make peace possible, and finally from differences in what is considered an adequate strategy for bringing the required changes about.

The international politics approach, the one for which I have least sympathy, takes existing courses on the U.N., the history of international law and world politics, adds to them seminars on arms control and conflict management and a semester abroad, and calls the composite a peace program. At its worst, this approach amounts to the appropriation of the rhetoric of relevance. Usually it is simply the creation, 10 years too late, of an adequate undergraduate program in international affairs.

Beyond International Politics

Of course, there are many scholars who believe that such a program constitutes the most scholarly and responsible approach to the problems of peace. They have much evidence and an enormous body of literature and opinion on their side. I would argue, however, that other forms of peace education and research raise serious questions about the adequacy of this approach. The international politics approach to peace education can best demonstrate its legitimacy not by continuing simply to dominate undergraduate international education but by taking seriously in a reorganized curriculum some of the questions and policy alternatives developed by other peace educators.

I have seen encouraging signs in the past year that just such a trend of reassessment is developing. In fact, a number of solid international-relations people have joined COPRED and have made important contributions to its self-definition and development. Political-science research, particularly in the area of transnational organizations, seems to be converging with peace research. Joseph Nye at Harvard and Chadwick Alger at Ohio State are among those who are doing exciting research and teaching along these lines. Northwestern's international-relations program is the first I know of that is focusing on "global society."

The world-order approach, which is closely related to the political-science and international-law traditions described above, grew out of the breakthrough work of Harold Lasswell and Myres McDougal at the Yale Law School and of Grenville Clark and Louis Sohn, the authors of *World Peace Through World Law*. World order has been pushed forward by Richard Falk of Princeton and Saul Mendlovitz of the Rutgers Law School. The World Law Fund has sponsored and published much of Falk's and Mendlovitz's work and is now working with a broader group of world-order scholars in this country and abroad. Princeton recently received a substantial grant from the Fund for Peace to develop a world-order research program within its Center of International Studies. The Fund for Peace is also in the process of establishing a consortium of universities doing world-order research and offering graduate training in this field.

The world-order approach does not have tightly defined boundaries, but its central concerns are identified in this statement about the Princeton program: "The term 'world order' refers to the development at the level of the international or global system of stable institutions designed to regulate large-scale violence and to achieve a just distribution of values." (A two-page outline of the world-order subject matter and methodology is available from the World Law Fund.)

World order is policy-oriented, first and foremost. This means that the development of theory and the highly sophisticated data gathering and analysis which characterize most contemporary social science have been given a lower priority than the invention and implementation of institutions, rules and procedures for improving very rapidly the world's capacity to deal with the problems of war, social injustice, poverty and ecological imbalance. This emphasis on institution-building also distinguishes world order from those approaches which stress the importance of changes in attitudes and life-styles and focus on individual human beings as the creators of worldwide social change. The world order approach offers a framework of analysis which links international law and organization with a radical value imperative and places both in a global futuristic context.

The establishment of university centers, institutes and courses on non-violence is another generally happy trend. Such programs as the ones established recently at Syracuse University, Kent State and Notre Dame should make important contributions to peace education because they deal directly with the following critical issues: values as the basis for policy and individual action, the role of individuals in the social change process, and the importance of justice in any conception of peace. The non-violence approach also presents a coherent, strongly argued alternative to the present system of national defense.

Non-violence is, of course, a moral and political movement with a compelling history. This accounts for much of its campus appeal but also for its major weakness as an educational approach. It does not always happen, but courses and programs in non-violence can be too narrowly focused. Careful analysis of alternative strategies for dealing with conflict are sometimes not adequately covered. Perhaps more important is the tendency of these programs to concentrate on community and national problems while failing to connect them directly with world problems. The emphasis on the individual in the non-violence approach can also obscure the key role of institutions and the necessity of fundamental changes in them. Such changes may be possible before large numbers of people around the world become supporters of non-violent alternatives.

Conflict Resolution

Another major approach to peace research and education, the conflict-resolution approach, began in the 1950's at the University of Michigan and has produced a significant body of literature and a large number of excellent scholars and political activists. Despite the unfortunate recent closing of Michigan's Center for Research on Conflict Resolution, this approach, which focuses on conflict at all levels from interpersonal to international, will continue to be the core of programs in all parts of the country. Institutes or programs in conflict studies already exist at the University of Wisconsin, the University of Washington, Michigan State University and Stanford, and there are probably several hundred psychology and sociology departments that cover some part of the subject in their courses.

Conflict resolution scholars have been far more concerned with research than with undergraduate teaching. The field grew up at the time of the quantification of the behavioral sciences and now boasts an impressive methodology, a specialized language of its own and an array of data banks and massive studies. The enterprise is based on the assumption that it is possible to identify causal relationships or patterns of events, conditions and behavior that produce violent conflict and that it is possible, therefore, to predict outbreaks of violence and devise strategies for preventing them.

Despite continuing theoretical advances and steadily improving data collection and analysis, a comprehensive, practical set of war prediction and prevention concepts still seems a long way off. As a result, conflict resolution teaching at the undergraduate level is difficult, often being too traditionally academic for many of today's students. (Interestingly enough, conflict-resolution scholars have themselves been prominent in a variety of activist enterprises such as the formation of Students for a Democratic Society, the Vietnam teach-ins and the university reform movement.)

Nevertheless, the conflict-resolution approach has important things to offer on such key peace subjects as negotiation and bargaining, conflict management, attitude change, misperception and elite decision-making. It is also the source of much that is valuable in the area of simulation, which is an increasingly accepted teaching tool, particularly in peace courses. Conflict resolution is already fairly well integrated with the more quantitative aspects of political science. The task now is to work out the linkages between its findings and the more normative and policy-oriented work of other peace researchers.

In addition to these basic approaches to peace research and education, there are several more general themes or clusters of academic activity which bear on peace education as it is developing today. I shall mention the main themes only briefly, but I do so because each could add an important and powerful dimension to peace education.

The first theme is futurism, which is a subject of great appeal to students. It is a line of inquiry that can add to the peace field a concreteness of vision and a sense of how much could be achieved in the next two or three decades. Elise Boulding has done important work in linking futurism with peace, as have the world-order people associated with the World Law Fund. (See *War/Peace Report,* January, 1970, for an article on the Fund's futuristic World Order Models Project.)

Another important factor is the development in recent years of what has been called "radical social science." With regard to peace issues, this has taken the form of active opposition to the Vietnam War along with critical scholarly work on such subjects as the military-industrial complex, the origins of the Cold War, U.S. interventionism and the need for a new China policy. A basic thesis of many in this group is that fundamental changes in American foreign policy, and thus in the international system itself, will first require major changes in our domestic institutions and in the distribution of political power. Despite the emotional and intensely immediate tone of much of this work, it does raise important long-term peace issues. In addition, the study of these materials provides students with opportunities for direct involvement in the subject matter.

The counterculture phenomenon, another influence on peace education, is a constellation of values, theories and random insights which cuts across various fields from education to politics to life-style. Counterculture ideas and perspectives raise questions about the need for fundamental social change in the United States, and they challenge traditional academic goals and teaching methods. These are critical questions not just because they are the current political reality of students' demand for relevance but primarily because they cut deeper, challenging accepted notions of peace, justice and human dignity.

Finally, there is the related movement for more participatory, action-oriented forms of education. Films, simulation games, independent study, field work, work-study projects, group activities, and changes in grading, formal requirements and class size are some of the prominent ideas and issues. More important than any single one of these is student participation in decision-making about all of them. Peace education projects at Haverford, Colgate, Pittsburgh, Colorado, William Paterson and St. Louis, to name a few, have had great success in student-faculty planning of peace courses.

Building on these traditions and trends, the transformation of peace research and education into a widespread enterprise with real bite must be pushed forward at two levels. Each college or university which plans to start a program or already has one should challenge itself to be creatively synthetic. At the same time, the leaders of the peace field should intensify their interactions and should devote considerable thought and discussion time to clarifying the parameters and priorities of the field.

At the local level, individual college or university peace studies groups can survey the entire field and devise a list of issues and substantive material that they feel must be covered in peace courses. Each participant in the planning should consciously try to stretch his own knowledge and perception of the peace question and should challenge the perceptions of his colleagues.

The procedure followed by the Colgate faculty in creating first their introductory course and now their full program is a sound model for any university to follow. Basically, the Colgate approach has involved broad participation in all phases of discussion by students and faculty. Involvement of people from several disciplines helped to insure against parochialism. Each participant recognized that he had to learn the peace field basically from scratch. Regular reevaluation of decisions and openness to basic changes in course content were established procedure from the beginning. A large number of people outside Colgate were consulted, and evaluations of syllabus and program ideas have been broadly solicited.

A number of programs designed by interdisciplinary groups actually combine two or more of the approaches described earlier. Manhattan College's peace studies major is a model program of courses in which the perspectives of history, religion, literature, social psychology, economics, international relations and government are brought to bear on the problems of war and peace. Manchester College in Indiana, with the oldest peace major in the country, has built its non-violence program on a solid base of international-relations courses. Haverford has had excellent results with a program that combines non-violence and conflict resolution. Kent State University's Center for Peaceful Change has established a three-fold program of academic study, research and public service. Still another variation is evolving at St. Louis University with a program that now involves several disciplines in the study of the structure of non-violent global and domestic societies. In order to provide information of peace studies activities and programs conducted by colleges and universities, the Center for Peace Studies of the University of Akron publishes an *International Peace Studies Newsletter* with a large circulation.[6]

Signs of Synthesis

At the national or intercollegiate level, several signs of movement toward synthesis, or at least engagement over these issues, appeared during 1971. The formation of COPRED was such an event in itself. COPRED's major accomplishment to date has been the stimulation of self-critical thinking in all of its meetings. The Conference on Peace Research in History has sponsored conferences, put peace research on the programs of professional meetings, and distributed important papers and bulletins of research-in-progress; it is developing a conference on war/peace curriculum in the summer of 1972, is launching an abstract service for peace research, and is seeking funds with which to create a full journal in which questions of scope and priorities could be argued out. One of the purposes of last summer's World Law Fund co-sponsored workshops was to think through the relationship between peace education goals and course content.

Ultimately, peace education is nothing unless it is credible. Despite the encouraging signs noted above, I must remain skeptical about its future precisely because I do not yet sense that there is a widespread understanding in the field of this critical fact. Changing the world must be the core purpose of all peace education. Diagnosing what is wrong with the world system is not good enough nor is simply explaining how it needs to change, as difficult as that may be. Ask three questions of each of the approaches described earlier and you will see what I mean: What does this approach have to say about the transformation of the world system? To what extent have these ideas been implemented and what blocks their further implementation? Is this approach adequate to the problem?

The credibility of the peace approaches does not depend on their ability to develop right now an obviously workable and comprehensive solution to the world's problems. Peace educators must demonstrate, however, that they recognize the full scope of the problem and are mustering all their resources for the hard, step-by-step push into the unknown. I simply do not sense that this is what is going on in the peace education field today. Peace educators show very few signs of becoming responsive to the setting within which political action is being and will be taken.

In keeping with my call for constructive dialogue, I conclude with a summary of my own current view of what would constitute a more comprehensive and powerful peace education program than exists anywhere today.

1. The *purpose* should be to involve large numbers of young Americans in some form of lifetime commitment to shaping a more just and peaceful world order through clarification of value perspectives and development of action strategies and goals.

2. The *key issues and subjects* should include the interrelated values of war prevention, worldwide economic welfare, social justice and global ecological balance; large-scale social change; alternative futures; transnational institutions and processes; tension reduction and conflict management; domestic institutions and processes as they affect foreign policy; and science and technology and their effects on global political development.

3. The *perspective or approach* should be explicitly and critically concerned with values; future time orientated; global and transdisciplinary.

4. The *teaching methods* should encourage student participation and interaction; use a variety of teaching media, and offer possibilities for testing and action outside the classroom.

World Law Fund
New York City

notes

1. Portions of this article are reprinted with permission from "Peace Education is Alive—But Unsure of Itself," *War/Peace Report*, XI (November, 1971), 14-18.

2. Inquiries should be directed to Allen Deeter, executive secretary, at Manchester College, North Manchester, Indiana 46962.

3. Inquiries should be directed to the World Law Fund, 11 West 42nd Street, New York, New York 10036.

4. The CPRH is an organization of historians and American Studies teachers committed both to scholarly research and to peace. Inquiries may be directed to the acting secretary-treasurer, Ralph E. Weber, CPRH, History Department, Marquette University, Milwaukee, Wisconsin 53233.

5. *To End War*, revised edition (New York, 1971); inquiries should be directed to the World Without War Council, 1730 Grove Street, Berkeley, California 94709.

6. Inquiries and information should be directed to the Center for Peace Studies, Warren F. Kuehl, director, University of Akron, Akron, Ohio 44304.

Was the Cold War Necessary? The Revisionist Challenge to Consensus History

Norman M. Wilensky

Nearly ten years ago, seventy-five distinguished students of American history participated in a poll measuring the performance of thirty-one presidents from George Washington to Dwight Eisenhower. Each participant in the poll helped to place the presidents into five general categories: "Great," "Near Great," "Average," "Below Average" and "Failure." One of the surprise rankings was the "Near Great" mark accorded to Harry Truman, ninth on the list. Only the five "Great" presidents—Lincoln, Washington, Franklin Roosevelt, Wilson and Jefferson—and three "Near Great" executives—Jackson, Theodore Roosevelt and Polk—preceded Truman. John Adams and Grover Cleveland, who immediately followed Truman, completed the "Near Great" group.

What qualities and achievements elevated Truman above many other presidents? He was, according to these historians, a strong executive who acted masterfully and farsightedly in foreign affairs. Summarizing the poll for his fellow historians, Arthur M. Schlesinger, Sr. noted that Truman "discharged impressively the awesome obligations devolving on the United States as the leader of the free world in the cold war with Soviet Imperialism." The Truman Doctrine, the Marshall Plan, the Berlin airlift, the Point Four program and the intervention in Korea "all constituted landmarks in an assumption of global responsibilities undreamed of only a few years before." Yet, less than a decade after the poll, this estimate is being dramatically challenged by historians of the Cold War.[1]

A recent book sharply critical of Cold War policies as well as Truman's role is Rexford G. Tugwell's *Off Course: From Truman to Nixon*. Because of Tugwell's credentials—he was a member of Roosevelt's "Brain Trust" and he is the winner of two major prizes for the writing of history—his latest book demands serious attention. Using Roosevelt's record and his probable postwar plans as a measure, Tugwell weighs the presidents who came after FDR and, except for Kennedy who had too little time, he finds them wanting; Eisenhower and Johnson but especially Truman allowed the nation to go "off course." "It had taken only two years after Roosevelt's death, and with Truman's mismanagement," Tugwell writes, "to turn two great victorious allied powers into aggressive enemies."[2] Far from praising the Truman Doctrine and the Marshall Plan as masterful or farsighted, Tugwell condemns them as the start of the costly and ineffective policy of containment. Although Tugwell admits that Truman cannot be blamed alone for the vast misfortunes of containment, he holds him responsible for the early phases of the Cold War, when the U.S.S.R. and China became America's enemies. That, Tugwell feels, "may be the most serious criticism that can be made of any American President except Buchanan, who allowed the Civil War to develop." Truman "was the President who kept on his desk that inscribed motto saying 'the buck stops here.' He cannot be exonerated; nor, to do him justice, would he want to be."[3]

Truman falls unfortunately short as Tugwell contrasts him with Roosevelt. Roosevelt understood the Russian wartime trauma, Tugwell insists, and he shared the Soviet fear of German recovery. Thus he allowed the Russians to fight the last battle for Berlin and he suggested the four-power occupation in order to keep Germany in disciplined subjection for as long as necessary. Other questions having to do with Eastern Europe remained to be settled, but Roosevelt felt he could handle them even though he foresaw a difficult time with the Russians, weary from war and suspicious of their capitalist allies. It was FDR's great attribute, says Tugwell, that he was an experimenter, not much worried if things went wrong temporarily. Roosevelt felt that something else could be tried until a tolerable situation was achieved. But when Roosevelt suddenly died Truman was "hopelessly unready." He had neither Roosevelt's sympathetic knowledge of Russian fears nor the ability to handle situations in flux. Indeed, nothing was tentative to the new president. "Truman not only considered any decision final, but belligerently regarded this as a virtue. It was his executive method. The way he put it was that he slept well after it was done and woke up to something else."[4] For Roosevelt, on the other hand, nothing was ever quite done; adjustments always had to be made. If Truman did not explicitly abandon Roosevelt's conception, Tugwell asserts that he did nothing to effectuate it. Almost from the outset of his presidency, Truman showed that implacable hostility toward the U.S.S.R. that "became the central principle of American policy in direct contravention of the Roosevelt strategy he professed to be following."[5]

Tugwell believes that Truman made five egregious mistakes, all of which reversed Roosevelt's policy and led to the Cold War.[6] The first mistake was the dropping of the atomic bombs on Hiroshima and Nagasaki. Tugwell suspects that issues other than Japanese defeat entered into the calculations to use the bomb. Perhaps the bomb was approved more easily because the Japanese were not white. Or perhaps it was used to prevent the Russians from participating in the Japanese defeat. Whatever the reasons, "they cannot have rested on saving American lives as Truman would persist in saying to the end of his life."

Disarmament was the second mistake. In the effort to control nuclear weapons, the opportunity to reach agreement was wasted as the Americans, who could have afforded to be generous, were instead irreversibly offensive. So the time passed when the threat of nuclear war might have been contained. "Opportunity for a mistake of this colossal size is not given to many men," Tugwell comments. "It was given to Truman, and it must be said that he made the most of it."

Containment is the third mistake since, Tugwell suggests, such policies as NATO only provided the Soviet Union with reason to build a vast new military, to hold tight to Eastern Europe and to penetrate into other areas in the Mediterranean and Asia. It might be, Tugwell concludes, that from the Russian view containment can be seen as a favorable policy.

Korea, the fourth mistake, was strategically unsound. Probably the Russians were not challenging the United States in this area which was only on the periphery of the American sphere of influence. But American intervention occurred under such a misapprehension, an error that ended as an occupation which had to be maintained for years.

Finally, Tugwell feels that assisting the French in Indo-China was Truman's fifth mistake. In Asia the pursuit of containment began by helping the French to re-establish their colonial power as the Japanese withdrew from Indo-China. In terms of what Roosevelt hoped to accomplish, Tugwell feels that this was about as complete a reversal as could possibly be imagined.

Could Truman's mistakes have been avoided? Yes, says Tugwell, if it is assumed that Russia and China could have been induced to remain allies for peace as they had been for war. Even if Roosevelt had been unable to deal sensitively with the Russians, Tugwell is certain that "Truman did not—and all his life was proud that he had not conceded anything."[7] Furthermore, the policy of confrontation with Russia, once begun, proved difficult for Truman's successors to abandon. Its costs by 1970 were a hundred thousand American lives and over a hundred billion dollars, a price hardly worthwhile, Tugwell insists, if it is suspected that Roosevelt, or other statesmen, might have made it unnecessary. "Seldom had people paid a higher price in dissension at home and lost opportunity abroad for decisions made in pursuit of futile aims."[8]

There exists a marked contrast between Tugwell's critical position in 1971 and those orthodox histories of the Cold War written in the late 1940's and the 1950's. The Soviet-American tensions of those years seemed to support the official version of the Cold War—that Russia was aggressive and that American firmness was therefore necessary. The breakdown of the Yalta agreements which had promised postwar cooperation, Russia's unwillingness to grant free elections in Eastern Europe, the menace to Greece, the coup in Czechoslovakia and the Berlin crisis lent credence to the idea that Communist ideology and ruthlessness were responsible for the break between East and West after 1945.

While the orthodox version of the Cold War stemmed partly from events abroad, it came as well from the liberal reaction to right-wing domestic politics. The fall of nationalist China and the Alger Hiss case added weight to Senator Joseph McCarthy's charges of subversion in the Roosevelt-Truman administrations. The right wing accusation was that America was losing the Cold War either because the Russians had duped American leaders or because traitors had betrayed the United States. Liberal historians felt, however, that the right wing wrongly assumed that American actions were decisive in shaping the postwar world when from the beginning the initiative in the Cold War had been in Moscow. The war itself, and particularly the need for Russian assistance, had left the U.S.S.R. in its dominant position in Eastern Europe. Nothing Roosevelt did at Yalta, or Truman at Potsdam, could have altered Russia's determined course. Containment was, therefore, not only a logical response to Soviet aggression, it was also a most successful postwar decision.

Another factor contributing to the orthodox interpretation of the Cold War was the conservative view of the American past that came to dominate historical writing during the 1950's. Historians of that generation found consensus and continuity in the American story and, along with other intellectuals, they celebrated the accomplishments of democratic capitalism and of a liberalism that seemed to have triumphed dramatically during the New Deal. As one historian has noted: "In their work, as well as in their public activities, some [liberals] even came to identify the protection of freedom with the advancement of the state's interests."9

Illustrative of the historians of the Fifties, Arthur Schlesinger, Jr., has reminisced recently about his mood when in 1949 he wrote *The Vital Center*.10 " . . . in the early stages of the Marshall Plan," he says, "I was still filled with the excitement engendered by that brilliant, generous and now, alas, forgotten undertaking. Moreover, the astonishing re-election of President Truman in November 1948 re-inforced one's belief in the prospects of liberal democracy; we regarded this as a triumphant vindication, against all odds and predictions, of Franklin Roosevelt's New Deal." Schlesinger also recalls that at the same time the onset of the Cold War forced the American liberal community to confront the phenomenon of Communism with more precision and responsibility than it had done. He wonders, too, whether the members of the younger generation who read *The Vital Center* will be surprised at the concern devoted to the problem of Communism. If so, he says, they must make the effort to put themselves back into the historical situation of the 1940's. "Perhaps," Schlesinger suggests, "it would help if, every time they see the word 'communism' in this book, they would read 'Stalinism.'" Stalin was running a cruel and terrifying dictatorship and "Communism in the 1970s is a very different thing from communism in the 1940s." Schlesinger is well aware that in the 1950's obsessive anti-Communism seized portions of the American government, and blinded many American leaders to the significance of the break-up of the world Communist movement which led the United States into "the frightful catastrophe of the Viet Nam War." But he still believes that it is essential to distinguish between rational and obsessive anti-Communism. "I note in the new generation a tendency to regard anti-Communism as *per se* an evil," Schlesinger writes. "I can only say that I have not the slightest regret for the campaign my contemporaries waged against Stalinism . . . ."

The orthodox interpretation of the 1950's still appears in the main in such widely read textbooks as those of John Lukacs and John Spanier, and since 1965 Charles Burton Marshall, Dexter Perkins and David Rees have continued to express the conventional view of the Cold War.[11] But other historians have rejected various aspects of the official doctrine. Following the example of the "realist" school of history established in George F. Kennan's *American Diplomacy* (1951), these historians question the fears and assumptions that guided United States policy.[12] They are critical of the legalistic-moralistic American tradition which prevented American leaders from understanding balance-of-power politics. In particular, they feel that American policy-makers did not understand that Stalin was more of a realist, determined to follow a spheres-of-influence policy, than he was an expansionist. Furthermore, containment lacked clear objectives which led the United States to overextend itself in a new policy of globalism after the Korean War. Nevertheless, these historians accept the basic premise of American policy after 1945, that containment was a proper response to Communist aggression. They are critical, not radical historians.

In disagreement with the realist and orthodox historians are a number of revisionists who have indicted the United States for precipitating the Cold War. They follow the lead of Denna Fleming who attributed Soviet suspicion and misbehavior to western aggressiveness in his book *The Cold War and Its Origins, 1917-1950* (1961). These revisionists emphasize that the justification for containment, the Soviet menace, did not exist at war's end and that weakness dictated Russian cooperation with the West. Of course, Western leaders, implacably hostile toward Communism, could not see the reality of Stalin's position, that as an ally Russia had the right to ask for friendly buffer states on her eastern border. Rather than accommodate the Russians, then, the United States used its overwhelming power to protest Russian hegemony in Eastern Europe and thereby placed Stalin in a defensive position which left him

164

no choice but to accept the Cold War. Furthermore for revisionists, who see a definite relationship between American domestic needs and her foreign policy, American imperialism is largely responsible for the Cold War. The Soviet-American confrontation followed American efforts to expand into various areas of the world, especially Eastern Europe, in order to meet domestic economic demands.

This reduction of the Cold War to economic causes has produced a more radical interpretation of American history. For some revisionists their criticism of American foreign policy is part of their reevaluation of domestic liberal institutions. They find both anti-Communist action abroad and reform efforts at home to be the natural result of an industrial society attempting to rationalize its own corporate capitalism. One important expression is that of William Appleman Williams in *The Tragedy of American Diplomacy* (1959). Williams argues that the United States since 1898 has deliberately continued the "open door" policy of extending American influence around the world. Since capitalism must have ever-expanding foreign markets to survive, this has even meant the expansion of the "open door" principle into areas under Soviet control. The Cold War, then, is only the latest phase in the whole course of twentieth-century American diplomacy.

At first, Williams' radicalism alienated the academic establishment, but his influence on other revisionists has become undeniably significant. David Horowitz in *The Free World Colossus: A Critique of American Foreign Policy in the Cold War* (1965), in basic agreement with Williams, characterizes American policy as counterrevolutionary because it was committed to the defense of a global status quo. He judges that the main purpose of containment was to crush any radical movement from threatening the will of the United States. In Gabriel Kolko's *The Politics of War: The World and United States Foreign Policy, 1943-1945* (1968), policies that once appeared enlightened—the Marshall Plan for European recovery and the Point Four program for aid to underdeveloped countries—seem almost imperialistic. He feels that the Cold War arose because Russia refused to let Eastern Europe become a part of the American colonial system. The disquieting theme that the origins of the Cold War lie in atomic blackmail elevates Gar Alperovitz's *Atomic Diplomacy: Hiroshima and Potsdam* (1965) to an influential place among revisionist histories.[13] Although his critique of liberal institutions is less radical than others, his careful scholarship adds strength to his conclusion that Truman got tough with Russia because the atomic bomb strengthened his hand. Truman even delayed his trip to Potsdam until the atomic bomb was developed, Alperovitz believes, in order to use the power of the new weapon to influence the Soviet Union.[14]

The nature of such criticism has understandably brought forth a sharp reaction. One historian, William W. McDonald, has complained that revisionists are guilty of reversing the roles of heroes and villains in the

Cold War. The revisionists "suffer from what one might describe as ideological myopia: American diplomats can do no right; Russian leaders can do no wrong." He also feels that the theme of America's "Open Door 'imperial expansion'" is highly debatable and that the revisionists have not shown that postwar coexistence could have been anything but antagonistic. Irwin Unger has called the revisionists bad-tempered, angry dissenters from America's current foreign and domestic policies. Charles S. Maier feels that the Marxian basis of the third-world perspective has serious analytical deficiencies. The Cold War represents to revisionists "a continuation of an international civil war in which Russian and later peasant revolutionary forces have successfully championed the cause of the oppressed in all countries, while the United States has become the leader of the world's elites." This, he asserts, overestimates the fragility of the capitalist order and overvalues the American contribution to counterrevolution as well as the will to impose it. Arthur Schlesinger, Jr., announced that the time had come to blow the whistle before the outburst of revisionism regarding the origins of the Cold War went much further. But he could not "blow the whistle," says Christopher Lasch. Schlesinger backed away somewhat from his position, admitting that although the revisionist interpretations did not really stick, revisionism was a necessary part of the historical process. ". . . it is good to know," chides Lasch, "that revisionists may now presumably continue their work (inconsequential as it may eventually prove to be) without fear of being whistled to a stop by the referee."[15]

Revisionists have, indeed, continued their work because the forces behind the reappraisal of American foreign policy and the origins of the Cold War are so great. Much of the impact on revisionists comes from the Vietnam war, which is for these historians the logical and unfortunate outcome of American Cold War policy. As Charles S. Maier suggests, Vietnam has so eroded national self-conceptions that many assumptions behind traditional Cold War history have been cast into doubt.[16] Also important as an influence on revisionists is their conviction that there is a moral issue in Vietnam. One historian has written: "The United States Government has tried hard to cover its moral nakedness in Vietnam. But the signs of failure grow day by day."[17]

What history is and what role the historian should play have an important bearing on the revisionist critique of the Cold War. Revisionists are convinced that the writing of history should not be used, as they feel it has since World War II, to buttress American policy; that has led to a distortion of research. Revisionists look instead, notes Walter LaFeber, for a vision of the past that will help them remake the present and the future. They hope, too, that history will offer a reinforcement of current moral values. "A faith in history is perhaps the most important and far-reaching of the revisionist views," LaFeber writes.[18]

A striking example of the revisionist concern for the proper use of history is Howard Zinn's *The Politics of History* (1970), which calls for "a higher proportion of socially relevant, value-motivated, action-inducing historical work." ". . . in a world where children are still not safe from starvation or bombs," Zinn asks, "should not the historian thrust himself and his writing into history, on behalf of goals in which he deeply believes? Are we historians not humans first, and scholars because of that?"[19]

Zinn deplores the dominant mood in historical writing in the United States which avoids direct confrontation of contemporary problems. Out of the enormous energy devoted to the past, only a tiny amount is directed to the solution of vital problems. Look at the pages of the historical reviews, Zinn admonishes, or at the tens of thousands of historical scholars who gather annually to hear hundreds of papers on scattered topics, yet "there has been no move to select a problem—poverty, race prejudice, the war in Vietnam, alternative methods of social change —for concentrated attention by some one conference."[20] Historians must challenge the rules which sustain the wasting of knowledge. No longer, Zinn maintains, can historians hide behind "disinterested scholarship" and "objectivity" and "publish while others perish." Historians, Zinn says, need to become critics rather than apologists and perpetrators of their culture.[21]

Zinn offers five ways in which history can be useful for those who "would rather have their writing guided by human aspiration than by professional habit."[22] History is not inevitably useful, Zinn admits, "But history can untie our minds, our bodies, our disposition to move—to engage life rather than contemplating it as an outsider." It can make us aware of the silent voices of the past and the present; it "can reveal how ideas are stuffed into us by the powers of our time. . . ." And, Zinn adds, history "can inspire us by recalling those few moments in the past when men did behave like human beings, to prove it is *possible*."[23] The guidelines for revisionist history which Zinn offers support LaFeber's contention that history is the way out for intellectuals who want change yet think it improbable in the near future.[24] The issue between revisionist and other historians of the Cold War is not the thoroughness of research. "Our values should determine the *questions* we ask in scholarly inquiry," Zinn states, "but not the answers."[25]

The age and educational experience of a number of leading revisionists also figure in their approach to history. Coming to intellectual maturity during the Cold War, young historians broke with the consensus of the 1950's as they became aware of poverty, racism, civil rights and Vietnam. One such group published essays in vigorous criticism of the historical consensus in *Towards a New Past: Dissenting Essays in American History*, edited by Barton J. Bernstein. At the time of the book's publication in 1967, the average age of the eleven contributors was only thirty-three. The authors sought explicitly "to make the past speak to the present, to ask questions that have a deep-rooted moral and political relevance." "... we have, by necessity," Bernstein wrote, "moved beyond objective history to the realm of values. In this venture we are following the practice, though not necessarily the prescription, of earlier generations of historians, and responding in a modest way to the call issued a few years ago to move 'beyond consensus.' "[26]

Some of the young revisionists of the 1960's reflect the influence of the so-called "Wisconsin School" of history. For instance, Gar Alperovitz, Lloyd C. Gardner, David Horowitz, Gabriel Kolko, Walter LaFeber and Robert F. Smith[27] received at least some of their training at the University of Wisconsin, where William Appleman Williams taught history. LaFeber suggests that part of the revisionist-orthodox split is along Eastern-Midwestern lines, and both he and Bernstein believe revisionists have been influenced by Midwestern populism and progressivism. Like Charles Beard, historian of an earlier generation, young revisionists trained or reared in the Midwest stress the impact of domestic economics on foreign policy, applaud the influence of public opinion on policy-making, condemn the concentration of power in a strong presidency and emphasize the relevance of history to the present.[28]

That the impact of the revisionist position is upon us is evidenced by many of the books displayed at the recent American Historical Association convention. Revisionism is in paperback as well as in anthology form, and it is sure to infiltrate history courses even at the introductory level. An excellent example of a collection is that edited by James V. Compton, *America and the Origins of the Cold War* (1972), which presents the views of both orthodox and revisionist historians. *Trends and Tragedies in American Foreign Policy* (1971), edited by Michael Parenti, examines "some long-muted dissenting notions and heretical views about the intent, purposes, and unhappy consequences of American foreign policy and the interests that shape that policy." Loren Baritz, general editor of Wiley's "Problems in American History," has added to that series Walter LaFeber, ed., *The Origins of the Cold War, 1941-1947* (1971). Irwin Unger has a broad scope in his collection *Beyond Liberalism: The New Left Views American History* (1971). A unique anthology is that edited by Thomas G. Paterson, *Cold War Critics: Alternatives to American Foreign Policy in the Truman Years* (1971). This is the first book to explore the beliefs and ideas of those who challenged American foreign policy during the early years of the Cold War. A book that focuses on individual policymakers during the Cold War is Lloyd C. Gardner, *Architects of Illusion: Men and Ideas in American Foreign Policy, 1941-1949* (1970). Two new works which approach the origins of the Cold War by reassessing Truman's rhetoric and policy decisions are Richard M. Freeland, *The Truman Doctrine and the Origins of McCarthyism: Foreign Policy, Domestic Politics, and Internal Security, 1946-1948* (1971), and Athan Theoharis, *Harry S. Truman and the*

Origins of McCarthyism (1971). Two other new books which promise to add to the revisionist critique are Jerald A. Combs, ed., *Nationalist, Realist, and Radical: Three Views of America's Past Diplomacy* (1972), and Joyce Kolko and Gabriel Kolko, *The Limits of Power: The World and United States Foreign Policy, 1945-1954* (1972). These are but some of the current books which indicate the growing popularity of the revisionist assessment of the Cold War.

The forces behind revisionism—the Vietnam war, the youth of critics, the new faith in history as a tool for change—have challenged the orthodox consensus, producing a great historiographical debate that will continue. New historians, trained in the late 1960's and 1970's, a period of rampant social unrest, are likely to accept revisionism, as LaFeber believes, not as an aberration but as logical and as fact. Christopher Lasch is sure, too, that increasingly William Appleman Williams, so influential on the radicals of the 1960's as well as on other revisionists, will become uncomfortable among those historians who demand that America rapidly rid itself of racism, poverty, imperialistic wars and ecological problems which threaten posterity. Whatever the specific course of argument, in the foreseeable future historians will have to come to grips with revisionism which has shattered so many of the assumptions of traditional Cold War history.

University of Florida

notes

1. Arthur M. Schlesinger, "Our Presidents: A Rating by 75 Historians," *New York Times Magazine*, July 29, 1962, 12. Truman is also included among the top presidents in the second edition of *America's Ten Greatest Presidents*. Richard S. Kirkendall has written an essay which adds Truman to the original list, thereby justifying the new title, *America's Eleven Greatest Presidents* (1971). Anticipating criticism, the editor, Morton Borden, writes: "To be sure, the inclusion of Harry Truman will be deplored by some—particularly the new breed of younger leftist scholars—but they would probably disagree with most of the selections." See p. viii.

2. Rexford G. Tugwell, *Off Course: From Truman to Nixon* (1971), 203.

3. *Ibid.*, 205. The poll of presidents, in agreement with Tugwell's judgment, ranked Buchanan 29th, last in the "Below Average" category, barely ahead of the two "Failures," Grant and Harding.

4. *Ibid.*, 201. Tugwell also says of Truman: "Someone must have told him, or he must have read—he was an assiduous student of American history and often expressed admiration for James K. Polk—that strong Presidents acted decisively. They were responsible; they make up their minds; they must not appear to have doubts. It was better to make mistakes than to hesitate and give the impression of uncertainty." See p. 222. The poll of presidents ranked Polk eighth and Truman ninth and for the same general accomplishments: forceful use of the executive office, especially in foreign affairs. Tugwell would no doubt disagree with this measure of presidential greatness.

5. *Ibid.*, 218.

6. "How It Went Wrong," Part V of *Off Course*, deals with each mistake. See pp. 181-222.

7. *Ibid.*, 214. Commenting on another recent account of Truman's presidency, Tugwell adds: "So, in fact, was Acheson. His *Present at the Creation* was one long rooster-crow over the results of his hard-line policy."

8. *Ibid.*, 205.

9. Barton J. Bernstein, ed., *Towards a New Past: Dissenting Essays in American History* (1969), viii.

10. Arthur Schlesinger, Jr., " 'The Vital Center' Reconsidered," *Encounter*, XXXV (September, 1970), 89-93.

11. John Lukacs, *A History of the Cold War* (1961); John Spanier, *American Foreign Policy Since World War II* (1967); Charles Burton Marshall, *The Cold War: A Concise History*

(1965); Dexter Perkins, *The Diplomacy of a New Age* (1967); David Rees, *The Age of Containment: The Cold War, 1945-1965* (1967).

12. A few examples are: Norman A. Graebner, *Cold War Diplomacy* (1962); Louis J. Halle, *The Cold War As History* (1967); William H. McNeill, *America, Britain, and Russia* (1953); and Paul Seabury, *The Rise and Decline of the Cold War* (1967).

13. Other revisionists of note are Walter LaFeber, *America, Russia, and the Cold War, 1945-1966* (1967); Ronald Steel, *Pax Americana: The Cold War Empire* (1967); and Carl Oglesby and Richard Shaull, *Containment and Change* (1967).

14. Martin J. Sherwin of Cornell has challenged Alperovitz in a paper, "U.S. Atomic Energy Policy and Diplomacy," delivered at a session of the American Historical Association on December 29, 1971. Sherwin stated that the dropping of the bomb did not alter policy; instead, it reinforced an atomic diplomacy developed by FDR that was hostile to the Soviet Union. While Truman had some choices open to him, the legacy of Roosevelt did not leave him a free agent. The thrust of Sherwin's remarks accentuates the American responsibility for the Cold War by enlarging Roosevelt's role. Thus, Sherwin revises the revisionists without discrediting them entirely.

15. William W. McDonald, "The Revisionist Cold War Historians," *The Midwest Quarterly*, XI (October, 1969), 47-48; Charles S. Maier, "Revisionism and the Interpretation of Cold War Origins," in James V. Compton, ed., *America and the Origins of the Cold War* (1972), 166-167; Christopher Lasch, "The Cold War, Revisited and Re-Visioned," *New York Times Magazine*, January 14, 1968, 26-27.

16. Maier, "Revisionism," 157.

17. Howard Zinn, *The Politics of History* (1970), 222. Chapter 13, "Vietnam the Moral Equation," contains a good discussion on this issue.

18. Walter LaFeber, "War: Cold," in James V. Compton, ed., *America and the Origins of the Cold War* (1972), 184, 175.

19. Zinn, *The Politics of History*, 1-2.

20. *Ibid.*, 23. The most recent annual meeting of the American Historical Association, held in December of 1971, supports Zinn's contention. A few of the 129 sessions did touch on relevant topics, however. For example, the revisionists were much in evidence at the session, "What is to be Done? An Agenda for Peace Research in History." Wilbur Jacobs of the University of California, Santa Barbara, called for a "radical, non-objective, new peace history." "It is almost our patriotic duty," he said, "to understand the forces threatening mankind." Charles Barker of Johns Hopkins insisted that "peace history is value-inspired history."

21. *Ibid.*, 5, 13.

22. *Ibid.*, 36. The five rules are discussed in chapter three, "What is Radical History?" They are: (1) "We can intensify, expand, and sharpen our perception of how bad things are for the victims of the world." (2) "We can expose the pretensions of governments to either neutrality or beneficence." (3) "We can expose the ideology that pervades our culture—using 'ideology' in Mannheim's sense: rationale for the going order." (4) "We can recapture those few moments in the past which show the possibility of a better way of life than that which has dominated the earth thus far." (5) "We can show how good social movements can go wrong, how leaders can betray their followers, how rebels can become bureaucrats, how ideals can become frozen and reified."

23. *Ibid.*, 54-55.

24. LaFeber, "War: Cold," 181.

25. Zinn, *The Politics of History*, 7.

26. Bernstein, *Towards a New Past*, xiii.

27. At the time of the present writing (1972), the oldest of these men is forty-two while the youngest is thirty-three.

28. It must be admitted, however, that other revisionists have an Eastern background. As Warren Cohen of Michigan State noted during the session on peace research at the recent American Historical Association meeting in New York: "I was born in this city and I didn't need William Appleman Williams or Gabriel Kolko to know the importance of economic interests."

Internationalism as a Current in the Peace Movement: A Symposium

It is apparent from the literature on the peace movement and diplomatic thought throughout this century that an exploration of the sometimes contradictory use of the word internationalism is in order. Not only has it been used for different purposes by competing factions of the antiwar movement and political leaders, but it has differing connotations for historians. This symposium is a contribution to a discussion of the term. Instead of asking for an abstract formulation, the editors invited several scholars to consider the roles of internationalist ideas in the peace movement in the hope that a functional definition might emerge, one which might stimulate formal analyses and eventuate in a working understanding. By way of opening the discussion, the editor asked Sondra Herman, the author of *Eleven Against War: Studies in American Internationalist Thought, 1898-1921* (Stanford, 1969) to identify some conceptual problems that arise from her analysis.

Sondra Herman

University of California,

Santa Cruz

From the last decade of the nineteenth century through the first world war of the twentieth, a small but prominent group of American intellectuals and peace advocates argued for a distinctive approach to foreign relations which they called internationalism. They represented a minority of the articulate public, probably a minority of the peace societies. They advanced ideas that were being heard also in Europe, and they debated the forms of international organization for years before President Woodrow Wilson took up their cause. When Wilson did use international ideals in his explanation of American mediation policy, and later of American war aims, he adjusted them considerably to the national interest.

These assumptions which touched so lightly national policy-making are familiar ones; progress toward peace is a real possibility, the internationalists held, and imperial rivalries intensified by the communications revolution have made international organization a necessity. In spite of the political independence of nations, which is natural, their economic, social and moral interdependence require new forms of political organization. Balance of power diplomacy, the traditional statecraft, cannot prevent wars.

Beyond these beliefs and a general sense of obligation to educate the public to them through concrete plans and models, the internationalists were united by very little. Specifically, the internationalists divided into two groups during the First World War.

One wing, the political internationalists (or institutionalists) advocated the development of legal machinery for the peaceful settlement of disputes. Some proposed a league to compel consideration of international disputes. They conceived of the world as an atomistic polity in which nations pursued their interests competitively. They believed that a world court of a League to Enforce Peace could civilize the natural aggressiveness of men, and that the rivalrous relations of nations could have a peaceful evolution.

The other wing of the movement included community internationalists. Although they did not ignore the possibilities of juridical and political organization, they did assert that such formal arrangements in themselves could never prevent wars. What was needed was the development of a more organic world consciousness, a sense of international community among the peoples of different nations. These community internationalists proposed such economic and social changes as the disallowance of trade advantages, international regulation of the world's food supply, international insurance for natural disasters, international control of the arms industry and of former colonies, and international health and educational programs. They believed that such activity would undermine contentious nationalism which itself was the distraint of collective security; but they did not say how the antagonistic nations could be persuaded to adopt such an approach.

The first question that arises about these two forms of internationalism is: How did the advocates of one type differ from the advocates of the other? I believe that the supporters of the legal-political methods—men such as Nicholas Murray Butler, Elihu Root and leaders of the League to Enforce Peace—had a different world view from that of community internationalists such as Jane Addams, Josiah Royce and Thorstein Veblen. The institutionalists held to conservative Darwinism, the Anglo-American understanding, and belief in American democratic capitalism, while the communalists expressed many doubts about the competitive ethic. The communalists interpreted human nature in more dynamic terms than the institutionalists did, believing that men defined themselves largely through changing relations with others. In brief, forms of internationalism reflected more general social philosophies.

Finally, it appears as though the social position of the communalists differed considerably from that of the institutionalists. The political internationalists either headed large organizations or associated themselves with the government. They thought in terms of making policy affecting many other people. Community internationalists identified themselves with the international community of scholarship or with the disinherited.

Applying this distinction to the history of American internationalism since the turn of the century raises questions such as the following:

1. How was the growth of internationalism just before and during World War I related to the expansion of American power, on the one hand, and the threat of revolution, on the other? For political internationalists the League of Nations became a vehicle of American influence in the world and the "road away from revolution." Was resistance to substantive changes in power relationships among nations, or among classes implicit in political internationalism from the beginning? Was political internationalism fundamentally an elaborate form of *Pax Americana*? Political internationalists believed that the spread of Anglo-American institutions and of capitalism aided the causes of peace in the world. Many internationalists were also enthusiastic expansionists in 1898, and this form of internationalism increased markedly with the growth of American economic influence abroad. On the other hand, there is little evidence that the institutionalists wanted the United States to become the world's policeman. They emphasized *collective* responsibility for peace-keeping.

2. Was internationalism a revolt against the nation-state? In particular, were the communalists seeking unrealizable goals? In some respects the communalists appear realistic. They understand very well the exacerbated nationalism of the war years. Yet they were overly hopeful of transcending national loyalties, if only certain conditions were met. Veblen's plan for a league of neutrals and Royce's plan for international insurance were never tested, but to some extent Jane Addams' proposals have been fulfilled in the work of U.N. specialized agencies. Do people in poorer areas of the world identify more closely with the U.N. under the impact of these agencies than citizens of richer nations do? Is there any evidence to suggest that extensive activity by world organizations on behalf of human welfare weakens fundamental national distinctions?

3. Is there evidence that fundamental positions in relation to foreign policy have social correlates? Is identification with an "inner" group or with the "establishment" important in establishing fundamentally conservative approaches to foreign policy?

4. What beliefs and identifications distinguished the American pacifist from the American internationalist since World War I? This is a difficult question in view of the fact that some members of the peace movement claimed the position of both pacifism and internationalism, but it is important in order to establish the legitimacy of their claims. Some plans

for international organization required the international use of force, and many internationalists willingly went to war in 1917 and 1941, in Korea and even in Vietnam. How exactly does their position differ from that of pacifists who also profess international goals?

5. Why did internationalism have such a limited appeal? Community internationalism hardly seemed to have a public at all, and political internationalism only developed a significant one when the League to Enforce Peace was organized, and more particularly when Wilson lent the cause his eloquent voice, before World War I. Why did internationalists fail to educate the public for the long-range commitment that internationalism requires?

6. How did internationalist movements abroad compare with American movements? Were they stronger by virtue of their association with socialism?

7. Did the Cold War kill American internationalism? Belief in the future of the United Nations appeared, superficially at least, quite strong and popular after World War II. Was this more than an emotional reaction to the war itself? Was it an acceptance of American responsibility in the world or an escape from it? When did this belief in effective U.N. action disappear? Did Americans begin to identify American police action with internationalism around the time of the Korean war? Has internationalism today become equivalent to American intervention, in popular thinking? There is a live peace movement today, of course, but is it characterized by the old-fashioned faith in international organization or international community?

Manfred Jonas
Union College

America's sense of uniqueness and of destiny, coupled with the facts of international life in the nineteenth century, promoted that unilateralism in foreign relations which is generally labelled isolationism. Paradoxically, it also encouraged speculation on the gradual evolution of a "United States of the World," in which nations would join together, democratically and under a system of law, much in the manner of the American colonies in 1776 and with similarly beneficial results. Historians, long fascinated by the isolationist tradition, have recently begun to turn their attention to this "internationalist" component of American thought and are attempting to trace its manifestations.

The results of their investigations, though often only implicit, are clear enough: aside from pacifist visionaries like William Ladd and Elihu Burritt, dabblers in international relations like Andrew Carnegie and Edward Ginn, and theorists like Josiah Royce and Thorstein Veblen whose primary concerns really lay elsewhere, there were virtually no prominent Americans prior to the First World War who can be meaningfully described as internationalists, and there was certainly no internationalist movement of any significance.

Benjamin Franklin, to be sure, published Pierre-André Gargaz's scheme for a European union with an approving introduction in the 1780's, and even speculated about an Anglo-French-American compact. Fifty years later, John Quincy Adams, John C. Calhoun and Daniel Webster, among others, judged the American Peace Society's essay contest on the subject of a Congress of Nations. Charles Sumner championed arbitration as a prelude to international confederation in the 1870's, and Andrew Dickson White and Captain Alfred Thayer Mahan led to the Hague Conference of 1899 an American delegation which carried with it a plan for the establishment of an international court. But all of these men would rank very high on any list of American nationalists, and their "internationalism" must therefore be taken *cum granum salis.*

The fact that they and other prominent and influential Americans lent their names and their efforts to schemes looking toward the formation of international assemblies and tribunals during the nineteenth century is actually neither very surprising nor especially significant. The American experiment, after all, was one of parliamentary democracy under law, and the dynamic of American society was provided by the belief that this experiment could be made to work at home and serve as a model for the rest of the world. Americans, moreover, looked favorably on the peaceful resolution of international disputes because they believed the maintenance of an extensive military establishment to be destructive of democratic government. In the abstract, therefore, the setting up of parliamentary or judicial bodies which might deal with disputes among nations as Congress and the Supreme Court dealt with disputes among the several states had considerable appeal, as did the notion that an international community and a recognized body of international law should be developed.

But Americans during the nineteenth century also had their sights set resolutely inward, and considered the problems of the world only incidentally, when at all. Even within the reform movement, the American Peace Society, the sole group with international overtones, had both a smaller following and a lesser impact than did organizations concerned with more immediately relevant issues such as education, prison reform and the abolition of slavery. The establishment of national consciousness and national unity, the maintenance of these in the face of conflicting sectional interests, particularly with regard to slavery, and the "road to reunion" after the Civil War were the central American concerns. In this context, "internationalism," though philosophically appealing, could be pursued only so long as it appeared to be an extension of, rather than an alternative to, the pervasive nationalism. Speculation about a "parliament of man" was possible, as was the advocacy of arbitration, but only so long as the results, both actual and expected, were seen as serving the national interest. What was pursued, therefore, was not internationalism at all, but simply a geographically expanded nationalism.

When America turned physically outward near the end of the nineteenth century, the situation did not change. The visible and tangible success of the American experiment, when measured in territory, wealth and power, heightened both national pride and national self-confidence. The United States entered the world arena after the Spanish-American War more convinced than ever that its ideas and institutions, or at least its version of Anglo-Saxon ideals and institutions, were destined to dominate the globe, and more confident than ever that this country could resolve any international problems it might encounter by itself and in its own way.

By expanding its trade and investments abroad and by becoming a factor in the power calculations of other nations, the United States was drawn increasingly into international discussions and contacts. Under the leadership of Theodore Roosevelt, who revelled in the limelight of the international stage, the United States mediated the Russo-Japanese War, sired the Algeciras Conference, promoted the Open Door in the Pacific, and claimed the role of international policeman in the Caribbean. But none of this should be confused with a turn to internationalism.

The archetypal American "internationalist" of these years, Henry Cabot Lodge, was an expansionist who recognized that American isolation had ended and, therefore, opted for a larger world role for the United States, flirted briefly with the League to Enforce Peace, argued eloquently that "nations must unite as men unite in order to preserve peace and order," and favored this country's "taking a suitable part and bearing a due responsibility in world affairs." But Lodge was primarily an American nationalist who fought the League of Nations because he correctly saw the conflict between the genuine internationalism inherent in the Covenant and his own views regarding national sovereignty and national independence. Indeed, the reservations he proposed were aimed directly at the elimination of those aspects of the League which might have placed international considerations above narrowly national concerns.

Woodrow Wilson and his followers, of course, were in theory prepared to give genuine internationalism a try, though it is doubtful whether even they would have been willing to surrender a significant portion of American sovereignty to·the League in actual practice. But it was precisely the internationalist character of the proposed world body, and the threat to the full and unimpeded exercise of national sovereignty which it represented, which made American participation unpalatable to a majority, not only of the Senate, but of the country as well. By contrast, American entry into the war itself, which could be justified in purely nationalistic terms, had won a far greater degree of acceptance.

The United States was prepared by 1919 for a certain amount of international cooperation, but on its own terms and within very narrow limits. It was willing to discuss matters of international concern with other powers, as it was to do at the Washington Conference of 1921, to participate in much, though by no means all, of the non-political work of the League, as it was to do increasingly during the 1920's, and to take the lead in a movement to outlaw war on moral grounds, so long as no positive action against future "outlaws" was specifically required. But it was not prepared at any time prior to 1940 to make binding commitments which suggested even remotely that this country would yield an iota of its sovereignty and independence to any international body or allow its policies to be directed in any way by the community of nations. As late as 1935, the United States rejected membership in the World Court, not because its sovereignty actually would have been impaired by such a step, but merely because joining might have opened the door, at least a little, to genuine internationalism.

Internationalism, if not actually a revolt against the nation-state, involves at the very least a rejection of the idea of absolute national sovereignty. As such it has been basically foreign to American thought. The establishment and maintenance of sovereignty was the keynote of Washington's Farewell Address and the basis for American actions certainly until World War II. Americans paid lip-service to internationalism on occasion, but generally envisaged nothing more than the voluntary cooperation of fully sovereign states, a visionary and unrealistic concept which masks the basic incompatibility of nationalism and internationalism. That a nation which, for nearly two centuries, only grudgingly yielded the alleged sovereignty of the individual states to the power of the national government should be unwilling to yield a portion of national sovereignty to an international organization is natural enough, particularly when no pressing reasons for doing otherwise could be convincingly advanced.

In practice, countries move toward internationalism only when there is either a widespread revulsion against nationalist excesses—as in Germany immediately following World War II, when a substantial number of the younger generation and even some of the political leaders began to see themselves consciously as "Europeans" rather than "Germans"—or when the belief is widely accepted that the nation alone lacks the power and the resources to protect its own interests effectively. Neither of these factors applied to the United States prior to 1940. As a result, the handful of philosophical internationalists could gain no following.

The expansionists, the advocates of a *Pax Americana,* and the believers in the natural spread of Anglo-Saxon institutions did not have to become political internationalists, and did not become so any more than did the "Hawks" of the 1960's. They could be, and largely were, ultra-nationalists profoundly suspicious of potential limitations on American sovereignty which might inhibit the developments they advocated. The pacifists, for their part, were internationalists only on those occasions when they regarded international commitments as a better guarantee than some form of isolation for the peace, not necessarily of the world, but of the United States. For most of them, these occasions were few and far between. And the great bulk of American leaders, and of the public, saw no need to embark on the troubled seas of internationalism so long as the security of this country was not directly threatened by events elsewhere in the world.

Internationalism on a substantial scale and of a sort that could be translated into policy developed in this country only after the fall of France raised the possibility of a physical threat to the United States which it would be difficult to counter unaided and alone. It was strengthened by the Pearl Harbor attack, the first foreign incursion on American soil since the War of 1812. This combination of events led not merely to entrance into war as in 1917, but, unlike in 1917-1920, to a general commitment to internationalism in some form. "This decision which we have made," Cordell Hull explained in 1944, ". . . was not a decision to make a mere sporadic effort. . . . We cannot move in and out of international cooperation and in and out of participation in the responsibilities of a member of the family of nations." The American commitment to the United Nations and to a long series of other international arrangements followed.

That commitment has survived the Cold War as well as the Vietnam tragedy. Indeed, a good case can be made that the "Doves" of the 1960's, the men now urging the United States to eschew the role of world policeman, including most of those frequently and erroneously dubbed "neo-isolationists," have a genuine internationalist outlook. They argue, after all, for the subordination of American power to the larger needs of the world community, for the substitution of joint action, within or without the United Nations, for unilateral American intervention, and for the realization that the United States alone—and the "alone" deserves special emphasis—cannot hope to solve all the world's problems. They are aware, moreover, that in the age of ballistic missiles and the hydrogen bomb, the United States can no longer assure its own safety without some international commitments.

The opposite of internationalism in terms of national conduct is unilateralism. The United States remained committed to unilateralism up to the Second World War. It opted for collective security after that, only to discover that the war had destroyed any meaningful "collective" and left this country in a dominant leadership role. Given the enormous power of the United States after 1945, the tendency to interpret internationalism simply as unilateralism on a global scale manifested itself at various times. To that tendency there is now substantial and effective opposition, spawned and sustained in large part by the unhappy consequences of American policy in Vietnam. The basis for a fruitful and genuine American internationalism therefore exists to a greater degree than ever before, and the discussion of its implications, in the realm of both theory and policy, is timely and essential.

| Robert A. Divine
University of Texas,
Austin | I believe that Professor Herman's distinction between political and community internationalists is valid for the period of World War II with which I am most familiar, but that it is of only limited significance. |

Certainly one can identify community internationalists for the war years such as Michael Straight, editor of the *New Republic* and author of *Make This the Last War;* Wendell Willkie, whose *One World* preached a popular if fuzzy brand of international cooperation; and Henry Wallace, perhaps the most eloquent preacher of a genuine world community.[1] The dominant element, however, was the political internationalist group—Sumner Welles, Cordell Hull, James T. Shotwell and his Commission to Study the Organization of Peace and John Foster Dulles, who headed up the postwar study effort of the National Council of Churches. Yet this group was split by a cleavage between "realistic" internationalists—those who accepted the necessity for continued national sovereignty and thus advocated only a limited role for a new international organization—and "idealistic" internationalists, who called for various forms of world government. During the war years, the realists clearly won out. The dream of a great association of nations based on the equality of all members in which each surrendered some of its sovereignty gave way to the United Nations Organization, in which control by the great powers (advocated privately by Franklin Roosevelt since 1942) became the central feature.[2]

My principal objection to Professor Herman's conceptual scheme is its failure to shed light on the actual course of American foreign policy. Important as community internationalists may be for a comprehension of the full range of internationalist thought, they had virtually no impact on public opinion or on the policy-making process. It was the interaction between idealistic and realistic political internationalists that provided the drama and the substance of the movement that led to the creation of the United Nations during World War II.

I find myself in substantial agreement with Professor Herman's characterization of the political internationalists as establishment figures who represented the prevailing configurations of power in twentieth-century America. Virtually without exception, they came from the ranks of Ivy League universities, New York law firms, American corporations and the philanthropic foundations. Realistic political internationalism was an expression of American capitalism, which desired a stable, orderly, non-revolutionary world for the peaceful expansion of American power and influence abroad. Professor Herman's suggestion that political internationalism was at heart an elaborate form of *Pax Americana* is a particularly penetrating insight. The Council on Foreign Relations, the Carnegie Endowment for International Peace, the Time-Life publishing empire built by Henry Luce—all worked for the goal of a world dominated by the large industrial nations cooperating together for the exploitation of colonial areas and the preservation of a global status quo.[3]

An understanding of the essentially conservative nature of political internationalism makes the transformation of the Wilsonian heritage after World War II into a blind defense of the Cold War not only predictable but inevitable. The refusal of the Soviet Union to fit docilely into its assigned role—most evident in the Russian insistence on creating its own security zone in Eastern Europe—undermined the United Nations. Reacting to Soviet intransigence, American political internationalists simply changed the collective security concept from a universal into a regional one. This fundamental alteration of the nature of collective security, foreshadowed as early as 1945 by Arthur Vandenberg's insistence at the San Francisco Conference on a regional loophole in the UN Charter, permitted the political internationalists to disguise the fact that the North Atlantic Treaty Organization was an old-fashioned military alliance and instead to portray it to the American public as a variant of collective security in the Wilsonian tradition.[4] Although some internationalists decried John Foster Dulles' formation of SEATO and CENTO in the 1950's, his proliferation of alliance systems in an effort to encircle Russia was but the logical extension of the new twist internationalists had given to "collective security."

When political internationalism is viewed as American imperialism in disguise, the reason for the lack of debate over the objectives of American foreign policy in the 1940's and 1950's becomes clear. The political internationalists who had supported the creation of the U.N.—Dean Acheson, John Foster Dulles, Arthur Vandenberg, Harry S. Truman— now became the advocates of a get-tough policy toward the Soviet Union. The few critics of containment—Walter Lippmann, Robert A. Taft, Henry A. Wallace—had all opposed the "realistic" form of political internationalism which had led to the creation of the U.N. Lippmann had championed a division of the world into spheres of influence during the war, Taft had warned repeatedly against an adventurous policy of international collaboration, and Wallace had been the foremost community internationalist, advocating a "people's revolution" that would usher in "the century of the common man." All three opposed the policy of containment in 1947 with varying degrees of failure—Lippmann's book *The Cold War* went virtually unnoticed until rediscovered by revisionist historians in the 1960's; Republican internationalists used the political popularity of Dwight D. Eisenhower to deny Taft the Presidential nomination so many in his party felt he deserved in 1952; and Truman and the Democratic internationalists smeared Henry Wallace as a Communist dupe in the 1948 election, thereby driving from public life the most outspoken and influential community internationalist.[5] By silencing these critics, the political internationalists established a Cold War consensus that ended meaningful discussion of American foreign policy for nearly two decades.[6]

In a very real sense, political internationalists transformed the Wilsonian concept of collective security into a justification for military alliances by which the United States assumed the role of world policeman. Historians might well find Professor Herman's insight into the conservative implications of political internationalism of crucial assistance in explaining how the United States came to deny its own ideals in the world after World War II.

Walter LaFeber
Cornell University

In the search for insight into the development and dilemmas of American internationalists, Sondra Herman's distinctions between "political internationalists" (or "institutionalists") and "community internationalists" are useful. One difference particularly merits emphasis. "Political internationalists" included prominent members of the American legal, political and corporate life; that is, they had risen successfully within the system by understanding how to control its institutions and make those institutions respond to their personal interest and, a logical extension, from this personal interest to what they perceived to be the national interest. In a real sense they were not internationalists at all, but nationalists who searched for an international arena in which American institutions could expand and prosper.

"Community internationalists," however, moved out of a reform movement that pivoted around the individual or around classes victimized by the American dream, rather than primarily focusing on national institutions. Indeed they sought to bypass such institutions by creating an international consciousness and supranational agencies which could work outside the traditional assumptions of nation-states. Such a bypass might have led to a fruitful journey had they tried to detour around domestic institutions of a third-rate power. Since they belonged to the superpower of the twentieth century, however, the "community internationalists" found themselves, if not in a series of political deadends, then establishing international agencies which scarcely touched the dynamics of the United States foreign policies and those of the other leading nation-states.

Such dilemmas are not new to American reformers. Their ability to repeat mistakes is eloquent testimony to their inability to understand the past. William Lloyd Garrison exemplified the dilemma in 1830 when he proclaimed, "My country is the world; my countrymen are mankind."

His country, of course, was not like the world, and his countrymen, especially in the South and Midwest, were atypical of, for example, the successful British abolitionists. Like many American reformers, Garrison loved an impassioned moral appeal, but it was valueless in terms of finding levers to make changes, for the nation-state was where the power was, and is, located. He was admitting, moreover, that his own nation was not in sympathy with him; Garrison consequently tried the traditional bypass of appealing to a larger world body which, unfortunately for him, had no substance or authority. When change finally occurred, neither Garrison nor the equally irrelevant Emerson or Thoreau played important roles. For good or ill, men such as Lincoln, Rockefeller and Root, who knew how to operate the nation's politico-economic institutions, forced the changes and reordered the society.

By the century's turn most American reformers drifted in the mainstream of the labor movement, Progressivism or anti-imperialist organizations, thereby working in fact within the assumptions established by the "institutionalists." Or else a few followed the course of Eugene Debs. But Debs does not fall into the category of either "political internationalist" or "community internationalist." He is of little consequence to the development of American internationalism, which may be one reason why he should be studied. While internationalists of various persuasions were assuming (or, more accurately, hoping) their country was the world, Debs set to work on the mundane but more useful task of analyzing and attempting to modify fundamentally the institutions of his home country. He apparently understood what few American reformers have comprehended: internationalism is the final, not the first step of reform; and internationalism, in the sense that reformers from Garrison through the 1960's student movements used the term, is irrelevant to the more fundamental need of altering, which means initially understanding, domestic institutions. With a few exceptions such as Debs, American reformers have successfully avoided the difficult problem of institutional change by emphasizing the individual (as Garrison, Emerson, Thoreau), attempting to alter the society by laboring outside its key institutions (as the Social Gospelers), or trying to leap over the problem to work on the supposedly more exalted level of international institutions.

The "political internationalists," or "institutionalists" (domestic as well as international) have not made such errors. Moving up within the domestic system, they understood that this arena's instruments of politics, finance, religion and education formed part of a larger theater whose stability and prosperity was necessary for their own and their nation's well-being. They therefore carefully defined their relationships to the larger theater. At first the "institutionalists" focused on the Western Hemisphere and the working out of profitable economic ties rather than entangling political alliances. Root's highly publicized tour of Latin America while he was Secretary of State exemplified this initial step. The

Mexican Revolution, World War I and the Russian Revolution forced an expansion of the policy until it became global in 1919. Again the dynamic was to be economic power, not politics, and when after the Paris Conference the League of Nations structure shakingly rested on a Franco-American Security Pact, and an Article X which some internationalists feared would commit the United States to fighting colonial wars for the British and French, many "political internationalists" belied their label and helped kill the treaty.

Between the wars Henry Stimson, who in many ways inherited the power and world view of Root, sought desperately for a makeshift series of alliances outside the League. This search finally collapsed during the critical months of the Manchurian Crisis in 1931-1932 when the British Foreign Office refused to cooperate in threatening the Japanese. As the League disintegrated, many "political internationalists" concentrated on restoring once again their domestic institutions within the larger framework of global stability. Historians persist in terming the interwar American policy one of isolationism. The results of such labeling have been interesting, particularly in the scholarly emphasis upon superficial political arrangements (while the economic and social substructures have been relatively neglected); and also in the picking up of the "isolationist" term by Presidents Johnson and Nixon to rationalize their own internationalism. These presidents have taken the word out of its proper 1930's context, but they are not to blame, for historians' simplistic use of the word allows a larger political misuse. (It seems particularly unfortunate that this traditional understanding of "isolationism," moreover, has prevented scholars from gaining sufficient insight into the impact which the American economic dilemmas of the 1920's and 1930's had on other societies. Such information would perhaps be helpful in comprehending the effect the United States is having in the worldwide Revolution of Autonomy which has especially shaken the former colonial areas of Africa and Asia during the 1960's.)

When the world again needed reordering in 1945 the opportunity was more propitious than any American internationalist had ever dared dream. With a monopoly of atomic power, unchallenged economic superiority, and two industrial heartlands of Japan and Western Europe dependent upon American beneficence, the Truman Administration, led in the foreign-policy realm by Dean Acheson, had the golden chance of making the world safe for the United States institutional system. Acheson's internationalism, however, reached only as far as American economic and military power allowed him to influence policy. This essentially meant that it reached to Japan and Western and Central Europe but not to the other areas represented in the United Nations. Acheson correctly understood that the international organization could contain neither the dynamic of American superiority nor the ensuing Soviet-American struggle. He consequently had few compunctions in cooperating with a crucial policy change in 1945 which removed postwar relief from the international agency of UNRRA and channeled it into bilateral agencies controlled by the United States; or in undermining the international organization with the Truman Doctrine and Marshall Plan that worked outside U.N. auspices; or in resisting Communist aggression in Korea, a three-year struggle in which the United Nations acted as an American surrogate; or, finally, in pushing through the Uniting for Peace Resolution of 1950 which created the fiction that the General Assembly (where Costa Rica, Albania, etc., voted equally with the two big powers) had by grace of the Resolution taken power from the Security Council where the world powers exercised a veto. The irony of this last event for the development of American internationalism might be greater than historians suspect, for it would be useful to see which American internationalist groups, if any, protested this veiling of reality and undermining of U.N. power. Since the Resolution rested on supposed democratic voting processes, and as it clearly was in America's interest to be able to bypass the Soviet veto in the Security Council, one can guess that very few internationalist groups in the United States understood, let alone protested, what Acheson did.

The pretension of working through the United Nations while actually weakening it could continue only until American unilateral power was blocked within and without the organization. This in fact developed during the 1960's in the battlefields of Vietnam, the council rooms of NATO, and the voting on the American resolution of whether both mainland China and Taiwan should be in the United Nations. This disciplining of American unilateralism, it must be noted, did not come primarily from American reformers and/or internationalists, but was imposed by other peoples in the world who used their own institutions to counter American power. With these defeats, which placed the United States in a world position closer to that of 1921 than 1947, the Johnson and Nixon Administrations reverted to policies reminiscent of the interwar era when, as at the Washington Conference of 1921 and the 1924 Dawes economic discussions, the major powers gathered outside supranational or truly global organizations and privately adjusted relationships of their domestic institutions to those of the few other major powers.

During the twentieth century the internationalist concepts initiated by Root had been unsuccessfully adjusted by Stimson, dazzlingly transformed by Acheson, and then narrowed and carried to one logical conclusion of unilateralism by John Foster Dulles and Henry Kissinger. Although several of these men, particularly Root and Dulles, believed at one time in the possibilities of international legal machinery, they either modified or dropped this faith when they perceived that such machinery might severely restrict American self-interest or, as between 1945 and the mid-1960's, the United States could go it alone without needing the machinery.

One constant throughout this drama of the "political international-ists" was their commitment to the primacy of American domestic insti-tutions. International organizations, in their view, were either to replicate or serve those institutions. Other nations in the world have refused to play the game according to such ground-rules. Unfortunately, American reformers have been in no position to be of much help in creating a more equitable international system. We now know enough about Jane Ad-dams to suggest that Eugene Debs is preferable as a historical example; for that matter, so is Henry Adams. Neither Debs nor Adams confused the priorities. And neither have the peoples in Southeast Asia, Western Europe and Latin America who have blunted American power. These peoples have agreed with the "political internationalists" such as Root that an equitable international system begins at home. After this point, unfortunately for the United States, their paths have sharply diverged.

Richard D. McKinzie
University of Missouri

Theodore A. Wilson
University of Kansas

Did the Cold War kill American inter-nationalism? Was belief in the future of the United Nations, which appeared quite strong and popular after World War II, anything more than an emotional reaction to the war itself? Was it an acceptance of responsibility in the world, or an escape from it? When did this belief in effective United Nations action dis-appear? Did Americans begin to identify American police action with internationalism around the time of the Korean war?

Sondra Herman's interrogations about American internationalism in the formative period of the Cold War are thoughtful and point to impor-tant issues. However, questions that emphasize the centrality of the United Nations are not wholly satisfactory, for they ignore a significant dimension of internationalist thought in this period. Commitment to the United Nations was, perhaps, the litmus test of America's conversion from isolation; but it did not reflect any serious interest in sacrificing national sovereignty to some larger concept of human loyalty or in supra-national approaches to political realities. Whatever faith in institu-tional internationalism American leaders possessed, the small group of visionaries who sat on the Department of State's planning committees, the political leaders who claimed responsibility for the nation's welfare and who had to explain their actions to the public hedged their loyalties from the beginning. For example, one month before the delegations assembled in San Franciso, the United States engineered a meeting in Mexico with Latin American nations for the purpose of developing much narrower schemes of regional cooperation. The obvious explanation is that Presi-dents Roosevelt and Truman's advisers lacked faith in the United Nations and viewed regional agreements as necessary insurance policies in the likely event that the United Nations failed.

185

The guardians of American national interests, of course, did not completely despair of working for peace through the United Nations. They viewed it as a valuable tool, as a useful, even necessary, forum for the reduction of tensions and promotion of understanding among the world's peoples. The United Nations was *one* means by which peace (some would add justice) would be gained; it was not an end in itself. Business spokesmen, many Congressmen, leaders of philanthropic and religious organizations, and "professional internationalists" shared this assessment of the United Nations' role. The Federal Council of Churches' Commission on a Just and Durable Peace, for example, urged in 1947 "greater use of the United Nations . . . as a place where the conduct of nations can be submitted to the moral judgment of world opinion."[1] For the Commission and others, the United Nations was not the "universal solvent" for which internationalists supposedly were forever searching. Senator Arthur H. Vandenberg, a staunch supporter of American participation in the U.N., never believed the organization was "created or equipped" to handle all or even most conflicts between nations. When Greece was torn by political and economic chaos in early 1947, Vandenberg said: "I am frank to say that I think Greece could collapse fifty times before the UN. itself could ever hope to handle a situation of this nature."[2] A year later John Foster Dulles, the architect of that internationalist, bipartisan Republican foreign policy that Vandenberg executed, wrote in a draft of the party platform: "We support the United Nations and will not by-pass it *in matters within its competence*."[3] It was not that Vandenberg, Dulles and the multitude of others who considered themselves internationalists were acquiescing fatalistically in the demise of earlier dreams; rather, the blow was not mortal, because the United Nations had never been the principal repository of their hopes for just and lasting peace.

Many, perhaps most, American leaders and spokesmen for the "important public" between 1943 and 1948 shared a view of the world—as naively emotional, utopian and obscurantist as the Wilsonian vision at its most extreme—best termed "economic internationalism." This group shared above all an aggressively nationalistic approach to international affairs, often consciously defining the needs of the world community in terms of United States interests and needs. This chauvinistic attitude was in large part the result of the Second World War, especially the global involvement thrust upon America by the war. Arthur Ekirch, Jr.. has observed with enviable perspicacity that by 1945 Americans had become "supremely confident" of the nation's strength and were "ill-prepared to accept any . . . challenge to United States world leadership. . . . In the fervor of their recent conversion from isolationism to internationalism, the American public was all too frequently blind to the fact that their own new views often only projected older nationalistic prejudices upon a world stage."[4] The productive capacity generated during the war had transformed the United States into a superpower, and American leaders, supremely conscious of America's economic preeminence, determined to use it to bring about universal peace and prosperity.

For a time, American leaders believed lasting peace was to be obtained by an all-out, aggressive effort led by the United States. "We must wage peace just as we have waged total war," President Truman told his friend Fred Vinson in the last months of 1945.[5] How did one "wage" peace, which Americans traditionally had negatively defined, as "the absence or cessation of war, strife, or discord"? It appears that what the President and his advisers intended when they spoke of "waging peace" was the implementation of an economic foreign policy designed to create and maintain a stable and prosperous environment in which universal peace would flourish.

The chief influences upon American internationalism were what happened to the great-power consensus and the open economic arrangements which were to undergird the United Nations. The importance of the collapse of the Allied wartime coalition is obvious. Since it was grounded upon the assumption of mutual trust, the United Nations' success, as Senator Vandenberg stated, depended upon "the temperature of Soviet-American relationships."[6] Antagonism born of the frigid breath of misunderstanding and political hostility combined with a second source of frustration: the inability of the United States to bring into existence a world economic order. This combination produced, during the critical formative years of the postwar era, a self-righteous and uncritical identification of international peace and harmony with perceived American interests.

An effort to realize an open economic world had been presaged by views about the causes of international strife developed during the long tenure of Franklin D. Roosevelt. Secretary of State Cordell Hull for many years had advocated a policy of international economic cooperation. Persuaded that conflicts of economic interests were the base cause of almost all international difficulties, Hull gathered around him a group of kindred spirits to draw up a blueprint for a stable, prosperous world order. Hull and his colleagues, and likeminded men throughout the government, possessed an economic vision of the postwar world.

It was believed a system of unrestricted international trade would ensure more efficient production of goods, higher living standards throughout the world, and thus bring about world peace, because every nation would have a stake in the economic well-being of every other nation. As Harry Dexter White stated some years later:

> The people of the United States and the United Nations have agreed on a program in which countries cooperate to maintain peace and prosperity. . . . This program recognizes that it is not enough to get countries to agree on political cooperation. That is important, of course. But we must

do more than that. We must support all our efforts for peace by providing an environment of stability and order in international economic relations. We must remove the economic causes of conflict. In such an environment, peace can flourish.[7]

When American planners talked of waging peace, they were referring to the task of creating a system of international trade which returned the world to that "golden age" before state trading arrangements and preferential tariffs.

Theoreticians at every level of government were agreed that the United States must take the initiative. They also were agreed in not foreseeing great problems of implementation. The problems the world would face after the war, these men assumed, would be primarily financial. Voicing the general opinion, Under-Secretary of State Will L. Clayton did not believe that the earth's resources were too meager nor available production facilities too devastated or worn down to permit rapid reconstruction and resumption of normal patterns of commerce. What was envisioned was a short period of rebuilding—two years at the most—followed by a return to a high level of commercial activity and universal prosperity. This would be good for America and good for the world, since prosperous nations were unlikely to disturb the peace. If such ideas appear hopelessly utopian in light of the economic shambles resulting from the war, it is not difficult to demonstrate that they permeated the administration Truman inherited in April, 1945.

No important bureaucrat opposed American participation in the United Nations or preached the virtues of tariff walls and economic isolation. Donald M. Nelson, FDR's War Production Board chief, believed that the interdependency of the United States with the rest of the world had come to be "a universally accepted premise." Nelson advised President Truman that returning soldiers would find jobs only if new markets could be found for American products; these markets could "only be found in countries whose purchasing power is growing, as a result of their economic development."[8] Another official stated bluntly that the United States would be turning out twice the volume of goods produced in 1939 and would "need to look to outlets for our products on a scale vastly larger than ever before." He concluded: "Closed factories, rusty plows, idle capital, and widespread unemployment breed war and revolution as well as depression."[9]

Awareness of these pressures did not in itself ensure that solutions would be forthcoming. American planners were confident that they had the key; unfortunately, neither they nor the political leaders who approved their program for waging—and winning—the peace realized, until it was too late, that the tasks of clearing away the debris of war and of reviving world trade overreached the capacity of the instruments Americans had constructed for these jobs. As well, U.S. planners failed to grasp that the creation of international financial institutions was only a partial response to problems that transcended temporary monetary maladjustments, problems that were political, psychological, even ethical in nature! The United States championed the creation of two institutions with limited powers, the International Bank for Reconstruction and Development and the International Monetary Fund. It was assumed that these agencies would be able to satisfy necessary requirements for readjustment to peacetime patterns of trade and essential economic development. It was recognized that relief for the victims of the war would for a time require substantial outlays by the United States. American leaders decided, therefore, that minimum relief would be dispensed through UNRRA, to be phased out when short-term reconstruction loans and the forces generated by the IBRD and the IMF to rationalize world trade brought full recovery. Had the anticipated postwar cooperation of the wartime Allies continued, had Congress been as generous as during the war, and, perhaps most significant, had that "golden age" of free and expanding trade that American planners sought to restore ever existed in fact, these policies might have worked.

That they failed was explained in part by the inability of Americans to understand that economic actions may have (or may be perceived by others as having) political motivations. American statesmen were entirely sincere when they stated that multilateral liberalization of trade would bring peace and prosperity to all the world. However, a policy to promote the free flow of goods and capital and to expand production, viewed from London, Moscow and elsewhere, would first benefit the United States. What country emerged from the war with unimpaired productive facilities? The United States. What nation possessed surplus capacity in almost every economic sector? The United States. Americans might claim reassuringly that the lead enjoyed by the U.S. was a temporary phenomenon and would disappear as the supply-demand cycle came into operation. But efforts to obtain an "open door" everywhere *before* reconstruction was accomplished were hardly reassuring, and the inability of the Roosevelt and Truman Administrations to grasp this fact heightened the tension between America and its erstwhile allies.

Even in late 1946 the Truman Administration was refusing to abandon the vision of a prosperous, peaceful world, believing that if "moral stamina" would suffice, the vision could be attained. Of course, it was not that simple. Victory over the Axis had created a new mood in Washington and in Moscow, and domestic priorities and interests forced American leaders to chart a new course. The American public longed to return to what was thought of as "normal" life; for many a prerequisite of "normalcy" was to have their wartime allies and enemies "get off the U.S. taxpayer's back." American leaders watched helplessly and in genuine puzzlement as domestic apathy and the deepening rift with the Russians upset their program for a peaceful, prosperous world. Plans in progress bogged down. It took Congress six months to authorize the British loan. When it did pass, the reasons were less that Britain needed the money and that aid would serve the economic aims of the United States than that the money would enable Britain to continue its stand against Soviet pressure in the Mediterranean and Middle East. The uncertainties of power politics delayed the opening of the IBRD until May, 1947, and U.S. support for the International Trade Organization faltered. By 1947 the nations of Western Europe were still in desperate trouble, spending a large part of their resources on relief instead of trade-generating reconstruction. Economic forecasters in the U.S. were saying that the reconversion of the American economy was complete, and that most of the savings of the war years had been released. In this atmosphere of crisis the Marshall Plan emerged from the Policy Planning Staff of the State Department. Its creators proceeded from radically different assumptions than existed during and immediately after the war. The Marshall Plan was, in one sense, a device to provide the assistance for Western Europe's reconstruction that should have been given—and Americans had thought they were giving—in 1943-1946. But the rationale for the Marshall Plan was political (anti-Communist), not economic. When the nations of Western Europe institutionalized their partnership with the United States by forming the Organization for European Economic Cooperation in 1948, the economic internationalists' vision of one world—prosperous and at peace—disappeared.

One result was a significant change in the approach of Americans to the solution of international conflict. Except for "purists" in the Treasury Department and some few others, American internationalists accepted the division of the world into two spheres and proceeded to erect new strategies upon that fact. Reflecting the change in attitude, a Treasury official wrote in August, 1947:

> The whole is the peace of the world which America is obliged to undertake. But it must be a peace in which the security of America is above all and in which we shall be able insofar as possible to help the rest of the world approach our standards of living, economic and spiritual. It is not our desire to change the political systems of others, but to retain our own which we hope others will approach and copy. . . . Therefore, we must always have in mind the strategic position of the United States in this power struggle between two great systems in order that we shall retain our supremacy and thus be enabled to weld together all of the world on some common ground.[10]

Emphasis was placed on Europe as a battleground between two competing economic and political systems. Economic internationalists were persuaded to abandon the dream of an open economic world in favor of an attempt to create a similar "environment" in that portion of the globe which was "free," i.e., non-Communist. Their emotional faith in the superiority of American institutions was transferred to a smaller stage, Europe.

It may be that the reduction in scope produced an intensification of the implicit self-righteousness and aggressiveness underlying United States policy, and that when events again forced Americans to think "globally," they automatically equated United States intervention anywhere in the world with the larger aims of internationalism. If so, the road to that assumption ran from the commitment to economic internationalism, to the idea of waging peace, which was so important in the years 1943-1948.

ROBERT A. DIVINE

notes

1. James MacGregor Burns, *Roosevelt: The Soldier of Freedom* (New York, 1970), 360; Robert A. Divine, *Second Chance: The Triumph of Internationalism in America During World War II* (New York, 1967), 62-66. Arthur Schlesinger, Jr., falsely labels Wallace a sphere-of-influence advocate on the basis of his postwar urging that Russia be permitted to control Eastern Europe. During World War II, Wallace proposed a broad internationalist program with no mention of spheres of influence. Arthur Schlesinger, Jr., "The Origins of the Cold War," *Foreign Affairs*, XLVI (October, 1967), 29; Henry A. Wallace, *The Price of Free World Victory* (New York, 1942).

2. Robert A. Divine, *Roosevelt and World War II* (Baltimore, 1969), 49-71.

3. For a suggestive analysis of the origins of the "corporatist" concept of cooperation among the industrial nations, see William A. Williams, "The Legend of Isolationism in the 1920's," *Science and Society*, XVIII (Winter, 1954), 11-20.

4. Roland N. Stromberg, *Collective Security and American Foreign Policy* (New York, 1963), 193-197.

5. Barton J. Bernstein, "Walter Lippmann and the Early Cold War," Ronald Radosh and Leonard P. Liggio, "Henry A. Wallace and the Open Door," and Henry W. Berger, "Senator Robert A. Taft Dissents from Military Escalation," in Thomas G. Paterson, *Cold War Critics: Alternatives to American Foreign Policy in the Truman Years* (Chicago, 1971).

6. For a provocative description of the failure of American intellectuals to criticize the Cold War, see Christopher Lasch, "The Cultural Cold War: A Short History of the Congress for Cultural Freedom," in Barton J. Bernstein, ed., *Towards a New Past* (New York, 1968), 322-359.

RICHARD D. McKINZIE AND THEODORE A. WILSON

notes

1. John Foster Dulles to Harry S. Truman, July 2, 1947, Box 1060, Official File 713, Harry S. Truman Papers, Harry S. Truman Library (HSTL).

2. Arthur H. Vandenberg to John B. Bennet, March 5, 1947, Arthur H. Vandenberg Papers, William Clements Library, University of Michigan.

3. Emphasis added. John Foster Dulles, "Confidential Draft of Republican Platform," June 6, 1948, John Foster Dulles Papers, Firestone Library, Princeton University.

4. Arthur Ekirch, Jr., *Ideas, Ideals, and American Diplomacy* (New York, 1966), 171-172.

5. Harry S. Truman to Fred Vinson, November 18, 1945, Box 68, Official File 20, Truman Papers, HSTL.

6. Arthur H. Vandenberg to Hamilton Fish Armstrong, April 2, 1946, Vandenberg Papers.

7. Speech by Harry Dexter White, "The Anglo-American Financial Agreement," Harry Dexter White Papers, Firestone Library, Princeton University.

8. Donald M. Nelson to Harry S. Truman, May 12, 1945, Box 52, Record Group 250 (Records of the Office of War Mobilization and Reconversion), National Archives, Washington, D.C.

9. Oscar Cox, "On Putting First Things First," n.d., Box 82, Cox Papers, Franklin D. Roosevelt Library.

10. "Memorandum for Secretary of Treasury," August 21, 1947, IBRD #3 folder, Box 56, John W. Snyder Papers, HSTL.

Date Due